L7

The Hunting Submarine

Crécy Books publications by the same author:
Operations Most Secret:
   S.O.E. Malayan Theatre
Path Of Duty:
   The Life of Bill Beytes
Stealthily By Night:

The Hunting Submarine

The Fighting Life of HMS Tally-Ho

IAN TRENOWDEN

CRÉCY BOOKS

This edition published in 1994 by
CRÉCY BOOKS LIMITED
First published in 1974 by
William Kimber & Co. Limited

© Ian Trenowden, 1974
ISBN 0 947554 39 4

Printed and bound by Hartnolls Limited,
Bodmin, Cornwall.

Contents

List of Illustrations

The officers of *Tally-Ho* on the bridge on their return from
the Far East   *(Imperial War Museum)*
Captain G.P. Claridge RN greets Bennington on arrival at
Blyth   *(Imperial War Museum)*
Tally-Ho berthed at Blyth with her crew mustered on the
bridge and casing   *(Imperial War Museum)*
Jackie Warner and Snoopy Thurlow in the snow
                              (Newcastle Chronicle & Journal Ltd.)
Tally-Ho officers attempt to spit-roast the 'bag' on a rough
shoot in Ceylon
Tally-Ho officers and crew in the forecourt of Buckingham
Palace in July 1945   *(Daily Sketch)*
Bennington with the winning Fleet Air Arm field gun team
                  (Crown copyright, by permission Controller HMSO)

LIST OF DIAGRAMS

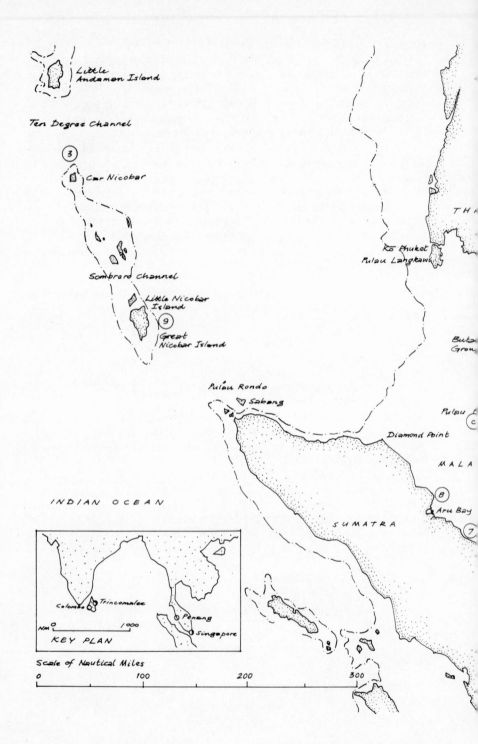

Little
Andaman Island

Ten Degree Channel

③

Car Nicobar

Sombrero Channel

Little Nicobar
Island

⑨

Great
Nicobar Island

T H

Ko Phuket
Pulau Langkawi

Buta
Grou

Pulau Rondo

Sabang

Pulau
ⓒ

Diamond Point

M A L A

⑧

Aru Bay

⑦

INDIAN OCEAN

SUMATRA

Colombo

Trincomalee

Penang

Singapore

NM⁰   1000

KEY PLAN

Scale of Nautical Miles

0   100   200   300

SKETCH MAP OF TALLY-HO
OPERATING AREA

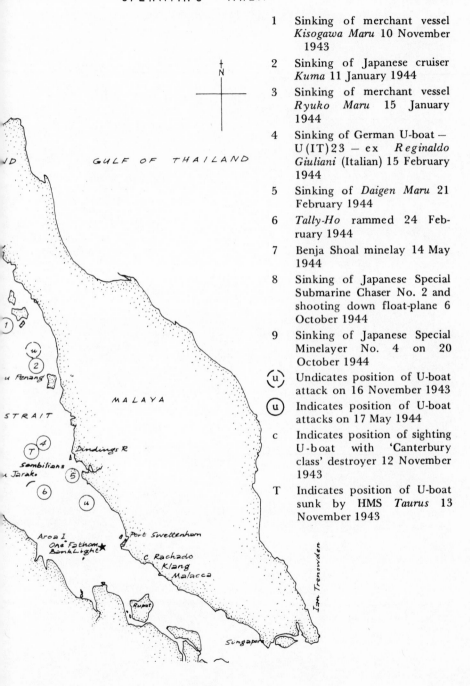

1 Sinking of merchant vessel *Kisogawa Maru* 10 November 1943

2 Sinking of Japanese cruiser *Kuma* 11 January 1944

3 Sinking of merchant vessel *Ryuko Maru* 15 January 1944

4 Sinking of German U-boat — U(IT)23 — ex *Reginaldo Giuliani* (Italian) 15 February 1944

5 Sinking of *Daigen Maru* 21 February 1944

6 *Tally-Ho* rammed 24 February 1944

7 Benja Shoal minelay 14 May 1944

8 Sinking of Japanese Special Submarine Chaser No. 2 and shooting down float-plane 6 October 1944

9 Sinking of Japanese Special Minelayer No. 4 on 20 October 1944

(u) Undicates position of U-boat attack on 16 November 1943

(u) Indicates position of U-boat attacks on 17 May 1944

c Indicates position of sighting U-boat with 'Canterbury class' destroyer 12 November 1943

T Indicates position of U-boat sunk by HMS *Taurus* 13 November 1943

For my son Mark

Acknowledgements

I wish to acknowledge my gratitude to the following all of whom served in *Tally-Ho* during her Far Eastern commission for their consideration and help to me. Their names are listed alphabetically after the captain's name:

Captain L.W.A. Bennington DSO and bar, DSC and two bars, RN (Retd), Lieutenant-Commander P.D.C. Bennett RN (Retd), J.C. Brighton DSM and bar, Sir Claude Fenner KBE, CMG, L.D. Hamlyn OBE, FIL, K. Lockyer, who suggested this book, P.D. Scott-Maxwell DSC and bar, Rear Admiral A.G. Tait DSC, Captain C.T.M. Thurlow DSC, Lieutenant-Commander S.A. Warner MBE, DSC, RN (Retd).

My grateful thanks are also extended to Rear Admiral P.N. Buckley CB, DSO, Captain R.W. Garson, RN Captain (Submarines) First Submarine Squadron, Captain P. Cobb RN, Captain (Submarines) Second Submarine Squadron and to Lieutenant-Commander G.H. Frere Cook RN (Retd), Curator the Submarine Museum HMS *Dolphin*, as well as to Lieutenant-Commander A.D.E. Pender-Cudlip RN, and the crew of HMS *Alliance* who were kind enough to take me to sea with them on exercises.

I should also like to record my thanks to:

The Central Reference Library, The Commonwealth War Graves Commission, The Guildhall Library, The Imperial War Museum, The Naval Historical Branch (The Ministry of Defence), The Public Record Office, The Submarine Museum, HMS *Dolphin*, Gosport, Hants, The Westminster Library and The Westminster Library, Maida Vale Branch, with its reserve stock of naval books and to Vickers Limited, Ship Builders and Engineers and Gus Britton, Research Archivist.

The greatest possible credit is due to Sally Mitchell who typed my manuscripts with unfailing good humour.

The unofficial badge
designed for *Tally-Ho*

SPECIFICATION OF PARTICULARS HMS *TALLY-HO*

Laid down: 28 April 1942
Launched: 23 December 1942
Completed: 20 April 1943
Class: 'T'-class
SIZE: 265 pp 273½ ft O/A x 26½ ft x 14¾ ft.
COMPLEMENT: 61
DISPLACEMENT: 1,300 tons (surfaced)
        1,575 tons (submerged)
ARMAMENT:
GUNS: one 4-in., one 20-mm. Oerlikon cannon
TUBES: six 21-in. (internal: bow)
        five 21-in. (external: 2-in bow, pointing forward:
        two midships, one at stern, pointing astern)
SPECIFICATION:
Officially described as patrol-type submarine for general service, saddle tank design, originally had equal of 42-day patrol.
PERFORMANCE:
Radius 9,000 miles @ 10 knots
FUEL OIL: 210 tons
TWO VICKERS DIESELS: BHP 2,500
SPEED: 15¼ knots (surfaced) on diesels
        9 knots (submerged) on electric motors
DIVING DEPTH: 350 ft
PENNANT No. P 317
BUILDERS: Vickers-Armstrong, Barrow-in-Furness

Introduction

Tally-Ho was a 'T'-class submarine which earned outstanding success in the Second World War. Her name was chosen by Winston Churchill, who may well have felt that the huntsman's cry on sighting his quarry was most applicable to a submarine. Indeed, events proved how appropriate was the choice. The boat's first (and unofficial) motto was *'Celeriter in hostem'* (swiftly among the foe).

It was not the first time that a ship of the Royal Navy had borne the name *Tally-Ho*. It had been given, during the First World War, to a requisitioned trawler, built in 1900 and displacing 216 tons.

The 'T'-class submarine of 1942 vintage carried a war crew of some sixty-five men and in the Far East made patrols of some four weeks' duration. It was not unusual for the whole four weeks to be spent without breaking radio silence. Once at sea the 'T' boat could receive wireless transmissions even when submerged, but she could not transmit unless it was really necessary. From the moment she had left port she would be entirely dependent on her own resourcefulness. Isolated from her friends she would discover that even our own over-zealous forces could be enemies.

Often her depot ship would learn that she still existed only when she presented herself at the rendezvous on return from a patrol. Some submarines failed to return and — apart from enemy reports — no one will ever know what happened to them. Survivors from submarines sunk in enemy waters were few and, in the Far East theatre, almost completely unknown.

During her first commission HMS *Tally-Ho* lived up to her motto in no uncertain terms. That commission lasted from 15 March 1943 until 26 February 1945 and included a particularly successful tour of operations in the Far East, principally in and around the Malacca Strait. Between November 1943 and November 1944 she sank a greater tonnage of enemy shipping than the total tonnage sunk by all other British submarines operating in that theatre; it amounted to more than twenty per cent of all warships and merchant vessels sunk in those waters during that period. Even so, at the end of her Far Eastern cruise her captain complained bitterly of a shortage of suitable targets. In fact – though at the time Bennington could not know this – by the autumn of 1944 (the year of the Japanese defeats at Leyte Gulf and in the Phillipines Sea) submarine sinkings by torpedo attacks, mine-laying and gun actions had obliged the Japanese to abandon the sea route to Burma through the Malacca Strait.

The Malacca Strait had been considered by many contemporary strategic experts to be too shallow for effective submarine operations, its waters were badly charted and in places so still that a periscope was apt to be alarmingly conspicuous. The strait was also ringed by enemy air bases. The restricted depth meant that accidental 'bottoming' – always a risk for submarines – was a frequent occurrence. The *Tally-Ho* crew once claimed that their captain could have manoeuvred a submarine in a goldfish bowl: in the Malacca Strait he very nearly had to do so.

Bennington, who commanded *Tally-Ho* throughout her first commission, was an extremely popular as well as successful captain and during his tenure of command *Tally-Ho* had exceptionally small turnover of personnel. Throughout the Far Eastern cruise Bennington shared the discomforts his crew endured, and, as much as any of them, he relished the single midday cigarette he allowed each man to smoke when the boat was submerged throughout the hours of daylight. (Submarines are always referred to as boats.) Discomfort on operational patrols was extreme. In the Malacca Strait it was necessary to submerge for about twelve hours in every twenty-four; in the Mediterranean, in summer, submergences of up to eighteen hours were quite usual. Without Schnorkel masts – the British version, 'snort', was not fitted to 'T' boats till after the war – the air inside the submarine became very foul and, of course, the diesels could not be run submerged. So impoverished of oxygen was the internal atmosphere that, by midday, when the majority of captains piped 'one apiece' – a single cigarette all round — it was necessary to light one's cigarette by the flaring match head as there was not enough oxygen to keep the matchstalk alight. By evening when it was time to surface, many crew members felt sick. In the course of a day in the Straits (Mediterranean), up to forty gallons of condensation would collect and a pressure of some inches water gauge build up. This usually caused a fog to form briefly in the 'fore-ends' on surfacing. As a result in the Mediterranean crews slept under oilskins.

Tally-Ho began her operations, in the even hotter Malacca Strait, without air conditioning and with her escape hatches securely fastened from the *outside*. Inside temperatures soared when the boat was submerged, prickly heat was rife. (In one boat a seaman had to have his hands tied to prevent him scratching his skin to ribbons; in another boat a seaman died of severe heat exhaustion.)

Half the crew had already served with Bennington in HMS *Porpoise* in the Mediterranean throughout the greater part of 1942 — the year our submarine losses in the Mediterranean were highest for the war. The remainder of his crew were for the most part from *Proteus* and had seen extensive service in the Mediterranean that year under another notable captain, Lieutenant-Commander P.S. Francis DSO, RN. Small wonder a crew compounded of such men should prove exceptional.

In the Royal Navy, whether in peace or war, the submarine commander will always have worked his way up in 'the Trade' starting 'fourth hand'. This term arose from the fact that submarines usually carried no more than four officers (plus an Engineer Officer). By mid 1943 this was no longer the case. Thereafter a fifth officer was 'borne additional', 'under training' or 'for extra watch-keeping duties'. It was, and still is, very difficult to become a good submarine commanding officer. In the Second World War many *good* submarine officers failed to make the grade in the 'perisher' (Commanding Officers' Qualifying Course).

Bennington possessed the qualities that enabled him to command not only his crew's loyalty but their admiration. He began his war in submarines and served operationally in them until January 1945. He had risen from the ranks, was modest of demeanour and had a reputation for being strict but fair with his

B

crews. At the same time he was human, avoided false modesty, eschewed histrionics and secured his crew's loyalty by his own example.

Throughout her war service *Tally-Ho* lost one officer, killed in action, and not a single rating. When the war ended, her usefulness did not; she went all over the world on good will trips and ended her service as a floating class-room. Not again, after Bennington relinquished his command early in 1945, did she see action. She was broken up in 1968 — after twenty-six years afloat — at about the same time as Bennington retired from the Royal Navy.

Today Captain Bennington DSO and bar, DSC and two bars, Royal Navy (Retd) is adamant that the story of the fighting career of *Tally-Ho* should not be a catalogue of his decorations. He emphasizes the qualities of his officers and crew — qualities on which he relied absolutely and never found wanting.

SOME TECHNICAL EXPLANATIONS

General Observations

The pressure hull of a 'T'-class submarine was a steel submersible cylinder some 260 ft long and 16 ft or so in diameter at its widest point. On the top surface, throughout its length, ran a narrow steel catwalk, the casing. This was perforated like a colander, so that it would present no resistance to the water when submerging. The bridge and 4-in. gun mounting had their own free-flooding casings. The casings were built up in light steel plate on a metal angle framework but were not armoured.

At sea, access from inside the pressure hull to the outside was through the conning-tower. When gun actions took place the gun crew would come up the gun tower. Both this, and the conning tower had upper and lower pressure hatches. For access in harbour the for'ard torpedo loading hatch was used for personnel as well as torpedoes, the engine room hatch for engine parts. There were also for'ard and after escape hatches.

On either side of the 'T'-class boat's pressure hull were her bulbous, steel, main ballast tanks. These filled completely when submerged and so were not used for 'trimming' or adjustment of attitude to take account of weight changes. Tanks for this purpose were provided throughout the vessel's length, and selective filling and emptying of them permitted very fine adjustment of 'trim' for varying depths, densities and weight distributions. Storage tanks were also provided for fuel oil, lubrication oil, drinking water and distilled water; trim changes were necessary to counteract changes in overall weight distribution as these commodities were consumed. Firing torpedoes also called for trim changes, extreme skill being necessary to prevent a 'T' boat, at periscope depth, breaking surface on firing a salvo, say, of half a dozen. To kill excess buoyancy and dive speedily, for tactical reasons the 'T' boat and all of her ilk had a quick diving tank known as 'Q' tank.

To further control her depth and attitude she had for'ard and after hydroplanes – horizontal rudders. The for'ard 'planes were used to regulate depth, the after 'planes to control the extent to which the vessel is bow down or bow up. No submarine is ever dived steeply – there is no point – to raise the stern bringing after hydroplanes, screws and rudders out of the water lessens the degree of control that can be exercised and does not speed downward descent.

For motive power the 'T'-class submarine had diesel engines to propel her on the surface at speeds between 7 and 16 knots; for submerged propulsion she had electric motors which gave speeds of from 1½ knots ('grouped down': electric motors in series) up to a maximum of 9 knots ('grouped up': with electric motors in parallel). The motors were powered by three batteries comprising a total of 336 'wet' cells, of which every cell weighed half a ton. The batteries had to be kept topped-up with water throughout any patrol. Leakage of sea water to the batteries had always to be avoided since this generated lethal chlorine gas. The energy provided by the batteries was by no means limitless. Fully charged it was enough for 1½ days cruising at about 2 knots or one *hour* at a top speed of 9 knots. Consequently after a brisk underwater chase and interception the 'T'-boat captain might find himself with very few amps left in the 'box'.

Wartime service in a 'T' boat was a particular strain on all the personnel involved. It was a life in which the constant contrast of boredom and monotony with excitement and fear, the remoteness, confinement, the foetid atmosphere in tropical waters, the danger and the discomfort made considerable demands on everyone's constitution. As well as resolution in fighting the common foe, the whole crew needed, in equal measure, the ability to get on with one another. Accommodation was so restricted that every inch of space had to be jealously husbanded. A curtain over the wardroom's low doorway was all that separated the officers from crew members passing for'ard and aft along the passageway outside the wardroom. Even a sliding door would have occupied too much space. The conditions in which they lived afforded little privacy to all save the captain who had a cabin to himself. The commanding officer's cabin was just under 6 ft by 6 ft, its volume was greatly reduced by the curvature of the pressure hull. In that space he had room for a wardrobe, desk, chair and bunk: it was his office as well as his bedroom. Though all might envy him the privilege, none would begrudge it.

The range of a 'T'-class boat at the time of the *Tally-Ho* Far Eastern cruise (after conversion of Nos. 3 and 5 main ballast tanks to carry fuel oil) had been increased from 6,900 miles to 11,000 miles. This was just as well as she was required to operate for four weeks in a patrol area 1,000 miles from her base in Ceylon.

Torpedoes

A 'T'-class boat carried five external 'dry' torpedo tubes, loaded before leaving port and thereafter inaccessible until fired by remote control. These were in addition to her original, designed, main armament of six internal tubes. These were 'wet' tubes, flooded before firing, loaded before any patrol and capable of being reloaded from inside the submarine; for which purpose six re-load torpedoes were carried. For maintenance the torpedoes had periodically to be 'pulled back' (withdrawn from their tubes) for the 'TI' (Torpedo Instructor or Torpedo Gunners' Mate) and his fore-ends team to do the 'routines' on them. The torpedoes, 21 in. in diameter and some 20 ft in length, were awkward to manhandle – each weighed 1½ tons – and quite valuable; in 1944 they were worth £2,500 each. In 1944 the 'T'-class boat began each patrol with seventeen torpedoes worth all of £42,500.

Torpedo Tube

The torpedo is fired from the tube by air impulse. If the air was allowed to follow the torpedo out of the tube a large bubble (discharge splash) would appear on the surface, giving away the position of the attacking submarine. This is overcome by the tube firing mechanism which cuts off the air impulse after the torpedo has been given its impetus but is still in the tube. An AIV (Automatic Inboard Vent) valve now opens allowing the air to come back into an open tank. The timing of the AIV valve being open also allows for the correct amount of water to come back with the air. This amount of water plus the water which fills the tube after the torpedo has left, compensates for the weight of the torpedo which has been fired, thus maintaining the trim of the boat.

Torpedo Firing

The torpedo in the tube is prevented from turning by side lugs which rest on the runners of the tube. A block of steel on top of the torpedo, called a top block, butts against the top stop which enters the tube and prevents the torpedo from moving forward. On the tube firing lever being pulled, the top stop is immediately lifted by air operation and the torpedo is free to move forward. On the torpedo being forced forward by air impulse, the air lever on the torpedo is knocked aft by the tripper on the tube. The air lever being knocked off, air from the air vessel in the torpedo is admitted to the engine, also to fuel bottle, gyro and steering mechanism and depth keeping mechanism. The engine turns with cold air at first, but after running off the number of revs set on the ignition delay gear, three hammers fall on three igniters located in the generator pocket attached to the induction ring of the engine, thus igniting the fuel/air gas mixture. The engine continues to run until the target is struck or until the range set on the torpedo is run off when the air is automatically shut off. The torpedo, having negative buoyancy, then sinks.

Attack Techniques

The choice of attack tactics was that of the commander of the submarine. The 'T'-class submarine usually fired her torpedoes at periscope depth, with her captain aiming them through the periscope; however, they could be, and were also frequently fired on the surface using a bridge mounted 'night-sight'. In addition to these two methods they could be fired, blind, using an Asdic* (now called 'sonar') firing bearing when below periscope depth or with periscope lowered.

The 'T' boat fired a 'hose-pipe salvo'. Most of her tubes were mounted for'ard and fixed facing for'ard. Torpedoes fired from the three sternward facing external tubes had a rudder adjustment so that they ran directly astern on firing. Thus, all torpedoes were fired in the same straight line. Hence the term 'hose-pipe salvo'. Early in the war experiments were made with a 'Ninety-bender' torpedo, designed to alter course 90° after firing but it did not prove satisfactory in service and was not generally adopted.

Director Angle

The degree of 'aim-off' that a submarine captain applied to allow for target speed was known as a director angle. It is that subtended between the track of the target vessel and that of the attacking submarine. The ideal director angle may be regarded as 90°. Acute director angles are referred to as 'fine': obtuse angles as 'broad'. (See diagram). A director angle was always specified Red or Green depending on whether it must be applied to port or starboard; e.g. a director angle of 30° Green or 30° to starboard.

Track Angle

The difference in bearing between target track and torpedo track, at the moment of firing, was known as a track angle. Whilst 90° was the ideal track angle; broad track angles (over 90°) and fine track angles (under 90°) were also used. A fine track angle was applicable where a captain was uncertain of an enemy's speed but had a good idea of the enemy's course. Conversely if a captain was uncertain of an enemy's course but did know the speed he might choose a broad track angle. Or he might well be obliged to use it to penetrate a destroyer screen.

It would have helped, of course, if an enemy being attacked

---

* From ASDIC: Anti-Submarine Defence Investigation Committee.

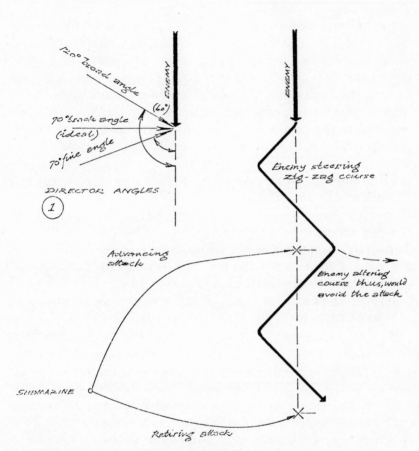

120° broad angle

(60°)

90° track angle
(ideal)

70° fine angle

ENEMY

DIRECTOR ANGLES

1

ENEMY

Enemy steering
zig-zag course

Advancing
attack

Enemy altering
course thus, would
avoid the attack

SUBMARINE

Retiring attack

2 TWO FORMS OF ATTACK ON A ZIG-ZAGGING TARGET
(Nowadays called 'a simulator')

would always steer a dead straight line on a constant heading: most enemies realised this and zig-zagged if there was any chance of their being attacked. Depending on circumstances, when attacking a zig-zagging opponent one may approach directly with an advancing attack or indirectly with a retiring attack. The presence of escorting vessels might materially effect the choice of tactics.

Advancing Attack

This offers the quickest means of getting to grips with the enemy. It is readily suitable for choppy conditions when a periscope's feather may be inconspicuous amongst wave crests, white horses and their following troughs. It provides a method of quickly getting through a destroyer screen if, for example, one is encountered ahead of a target vessel or convoy. During its penetration of the screen the submarine will probably present only its smallest end-on aspect.

Retiring Attack

This offers a more leisurely approach and might well be more appropriate when approaching an unescorted target or manoeuvring to outflank a destroyer escort.

In making a periscope observation it was always prudent for the submarine captain to raise his periscope only when proceeding at slow speed. If a vessel is moving at speed the periscope wake or 'feather' is always larger and more conspicuous. When manoeuvering to a firing position the captain of any Second World War submarine had also to allow for a time lapse of about 1 knot per minute when he wanted to increase speed and a somewhat more pronounced 'coast-on' effect when reducing way.

Whether his attack was successful or not the submarine captain could usually expect an enemy counter-attack. There is no record of any submarine captain in the Royal Navy being deterred by this prospect.

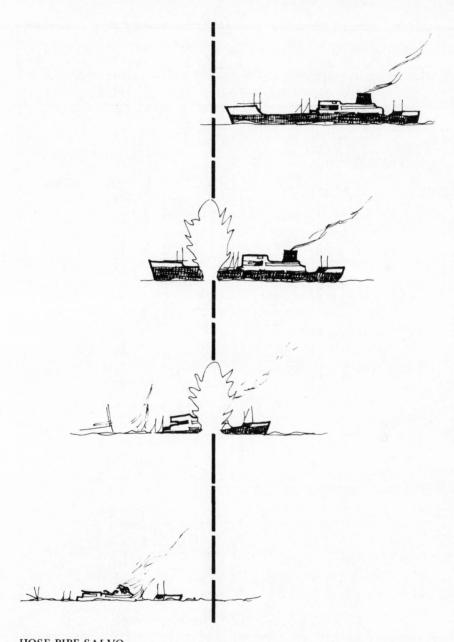

HOSE-PIPE SALVO
All four torpedoes are fired on the same line: it is the target vessel's movement that spaces them out.

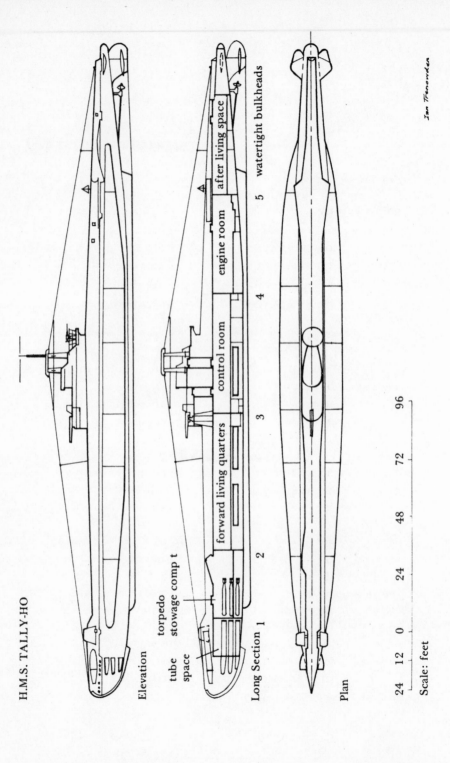

H.M.S. TALLY-HO

Elevation

torpedo
stowage comp t
space

tube
space

Long Section 1

Plan

forward living quarters

control room

engine room

after living space

watertight bulkheads

1   2   3   4   5

Scale: feet

24 12 0   24   48   72   96

Ian Frenawden

First Blood

Tally-Ho slipped and proceeded from Colombo at 1730 on Tuesday 26 October 1943 on her first war patrol in the Far East. She was almost brand new: her first commission being barely 230 days old. Just long enough, in fact, for her to have 'worked up' in home waters after completion and for her passage to the Far East.

As her slim bows nosed from her berth, the sun was already low in the sky. Even so, the heat seemed to shimmer up from the water and from the metal deck plating of her bridge. Bennington, the captain, was on the bridge as she left port, as was usual. He wore an oldish, peaked cap — retained solely for watch-keeping — which afforded some shade for his eyes at this crucial moment of clearing the harbour jetty.

The bridge breastwork on which he leaned — carefully, for it paid to avoid those parts which would have become most heated under the noonday sun — was not armoured. Large areas of it, of necessity, were brass to avoid interference with 'Faithful Fred', the ship's magnetic compass; Bennington had no illusions that they would stop even certain calibres of bullet which were being used in that theatre. This did not worry him: he fully intended to do his most important fighting submerged.

From where he stood he could readily perceive the humps and bulges which spoiled the symmetry of the casing that ran the length of the submarine and which, inevitably, must detract from her performance submerged. Their presence was due to the installation of the extra, external torpedo tubes which had been added to the 'T'-class boat since the prewar design. Thirteen of these boats had been laid down before the war; less than half had survived and were still afloat at that time. The present version (built by Vickers Armstrong Ltd at Barrow) was, admittedly, uglier and somewhat slower than the original had been, but it packed a harder punch. Eleven torpedo tubes, with a possible six reloads, gave a formidable total of seventeen torpedoes expendable during her three-week patrol period.

Tally-Ho and her silhouette had further suffered by the addition of a circular 'bandstand' platform just abaft of her conning-tower. This was to take the mounting for a 20mm-calibre Oerlikon cannon, the addition of which was becoming a standard modification to all submarines at that stage of the war. The Oerlikon was one of the, then, latest automatic weapons and was currently enjoying great success on surface vessels against both air and surface attacks. With the 4-in. gun (quick firing, semi-automatic Mark III), mounted inside a swivelling shield on the gun sponson just for'ard of the conning-tower, the Oerlikon completed the submarine's surface defensive and offensive armament. The 4-in. gun's design was virtually unchanged from that which had fired the first shot of the 1914-1918 war, on board the destroyer HMS *Lance* on 5 August 1914. It was something of a contrast, with its heavy solidarity, to the almost elegant, slim-barrelled Oerlikon cannon. Even so it was a proven weapon, and, with the tactical advantage of surprise – always a submarine's prerogative – allied to a well trained crew, it could be a devastating one.

None the less, the submarine's silhouette still retained a certain wicked grace, which the overall, matt, slime green, camouflage paint – usual for that theatre – might impair though not eliminate. The paintwork was as yet unmarked. Although, in her service to date, *Tally-Ho* had travelled as far north as the Arctic Circle, and as far south as her present position, she had still to see action, and her captain was determined she should find it; no matter how long it took.

The captain, Leslie William Abel Bennington, was thirty-one years old and had been promoted Lieutenant-Commander on the passage out to Ceylon from Aden. He held the Distinguished Service Order and Distinguished Service Cross, both gained in submarine service since 1939. His first posting to submarines had been in 1934 so that he had seen considerable service in submarines by the time the war started. His left hand, now resting on the bridge coaming in front of him, bore witness to that service. An accident with a periscope wire, way back before the war, had permanently deformed the nail of the third finger; resulting in a slight convexity of profile and a rather horny appearance. Beyond being somewhat difficult to trim, it had given him no particular trouble.

Bennington was a little above average height, his head frequently bent forward in the slightest of stoops. He was of slim frame, his face lean, composed and clean-shaven, even a trifle drawn. On the whole he had the appearance of a scholar or a cleric — which belied the man of action. He was darkly tanned — no one who served out here could avoid that. His tropical kit of shorts and singlet revealed a wiriness of leg and arm which had stood him in good stead on playing fields. He had played hockey for the fleet and before the war had captained the Mediterranean Fleet soccer team. All his actions were marked by a decisive quickness of movement.

Beyond an occasional steering order to the helmsman, Bennington did not speak. He was not given to talkativeness, and spoke neither of his home nor his back-ground. So that it was not widely known that he had joined the Royal Navy some 16 years before, as a boy seaman, just prior to his sixteenth birthday.

This was a background frankly unusual for 'the Trade', as the Submarine Branch was known to the rest of the Royal Navy. It was characteristic of Bennington that he chose to keep silent about his beginnings in the Service; many a lesser man might have chosen to capitalise on the uniqueness of his selection. Unique, certainly, it had been. On 1 September 1933, Able Seaman Bennington, acting Leading Torpedo Operator, had been promoted to acting Sub-Lieutenant. Only six others from the entire naval division had been so treated.

The peacetime Submarine Branch had been even more tightly knit than the rest of the Royal Navy. This meant that Bennington had known well, as friends, the majority of submarine commanders and officers who had already been lost in action, to say nothing of those who had perished in a rare, prewar submarine accident. Bennington's first submarine service, after the initial course, had been in L69 ('commanded by Lieutenant-Commander Guy Howard Bolus RN, who lost his life while in command of the *Thetis* which sank on diving trials on 1 June 1939). The shock to the British nation was the greater for the tragedy occurring in peacetime and when the international situation was giving rise to uneasy speculation.

When war began, Bennington was serving in *Swordfish* under Lieutenant Cecil Bernard Crouch RN, whose war service earned him the DSO and bar. Crouch went on to command the salvaged and recommissioned *Thetis*, renamed *Thunderbolt*, and died when that ill-fated boat was lost in the Mediterranean.

Far too many of Bennington's peacetime friends and brother officers of the Submarine Branch had been lost. It wasn't good to brood upon such things. Nor, perhaps, was it good to brood on the immediate prospect of the patrol ahead.

From Ceylon *Tally-Ho* would be operating in Japanese-held waters along the Malacca Strait and around its many islands. In that area where shallow waters made submarine operations particularly difficult, it seemed that the shallowest were where targets could most likely be expected.

To Bennington, after his experience in the Mediterranean, it was going to be interesting to discover what technique proved most effective in these, to him unfamiliar, waters. The Mediterranean was well charted; these waters were not. In the Mediterranean the Axis forces had enjoyed air superiority and submarine captains had been forced to rely on a technique of waiting submerged outside their harbour bases for a target to appear. In his fourth year of war Bennington felt he knew the ways of the Germans and Italians fairly well. But now *Tally-Ho* was off to face not only unknown seaways but also to face an unknown foe. He knew relatively little about the Japanese. Rumour had it that they were ruthless and wily adversaries. Most of this, however, was speculation.

The intelligence reports that he'd read were less likely to contain speculation. They had simply, and baldly stated that Japanese warships would be considered overcrowded by Royal Navy standards and that the living conditions were harsh as well as uncomfortable. Japanese crews could be expected to be tough, well accustomed to battle and probably resolute foes. Whether they would be more cunning than Germans or Italians, as submarine hunters, remained to be seen.

One thing was certain in Bennington's mind: there could be no surrender to the Japanese. Their reputation for speeding opponents to the next world by summary decapitation was already firmly established. So that he'd had no qualms about securing the submarine's escape hatches from the *outside* with salvage clips. This had been one of the modifications carried out in Port Said, where they'd stopped for a brief period of acclimatization on their passage out to Ceylon.

Many submarine captains had done the same thing in the Mediterranean where the extreme depths to be encountered precluded escape by DSEA (Davis Submerged Escape Apparatus). There had been one or two cases of submarine escape hatches lifting under depth-charge attacks in the Mediterranean. It had happened to *Porpoise* once, off Crete. The attacks had started at breakfast time on 19 August 1942, and Bennington and his crew had been on the receiving end of over 100 depth-charges during that patrol. When the first one had exploded, Bennington had seen a tea cup, on the control room floor beside him, rise two feet and smash in mid air. The attacks had gone on for hours. When they ended the battery cells had been cracked, leaking electrolyte and releasing choking fumes. When *Porpoise* had surfaced, after being down for nearly seventeen hours, her whole crew had been breathless, lethargic and on the point of vomiting. The stock of distilled water, carried for battery topping up, had almost completely been used up in damping down the batteries. The battery tanks had been filled with smoke. Topping up the batteries, through the access hatches, had been a frightful job involving moving all the furniture in several messes. They'd been lucky to get away with it.

At the height of the attack the fore hatch had lifted after a particularly near explosion, and much water had been taken on board. This had been despite the efforts of the 'TI', stalwart Joe Brighton, and the fore-ends crew, who'd immediately fought to get the hatch reseated and the clips replaced. Even with their efforts, which had been prompt, it had been a near thing. And once *Porpoise* had surfaced, their troubles had been far from over. They were in an area known as 'bomb alley', could not submerge, and were three hundred miles from a friendly port. They'd have been hard put to make it had air cover and a surface escort not been available. Bennington was not going to take the same risk again.

Not that he was suicidally inclined. He'd made sure his crew were in no doubt on that point. Having cleared the lower deck he'd addressed his assembled officers and ratings and explained that he was determined to survive; also that he was convinced that the best way to do it was with the escape hatches secured. There had been no arguments: no captain can decide a wartime submarine's policy by committee. He didn't find it strange that he should take it on himself to decide such things for the whole crew nor that they should accept his judgement.

Having secured the escape hatches there had been no point in retaining all the DSEA sets. Regulations had required that one third spares be carried in addition to a set for every member of the crew. Accordingly they'd discarded eighty-two which were now stacked in the First Lieutenant's cabin aboard the depot ship, together with their steel storage boxes, their safety seals still intact, leaving no room for the First Lieutenant. Six sets only had been retained for shallow diving purposes. They might come in handy for freeing a fouled screw or inspecting parts of the hull below the water line.

To be taken prisoner from a submarine was rare but not unprecedented[1] and Bennington was determined that he would never go 'into the bag'.

There had been internal modifications to the *Tally-Ho* in Port Said. Bedding had been dumped and camp beds had been embarked. They were a considerable success; they exactly fitted the bunks and allowed for air circulation around the sleeper's

---

[1] It had happened to one of Bennington's close friends. Lieutenant-Commander Peter Noel Buckley RN, in command of *Shark*, had been patrolling north of Stavanger on 5 July 1940 in a region where there was virtually no dark period in the whole twenty-four hours. Caught on the surface charging batteries, he was repeatedly attacked — in the first ever series of attacks when aircraft dropped depth-charges — and *Shark* became crippled and unable to dive. The attacks continued, but only after bringing down one aircraft and when all her crew were wounded and all her ammunition expended did *Shark* reluctantly prepare to scuttle. After the Germans had embarked her crew in a trawler the gallant vessel foundered when her captors attempted to take her in tow.

body. There had also been Engineer Officer Scott-Maxwell's modification of Nos. 3 and 5 external ballast tanks to carry extra fuel oil. Scott-Maxwell had been enthusiastic when Bennington had suggested this. Scott-Maxwell was a Temporary Lieutenant (E) RN. Prewar he'd trained as a marine engineer, and had enlisted in the RNVR in the first week of the war. Consequently Bennington's views on the Royal Navy and his own were probably diametrically opposed. For Bennington, the Navy had been the whole of his adult life. For Scott-Maxwell it was the way of fighting the war. Nor did the contrasts end there. Scott-Maxwell came from a landed family in Scotland. Bennington had grown up near Poole Harbour in Dorset: his family was not rich. From such beginnings had Bennington's love of sailing and flair for seamanship derived as had his preference for small boats as opposed to men-of-war: one point, of course, on which Scott-Maxwell thoroughly agreed with him. Despite the differences of background and temperament the two got on well together. They thought alike on most fundamentals and were prepared to respect one another's points of view on details.

The task of modifying the ballast tanks had provided Scott-Maxwell with a creative engineering task; something which had been lacking from the day-to-day duties of a submarine engineer officer. The modifications, duly completed, proved highly successful. One thing only had been lacking — official approval. Admiralty disapproval had been strongly voiced and most eloquently. The additional fuel oil was for use on passage to the patrol area. Once arrived at the 'billet', as they called it, the remaining fuel in the tanks could be flushed out and the oil replaced by sea water. Of course, the oil in the ballast tanks might mean the vessel initially trimmed low on the surface and lost something of her mobility. Bennington, however, was quite satisfied that this last, slight disadvantage could be overcome by seamanship. For the duration of patrol required in this theatre, the modification seemed only common sense. Eventually this belief would be ratified by official conversions to other boats.

In the Mediterranean the patrol duration had been three weeks. Out here, it was generally longer. Passage to and from the patrol areas alone involved sailing over 1,000 miles each way. Even that

c

was pretty normal by Mediterranean standards, boats operating from Alexandria or Beirut, around Malta or up into the Aegean must have done at least that. The German boats which were said to be operating from Penang had probably come out from Germany round Africa. That meant they would be about 10,000 miles from home base. Bennington didn't mind admitting that the German submarines operating from Penang were of particular interest to him. Sinking German U-boats out here would be every bit as useful as sinking them anywhere else.

Bennington passed the order to go from harbour stations to passage routine, and the special sea-duty men mustered on the casing went below. The helmsman went below and steering of *Tally-Ho* proceeded from the control room helm position. Bennington increased the bridge look-outs to four. This meant every man had to watch only a 90° quadrant of the horizon. Bennington was an individualist in his policy regarding look-outs. He'd have anyone on the bridge for this duty if suited for it, regardless of age or duty normally undertaken. 'Chiefy' Powell was a case in point: as Chief Engine Room Artificer, his position was in the engine room. As one of the oldest men on board – almost Bennington's age – he could hardly be expected to have the eyesight of a twenty-year-old. Bennington, however, was right: Chief ERA Powell had exactly the degree of application look-out duty required. He often saw what younger men missed, and he welcomed the chance to be on the bridge, a chance he'd not had under previous captains.

Powell's ability as a look-out did not surprise Bennington. He'd remarked a similar ability in himself: he sometimes saw aircraft, masts over the horizon or other vessels before any of his look-outs. Woe betide them when he did! It was their job not the captain's. But he was shrewd enough to realise that the reason his observation was so acute was because he understood the importance of vigilance. It was not just a question of good eyesight – although he seldom met people who could see better than he – it was rather a question of knowing *why* one *must* see. It was like periscope duty: one had to be quick but thorough. To stop, refocus and ponder during an 'all round look' – a 360° sweep – increased the possibility of others seeing one's periscope or its attendant 'feather'.

An hour after leaving harbour *Tally-Ho* was near the end of the swept channel in the harbour approaches. The briefest possible exchange of signals ensued and the escorting trawler took her leave. There was always a risk of mines laid by marauding enemy submarines here and it paid to follow the trawler carefully and not stray. At this point Bennington gave the order 'Open up for diving'. This meant a lengthy and complex procedure whereby the First Lieutenant and the Outside ERA went right through the boat and checked everything possible that would be involved in the diving process: vents, hydroplanes, cotters and their removal: the works! After that a dive in slow time would follow to catch the trim.

The exercise had purpose; it was so thorough it did not have to be repeated often. Number One, the First Lieutenant, was responsible for trim; the 'Outside Wrecker', as that particular ERA was called was responsible for all machinery apart from the engine room and torpedo tubes. Fine adjustments to be certain of catching the essential trim if one submerged suddenly were all-important. A submarine's best tactical advantage lay in its ability to attack submerged: that was the chief principle in submarine warfare. Submergance to avoid pursuit was entirely secondary. Few people outside the Submarine Branch, in Bennington's experience, seemed capable of understanding such niceties.

Tally-Ho proceeded smoothly on the surface, having successfully completed her trim dive; there would be plenty of time to submerge later, hundreds of miles nearer to enemy territory. In the meanwhile it paid to cover the passage route as quickly as possible and cut down the time until coming to grips with the enemy.

Bennington found his thoughts turning again to the German submarine crews operating from Penang. The submarine base there had been constructed by the Japanese assisted by German naval personnel. The Germans would be from various merchant cruisers and from blockade runners. The German U-boat crews, it was said, lived in comparative comfort in local schools and hotels requisitioned for the purpose. Between patrols they would spend weeks in convalescent quarters in the cool of the hills. Bennington did not know it but, at this time, Penang never having suffered an attack, the German boats lay in unprotected berths at Swettenham Pier.

For victualling the German boats a modern and well-equipped factory had been provided. It was necessary, since it was virtually impossible for Europeans to exist on the provisions supplied to Japanese U-boats. The factory turned out essential preserves such as tinned bread, pressed meat, vegetables and fruit. So sure of their invulnerability in Penang were the Germans and Japanese that there was virtually no anti-submarine organisation or appropriate vessels around Penang. No wonder Allied High Command wanted submarine patrols in the Malacca Strait. The prime objective of such patrols was attacks on the extended enemy shipping supply routes for carrying food, fuel oil and aviation spirit to Japanese forces in Burma. In addition British submarines operating from Ceylon were able to strike at enemy warships and naval bases in the Malacca Strait — for a time they were the only part of the British Far Eastern Fleet able to do so. Bennington was instructed to concentrate on the destruction of supply ships unless tactical movement of warships was expected. In that case the priority was for the destruction of destroyers or anything bigger. Warships escorting shipping, however, could be attacked, depending on the circumstances. In addition to these provisos enemy submarines could be attacked, 'provided their hostile character' could be established 'beyond reasonable doubt'. It was a neat turn of phrase and, in these waters, not too difficult to put into action. In this area warnings were transmitted where our own and other submarines would be operating — this was a little different from the way things had sometimes been in the Mediterranean; here one never knew whether a submarine was in fact a U-boat. Therefore, in view of the flexibility of Admiralty instructions, U-boats were by no means excluded as prime targets.

Early in the war Winston Churchill had declared that the word 'submarine' might only be used to describe British and Allied craft. All enemy submersibles, therefore, by 1941, be they German, Italian or Japanese were 'U-boats'. The order had the authentic Churchill stamp about it: it allowed for no compromise and so one was glad to accept it.

The first excitement of the patrol occurred quite early

on – later the first day, to be precise. Not for nothing would
Bennington write in his patrol report:

This patrol was the most exciting the Commanding Officer
has ever done.

Just before sundown, as they were proceeding on the surface,
one of the for'ard look-outs suddenly glimpsed movement in his
field of vision. The drill was for a look-out to sweep the horizon of
his allocated quadrant, using its line as a datum to neatly bisect
the lenses of his glasses. In these latitudes there was a compli-
cation; seldom was there a distinct horizon. The look-out had also
to scan the sky. For sky search the glasses were of no use: it took
too long to focus on the moving speck of an aircraft. In any case it
was usual to dive if any aircraft were spotted. That lesson had
been learned early in the war – and had been neatly summed up
by one British submarine captain who had signalled his estimated
time of arrival to his base, with the following proviso: 'Friendly
aircraft permitting!' As well as the horizon and sky the look-out's
responsibility included the surrounding sea in the foreground.

So it was that a movement glimpsed from the corner of his eye
caused the look-out to turn and focus his glasses. Rapid though
the reflex was, Bennington's action was quicker. Pausing only to
shout the order 'Dive!' he closed the cock to shut off the
voice-pipe. In the briefest of pauses all four look-outs disappeared
below. A man didn't climb down the conning-tower ladder in the
accepted sense. He simply gripped the ladder's sides and went
down in a controlled slide, using his hold on the ladder's vertical
sides to control the speed of descent. Bennington did not hurry to
the same extent. By his standards there was plenty of time.
Although the opened vents of the main ballast tanks were already
noisily fountaining up spray like a whale's out-blowings, *Tally-Ho*
would still have a good forty seconds before she submerged.
Bennington had glimpsed what he thought was a torpedo
track – it certainly looked very much like one – but of far greater
urgency was what appeared to be an aircraft approaching in the far
distance. He would never dive on a suspected torpedo alert (an
unimpaired view was essential at such a time) but one didn't
quibble about aircraft, one immediately acted. A last glance before
going below indicated that the torpedo – if torpedo it had

been — had failed to run true. With the water already lapping the sides of the conning-tower, Bennington closed the upper hatch over his head, forced on the clips and rammed home the pins.

The habit gained during ten years in submarines persisted; Bennington was careful to complete the drill and sing out the accustomed litany. 'One clip on, both clips on; one pin in, both pins in.' Failure to do that could result in the crew below shutting the lower hatch — that was their duty — and one would be left in the conning-tower, between the two hatches, to drown. That would never happen in *Tally-Ho* whilst Bennington was alive. In 1940 a submarine had been strafed by a German aircraft and the captain killed by machine-gun fire. With his body blocking the upper hatch the submarine had been unable to dive.

Below a practised routine was put in operation when Bennington initiated the diving signal. The first man down the tower pressed the klaxon twice; a single blast would have been ignored. The twin klazon sound summoned the crew from 'patrol routine' to diving stations. At patrol routine only one third of the crew were on duty, the crew being divided into three watches traditionally referred to as 'Red, White and Blue'. At 'diving stations', however, every member of the ship's company had a duty. The Coxswain was at the after hydroplanes, controlling depth; 'Simmo' the Second Coxswain was on the fore 'planes; the First Lieutenant would be by the blowing and venting panel, his eye on the trim. In a submarine diving stations is also 'action stations'. (Indeed, much later on when they were rammed, Bennington, with no intention of diving, brought everyone to action stations. Had he dived he knew they were all done for.)

Bennington made it a habit always to dive on the klaxon. Except, of course, for the rare occasions, like just after leaving Ceylon when they had opened up for diving and gone down in slow time. That had served its purpose. Because of that Bennington had no doubt that when he gave the order the Outside ERA would be set to open the vents of the main ballast tanks and they'd go down without any fumbling. Because of that, too, the 'planesman had neatly caught the trim just below periscope depth, as 'Q' tank was blown.

So now *Tally-Ho* submerged in double quick time. (One resists the temptation to call it a 'crash dive'. This is purely a journalistic expression. One dive is the same as any other.) 'Periscope depth!' Bennington snapped immediately afterwards, acting in the knowledge that a submarine's best offensive is submergence. Bennington used the periscope to make a quick sweep of the horizon. His 'all round look' revealed no sign of any enemy; on the sea or in the sky.

Bennington was interested to know whether the Asdic operator had picked up any hydrophone effect ('HE' as it was called). From its characteristics could be ascertained the vessel's type of engine, be it reciprocating or whatever. Good at the job though George Backman was, he could hear nothing. 'Set's not on the blink, is it?' queried one of his shipmates. George simply gesticulated for silence without replying; he had to listen. In any case, a set likely to be unserviceable would not be his. The suggestion was virtually an insult.

George Backman's expertise failed to produce any Asdic indication of an adversary's whereabouts. As the search proceeded, Bennington was thoughtful. He had been wondering how near to Colombo the enemy's submarines operated. The suspected attack appeared to give a fair indication of this. As soon as he was certain that the Asdic search was fruitless he gave the order to stand down from diving stations and go to 'watch diving'.

Surprisingly two further torpedo alerts occurred on the outward passage to the patrol area on 1 and 3 November respectively. Once out of sight of Great Nicobar Island *Tally-Ho* proceeded on the surface. The Nicobars had been occupied by the Japanese since early 1942, and one took no risks of compromising the secrecy of an offensive patrol. *Tally-Ho* proceeded southwards down the Malacca Strait making for Penang. As she neared the busier enemy shipping lanes Bennington was careful to surface only at night. It was at night, with the moon scarcely visible, that *Tally-Ho* first approached Penang, North Entrance.

Bennington had taught himself to sleep on the bridge at night. He'd begun this policy in *Porpoise*, in the Mediterranean. It hadn't been easy: it demanded an unusually high degree of fortitude. 'Sleeping' was perhaps an overstatement. Frequently at night it was necessary, tactically, to zig-zag on a continuous wheel. This meant that every so often the night stars would whirl drunkenly above one's head as the heavens switched their orientation every time the helmsman put the wheel down. It paid dividends, however, for each time the officer of the watch breathed the words 'Captain, sir' he was not only on the bridge but his eyes were already attuned to night vision. Apart from passing discomfort and appalling retrospective backache, he felt it was well worth the trouble involved.

In the early hours of 2 November *Tally-Ho* had first approached Penang, North Entrance. 'Captain, sir. Lots of small lights ahead.' Bennington was on his feet in seconds. Ignoring the officer of the watch's suggestion to dive quietly without the klaxon, he decided to move in closer and see what went on. Disappointment awaited him: the lights were those of fishing boats. Bennington was reminded of the early Biscay patrols in 1940: fishing boats had been a nuisance then. Here, however, the boats were smaller — many of them open boats, like skiffs. A number of them showed no lights at all. Those that did carried only a single white light. Reflecting that it must be a hell of a way to make a living, Bennington altered course away slightly, in the direction of Sumatra. The unlit boats had been perilously difficult to see and avoid; had *Tally-Ho* blundered in among them the balloon would have gone up and a week's careful passage from Colombo been wasted.

Bennington made it his practice never to complain, no matter how many times the officer of the watch disturbed him at night. There could be no comfort in being allowed to slumber on — and be sunk the one time that the officer of the watch elected not to trouble the captain.

Tally-Ho remained outside the North Entrance to Penang Harbour the whole of that day and the next, submerged at periscope depth. On the first day nothing of interest was sighted. Bennington was convinced if he waited long enough his patience would be rewarded. The following day a 300-ton Japanese submarine chaser appeared on patrol. Bennington shadowed her carefully; she had, it appeared a set routine. She would remain stopped in one position for up to two hours, apparently listening. Then she would shift position — not more than about two miles — and resume her listening watch. As no Asdic transmissions were picked up during her stopped periods, she must have been listening on hydrophones. At one time she was only 600 yards away from *Tally-Ho* but failed to make contact. Bennington was pleased because, to him, it suggested sloppy training and ill prepared anti-submarine defence at Penang.

At 1735 the same day, the officer of the watch, carrying out a periscope watch, reported a small object close inshore. Bennington took over the after search periscope. The object, difficult to identify against the thickly wooded shore, might be a U-boat. 'Reciprocating engine, sir,' came the Asdic operator's report. 'Can't hold her I'm afraid: too many water noises inshore.' Undeterred Bennington tried to work round to the enemy's starboard side to deliver an attack. This meant moving seawards, away from Penang. After an hour's stealthy manoeuvring Bennington was able to get a clearer view of his quarry. It was a large trawler. Bennington speculated that her sudden appearance, coast crawling, was probably connected with some movement to the south of Pulau Kendi Island.

Again there was nothing to do but wait upon events. The night passed slowly and the whole of the following day. The monotony was relieved only by the sighting of a small merchant vessel in the afternoon. She was only 150-200 tons and therefore not worth a torpedo. Bennington broke off his pursuit intending to regain contact after dark and sink the vessel by gunfire: if a dozen 4-in shells would put paid to it, why waste torpedoes?

An hour later came a sighting which put out of mind the little piddling coastal freighter; only 2,400 yards away and broadside on was a German U-boat. It seemed too good to be true. The silhouette was unmistakeable, fine and clear-cut: had it appeared an hour later there would have been insufficient light for a periscope attack. Seven minutes after first sighting her, Bennington fired five torpedoes without a single hit. It seemed unbelievable. He had lowered the periscope directly on firing and turned to receive the Asdic report that his torpedoes were running true. Then, astonishingly, in silent disbelief he heard a report he'd never received before: 'One coming back, Sir!'. There was barely time for angry speculation on why £2,500-worth of valuable war material had suddenly acquired a will of its own and gone 'rogue'. There wasn't even time to go deep. With anxious care George Backman followed the torpedo's position by Asdic, as it passed along the port side of *Tally-Ho*. For what to him was an eternity it seemed impossible that it would not hit.

For Joe Brighton, Torpedo Gunners' Mate, the moments were doubly agonising. He and his fore-ends crew had prepared that torpedo, done regular routines on it, lubricated its internal mechanism with special oils, greased its exterior and humped its one-and-a-half tons weight about the 'tube space. Finally they'd loaded it, in good faith, and now this. . . . He looked around him, the other members of the fore-ends crew, Glanville, Charnock, Ianto Griffiths, Fulford and Boy Seaman Medhurst were all thinking similar thoughts. Joe knew the work had been done well, there was no reasonable explanation for the fiasco. Bennington neither asked questions nor complained. Naked, except for khaki shorts, in the control room's stifling heat he ordered the periscope to be raised; post mortems could wait[1]; there were more important things on hand.

The U-boat's behaviour also proved vexatious. She remained on the surface and was swiftly swallowed up in the gathering gloom. Inevitably, the submarine chaser appeared again, and *Tally-Ho* took instant evasive action. This ended further attempts to trace the U-boat. Ironically, it turned out to be the only clear night of the patrol with, later on, a full moon high in a westerly sky. Despite an unabating watch nothing was sighted.

The following day dawned gloomily with torrential rain. The submarine chaser reappeared. Today it seemed more purposeful in its movements. After the first hour of its search, it was stationary on *Tally-Ho*'s port quarter, only 300-400 yards away. Then came an alteration of course towards the submarine. Bennington countered this move by going to a depth of 70 feet and edging

[1] Questioned by the author, Bennington explained: 'We had torpedo gyro failures on several occasions when we were chased by our own torpedoes. In one instance we had hit a ship . . . our torpedo, a "rogue" came back at us and passed very close. . . . Roughly speaking, the fault was due to a friction plate not operating properly.' He indicated with his hands how a car's clutch plates engage. 'It was a new type of air blast gyro. . . . We never had that sort of trouble in the Med.'

away at slow speed with both motors grouped down. After ten minutes two patterns, each of four depth-charges, rained down. They were not particularly accurate; just close enough to break the glass of one of the depth gauges. Two further patterns followed, their accuracy rapidly falling off. *Tally-Ho* moved away, but only far enough to break contact and be out of range. Bennington found himself thinking that these Japs were, perhaps, not too bright: he would have never escaped so lightly from the Germans or Italians, in the Mediterranean.

All in all, his first impression of the Penang anti-submarine organisation seemed most encouraging. There had been no evidence of shore mounted hydrophones or searchlights nor yet of radar. Impudently he brought *Tally-Ho* to periscope depth to check on the submarine chaser's position. She was a mere 3,000 yards away, lying stopped, and, he suspected baffled. He'd have dearly loved to send her to the bottom with a single torpedo but five had already been wasted and as a target she didn't justify even one.

Again *Tally-Ho* waited. Barely sixty-five minutes later she was chasing a 1,500-ton merchant ship along the ten-fathom line close inshore. The sight of a float plane, a German Arado 15, from Penang had attracted Bennington's attention and at once suggested that it might be escorting a merchant ship while no doubt searching for him. The news of an enemy submarine's presence would, of course, be being broadcast from Penang. That didn't worry Bennington: what did upset him was the fact that she was too close inshore for him to mount an attack. Slowly – and infuriatingly – she slipped out of his range and into Penang Harbour.

An hour later he fired two torpedoes at another merchant ship. This time he closed the range to 700 yards hoping to overcome the torpedo faults. Again two misses, both due to faulty torpedo running.

Joe Brighton couldn't help thinking that perhaps this wasn't his place. Bennington obligingly moved the patrol up north towards Butang, in the hope of getting a second chance to attack the larger vessel should she put out from Penang. He had to admit that, by now, the Japanese must be too well aware of his presence for him to expect another target close to Penang.

Two days later, on Wednesday, 10 November 1943, at 0525 he sighted smoke. Confusing mirage conditions were then occurring and it was nearly an hour before he was convinced that it was the freighter of two days before. He decided to keep *Tally-Ho* on the surface although it increased the risk. In such tricky light conditions he reckoned a periscope depth attack was probably out of the question. As soon as the enemy was within 2,500 yards range he fired two torpedoes, spread over two ships' lengths. He dived after firing and two minutes later there were two explosions. Through the periscope he saw the second one blow the target to pieces just before the Asdic operator's cry, 'One coming back, sir'. There was nothing for it but to dive deep to safety. On rising to periscope depth he saw smoke and burning oil on the surface and smoke – still visible two hours later. There could be no doubt about this, the first confirmed sinking by *Tally-Ho*.

No one knew it then, of course, but the enemy freighter was the *Kisogawa Maru* (1,914 tons), a water tanker converted to carry fuel oil. Now *Tally-Ho* could make for home knowing something had been achieved. Even Joe Brighton cheered up though the torpedo failures were still worrying him.

On the return passage, at 0118 on Friday, 12 November, Bennington was wakened when a vessel steering an opposing course was sighted. A slight alteration of course put *Tally-Ho* in a position where she presented only the smallest silhouette to her potential adversary. Certainly the strange vessel didn't seem very big, she looked rather like a jolly little Canterbury-class cross-Channel packet. There was something jogging around in her wake. Closer examination revealed a Japanese destroyer escorting a U-boat. *Tally-Ho* manoeuvred to within 5,000 yards range trying to get into an attacking position, using the heavy rain clouds in the far distance as a background.

Suddenly the destroyer altered course towards *Tally-Ho* and switched on a red masthead light. 'My God,' said Bennington, 'I do believe she's going to signal us. Yeoman to the bridge.' Ginger Facer hurried to the bridge and decoded the following signal 'G, XE, NR'. There seemed no point in hazarding an answer. The next developments are best described in Bennington's own words:

Tally-Ho altered course away and increased speed and pretended to be a small cloud. The escort declined to accept this and gave chase.

Reluctantly Bennington gave the order to dive and *Tally-Ho* went to 200 feet but received no depth-charges. While visibility had been good enough for a surface attack, it was too poor for one at periscope depth. Bennington was tempted to return towards his Penang patrol area and dive ahead of the U-boat. That way he'd probably make certain of her in a close-range attack. But this would have meant taking a chance. The British submarine *Taurus* would be entering the area in scarcely an hour from that time, and unless he could contact her by wireless telegraphy, *Taurus* would assume *Tally-Ho* to be hostile. Bennington decided not to stay

Later that day, proceeding homewards, *Tally-Ho* sighted another U-boat. Again it was surfaced; again Bennington gave chase at periscope depth but lost his quarry when it disappeared at speed in a cloud of exhaust smoke.* The incident reminded Bennington of the abortive U-boat sightings during her Biscay patrol on passage from England to Gibraltar. At all events the passage to the Far East seemed to have been worthwhile. Given reliable torpedoes *Tally-Ho* could be effectively used out here — if only every patrol were like this one!

The torpedoes were later investigated. Those still unfired were examined and found to be defective. Poor depot ship maintenance was the cause. Joe Brighton was completely exonerated; which was no surprise to Bennington who knew his TI was careful, methodical and experienced in his job. Bennington had ascertained the full facts from Joe, put them in his report and, as a good captain, backed Joe up to the hilt. He had also suggested ways in which similar trouble might be avoided on future patrols. One of the snags arose from the fact that torpedoes were frequently embarked whilst a submarine's Torpedo Gunner's Mate was absent on patrol leave. The depot ship torpedo staff, therefore, would complete the first routines on the torpedoes. If these were not properly carried out not even Joe's regular care and routine could ensure satisfactory results. The problem needed very careful appraisal. Basically like miniature submarines, torpedoes are

* The U-boat, *Tally-Ho* attacked, was almost certainly *U-178* (Kaplt Wilhelm Spahr) her logbook records seeing a torpedo track astern at that date and time. *Information from Karl-Heinz Wiebe her Engineer Officer.*

complex mechanisms having many complex parts. Climatic conditions played hell with the viscosity of the special lubricating oils.[1]

Tally-Ho was back at Colombo Harbour on 17 November, secured to the depot ship *Wuchang*. Conditions on the trip had been hard. *Tally-Ho* was without air conditioning equipment and temperatures in the engine room, submerged, were over 90°. On the surface, at night, it was reasonable to expect the atmosphere down below would have been pleasantly cool; but battery charging raised the inside temperature above even that of submerged cruising. In addition, the contrast between the submarine's interior temperature and that on the bridge was such that going up on the bridge to keep watch meant risking a chill if one did not put on warm clothing.

Everyone sweated profusely and it was hard to avoid prickly heat. The skin irritation it produced was almost unbearable and scratching produced boils and septicaemia. Ginger Facer was perhaps the worst affected; as well as the discomfort, he particularly feared he might be prevented going on the next patrol.

Bennington felt his crew had done him well under difficult circumstances. He summarised everything in his patrol report. It had been a relief to find that aircraft activity had been on a very small scale, unlike in the Mediterranean. Apart from near Penang, only one aircraft had been sighted and that had been off Lem Voalam. He also felt that the observations he had been able to make on the anti-submarine technique of vessels operating from Penang would be of use to others on future patrols.

As a final commentary on this patrol he closed his report with the following words:

> The food was good and on the whole the weather was not too bad, but the torpedo failures were discouraging. One cannot help feeling sore about the torpedoes. To be chased 3 times in a patrol by one's own maddened torpedoes is surely an aspect of war that would lead one's mother to write a stiffish note to the Prime Minister.

[1] At least one report suggests some of *Tally-Ho*'s torpedoes may have been badly assembled in the factory.

CHAPTER TWO

Recreation and Frustration

Secured alongside *Wuchang* in Colombo Harbour, on completion of her first war patrol in the Far East, at least half the crew of *Tally-Ho* were wondering how best the forthcoming rest period might be spent. 'Rest' is perhaps a misleading word — the majority were actively planning what they hoped would be a memorable 'run ashore'. Two of these were 'Snoopy' Thurlow and 'Jackie' Warner. Thurlow was nicknamed 'Snoopy', after the ship's cat, the first Snoopy (brought aboard by a carefree stoker returning from shore leave immediately prior to sailing), had thoroughly wet him through an unbuttoned Ursula suit.

Lieutenant Christopher Theodore Martin Thurlow RNR and Lieutenant Sydney Alfred Warner RN were both twenty-three years old and high spirited. They were good friends with similar interests and were both fond of a good time. They were Third Officer and 'Fourth Hand' respectively. Thurlow therefore at sea did the navigation, Jackie Warner as Torpedo and Gunnery Officer was responsible for armaments. Their duties coupled with day-to-day watch-keeping meant that the four-week patrol period was passed in a rigorous routine that permitted virtually no time for relaxation. Four hours sustained sleep was the longest period that the schedule permitted an officer at any one time. Small wonder that in a young man the human mechanism must react against patrol routine once he was in port.

Some of the effects of a patrol on the constitution were immediately obvious, such as experiencing extreme fatigue after toiling up the long ladders in the depot ship; the ingrained reflex that precluded sleep for longer than four hours at a stretch — no matter how tired one was. The more sinister mental erosion a patrol induced was less obvious. No one ever spoke of it; it was not necessary to do so: it was enough to know how to avoid the trouble. The popular method of therapy could be summed up in five words — drink up or crack up! Drink assisted relaxation. Some no doubt could and did achieve perfect relaxation without alcohol; the majority found it helped. The essential thing was to void one's mind of what had happened on the patrol and what might happen on the next patrol, until it was time to go to sea again.

Drink was *not* a craving — rather it was a catalyst. At sea the wardroom would be totally dry: the well-appointed wine cupboard was kept locked. It was unnecessary for Bennington to issue categoric orders about this for his officers knew him well enough not to suggest the supply be broached while at sea. It's function, as was well known, was for the entertainment of visitors in harbour. None the less, at the end of a patrol the officers found they had willy-nilly saved up a sizeable ration of gin. Herein, felt Snoopy and Jackie, must lie a foundation on which to build a successful run ashore.

Thurlow and Warner left *Wuchang* as soon as they reasonably could after *Tally-Ho* had berthed alongside her. This was not because they spurned the particular comforts of the depot ship. *Wuchang* was a former Chinese river steamer and having been built in the tropics was cooler and more comfortable than some of the other larger submarine depot and accommodation ships. Even so, Jackie and Thurlow argued that it was common sense to escape the heat at sea level. They therefore took off for the cooler mountain air of Kandy, after the briefest of pauses to change into 'running ashore' kit and to ascertain how long they had at their disposal. Naturally they took with them their share of the gin.

Kandy, some sixty miles from Colombo, was as far as one could reasonably hope to travel in Ceylon during a patrol leave. Transport would be a question of organisation: there was bound to be service transport leaving for Kandy. They were soon fixed up and *en route*. Hard work deserved hard play.

Bennington also planned to spend his patrol leave in the hills. But he did not leave the same day as Thurlow and Warner. As commanding officer he had responsibilities to discharge before he could set about relaxing. In due course, however, he accepted an invitation to spend his leave on a tea plantation with a planter. As captain he needed peace and a respite from his crew. Whilst he acknowledged to himself that his crew were of the best, it was vital to a successful working relationship for him to relax away from their company. As well, some of the crew would take advantage of his temporary absence to share out their illegally hoarded rum ration. Rum was issued for immediate consumption; however, 'tot-bottling' was a tradition going back to Nelson's days.

Jackie and Thurlow expected to stay ten days. They already knew of the principal sights to be seen in Kandy such as the sacred elephants, the Buddhist Temple of the Tooth, the Botanical Gardens. But Kandy in wartime had other attractions. It was full, they were told, of SEAC (South East Asia Command) big-wigs and American Liaison Service personnel including, in particular, a great many members of the American Womens' Services. These factors gave a prospect of parties galore. And Jackie and Thurlow exhibited a naïve enthusiasm in their quest for parties. Everywhere *Tally-Ho* had stopped on the way out there had been parties. In port away from home, parties – preferably attended by pretty girls – were what was needed. Romantic attachments were something quite different. Thurlow had been married just over twenty months, Warner had a fiancée back in his native Harwich. Those romances were the real thing; so until the commission was over there could only be parties. . . .

In Kandy they installed themselves in the Grand Hotel. Before long they were fraternizing with American officers and almost at once the first party invitation materialised. The gin, of course, had helped. That had been part of the plan.

The party was a Thanksgiving Ball. Jackie had an idea that it was customary for Americans to celebrate Thanksgiving with fireworks. So for the occasion he managed to procure a supply of small Chinese rockets. Being small they were not difficult to conceal. So, armed with the fireworks and a bottle of gin, Jackie and Thurlow set off for the ball, which was held at the American Club. On their arrival the two British officers were well received and made to feel as guests should. Their tropical white uniforms were a novelty amid the American khaki. The girls all appeared pretty, pleasant and friendly, their dresses made bright splashes of colour on the crowded ballroom floor.

D

Warner and Thurlow were asked a number of friendly questions about submarine patrol routine. The one that Thurlow liked best was: 'Do you wear full uniform when you go to diving stations?' It showed a touching naïvety about the facts of life in a submerged boat in the Indian Ocean. He could not resist the reply, 'No, you just wear a towel round your waist — you can easily tell the captain — he's got the cleanest towel!' Altogether it was an agreeably relaxed evening with cool drinks, dancing and good--humoured badinage.

Jackie, seated at a small table conveniently close to the dance floor, decided that for the celebration of Thanksgiving the evening was a shade too decorous. He surreptitiously ignited the first rocket, which flared, spluttered and seconds later was on its way. It weaved an erratic path through crowded dancers, scattering couples and showering cascades of sparks. In quick succession Jackie launched a further three. These, however, ended their travel by exploding in wreaths of dense, choking smoke. Jackie's well-intentioned co-operation in saluting the American holiday had not gone as planned. Not surprisingly he and Snoopy were assisted from the club.

Next day, shortly before lunch, they were approached by an American officer whom they'd met the night before. 'Do have a drink,' suggested Jackie. The American firmly, but not unkindly, refused a drink, explaining that he was on a mission: to request them to leave Kandy. He personally had enjoyed the party; but, well, he was sure they understood. . . . When they went upstairs to pack, Jackie had only one regret: 'Just think,' he said to Snoopy, 'what we could have done for the Fourth of July . . . for Independence Day!'

Before long the two friends found themselves at the rest centre at Dijatalawa. When, quite soon, the gin ran out they were reduced to drinking the local arrack which produced some dreadful hangovers. They concluded that perhaps leave had lasted long enough. They returned to *Wuchang*.

Back aboard *Tally-Ho* Bennington, relaxed and undeniably eager to be away, was occupied with the depot ship specialists, seeking to ensure that the torpedoes would function properly on the next patrol. Joe Brighton had the whole matter at his finger tips, almost as if he hadn't left the fore-ends for his patrol leave. Next time there shouldn't be any hang-ups. If only they might have many target sightings as in the previous patrol! Jackie was soon checking the number of 4-in high explosive and semi-armour-piercing shells embarked for the coming patrol. But first, he and Snoopy regaled the breezy and confident John Milton ('Steady') Steadman RNR with a description of the *débâcle* at Kandy. Snoopy and Steady had served together in *Porpoise* and had always been close. Engineer Lieutenant Scott-Maxwell was busy. He moved hither and thither saying little, with his dry Scots composure, but his eyes missed nothing. If the machinery was to let them down on the forthcoming patrol it wouldn't be his fault. Lieutenant Michael Gardiner ('Nobby') Clark RN (all Clarks are Nobby in the Royal Navy) came aboard and completed the team of officers. A South African, about the same age as Warner and Thurlow, he had joined *Tally-Ho* just before the last patrol, coming from *Taurus* then on passage to the Far East. He was a likeable man and, like Scott-Maxwell, a capable, composed and often silent character.

Steady Steadman, the *Tally-Ho* First Lieutenant had seen service before the war in the Mercantile Marine, and had travelled extensively with the British India Line of which his father was a director. In the course of his travels he had become a Mohammedan. Joe Brighton vows that Steadman kept a prayer mat in the fore-ends and that he once strongly objected to a seaman's having taken a 'caulker' (snooze) on it. Steadman, Thurlow and Bennington were together for over two years — a period which includes service in both *Porpoise* and *Tally-Ho*. Steadman had acquired some 'spare bod' service in *Osiris* before joining *Porpoise*. He claimed that it was unwise to go ashore unarmed in the tropics and was acknowledged to be a fair pistol shot. At one stage in his career, in a moment of hilarity, he shot out a street lamp in Colombo, a prank with lost him some months seniority. His breezily extroverted manner made him almost a caricature of the young RNR 'hostilities only' officer. He was soon to be decorated for his service in *Tally-Ho*.

It will be recalled that on 12 November 1943, *Tally-Ho* had been obliged to break off shadowing a Japanese U-boat because

Taurus — Nobby Clark's former boat — was expected in her area later that same day. *Taurus* in fact entered the area a bare hour after *Tally-Ho* had left it. What is more, the following day *Taurus* caught up with and sank a Japanese U-boat. The circumstances of the attack suggest most strongly that the U-boat was that first encountered by *Tally-Ho*.

Taurus, commanded by Lieutenant-Commander M.R.G. Wingfield DSO, RN, had attacked and sunk the Japanese U-boat I 34 thirty miles due west of Pulau Pangkor. That put her 130 miles south east of where *Tally-Ho* had sighted the U-boat and her 'Canterbury-class' escort. The course and speed seemed to fit. The sinking by *Taurus* was something of a milestone: I 34 was the first Japanese U-boat to be sunk by a British submarine. Thus Mervyn Wingfield and *Taurus* achieved an important 'first'.

Nor did they escape easily after their signal success. The following day, a mere twenty miles from where the sinking had taken place, Wingfield found himself under a determined attack by a Japanese submarine chaser. *Taurus* was obliged to dive quickly and deeply. By all accounts she went down rather fast and at an extremely steep angle. As a result she stuck fast on the bottom. At that stage her attacker inadvertently became the saviour. Explosions from the pattern of depth-charges dropped closest to *Taurus* loosened the grip of the silt on the submarine's hull and with one or two bounces *Taurus* sprang free.

Wingfield at once decided to surface and fight his adversary. After a quick reconnaissance at periscope depth, it was clear that she did not merit a torpedo. He therefore surfaced for gun action. The first salvoes from *Taurus*, fired at point-blank range, were on target. Wingfield was obliged to break off the engagement when attacked by a Japanese aircraft, no doubt summoned by radio to assist the submarine chaser. *Taurus* again dived deep, but Wingfield glimpsed through the periscope, the Japanese vessel, gunwales awash, badly damaged and sinking. It had been a memorable first war patrol in the Far East for *Taurus*.

During the last few days that *Tally-Ho* remained berthed alongside *Wuchang*, Bennington spent much of the time aboard the depot ship *Adamant*. As he did not discuss his visits, it was generally supposed that they were connected with matters of routine administrative nature. The truth was that *Tally-Ho* was becoming involved in cloak and dagger activities. While *Tally-Ho*, alongside *Wuchang* was making preparations for her next patrol, Colonel Christopher Hudson arrived in charge of an Intelligence Unit of Force 136. By an odd coincidence he was one of Scott-Maxwell's oldest friends.

Intelligence were keen to have agents operating on the Malayan mainland. The terrain was unsuitable for dropping agents from aircraft by parachute. The submarine therefore seemed to offer the most feasible answer in spite of the difficulties to overcome. The hazards were considerable and the precision required for navigation, timing and general judgement necessitated that Captain H.M.C. Ionides, Captain (S) of the Fourth Submarine Flotilla, in *Adamant*, allocated his most experienced crews for the duty. In order to avoid compromising the secrecy of a special operation, attacks on enemy shipping were forbidden for twenty-four hours before and after a special operation — which also tended to limit the field for action; even after the statutory time limit had elapsed, attacks could not take place close to the scene of a special operation for fear of exposing the agent. In such circumstances a submarine's patrol effectiveness was severely curtailed.

However, the submarine captains and crews had every sympathy for the agents who were all volunteers. For the most part they were former planters, many of whom had already escaped from Japanese captivity after the Malay peninsula had been overrun. The nature of the warfare they were conducting, the type of courier who would carry the agents' messages, and the lack of codes and modern espionage facilities meant that the operations of Special Operations Executive in this theatre had to be conducted with less secrecy and by more insecure methods than those of their European counterparts. Inevitably, the agents ran the risk of torture and execution if captured.

To limit the risk of information falling into the hands of the enemy, none of the participants of a special operation was in possession of all the facts relative to it. For example, whilst Bennington would be aware of the location of three possible rendezvous zones where agents were to be delivered and from which they were to be picked up, he would be ignorant of the precise nature of the operation to be undertaken by these agents. Nor till long after *Tally-Ho* had sailed would the choice of rendezvous be identified. A wireless signal in code would notify the submarine whether it was (a), (b) or (c): certainly the coordinates of the rendezvous's position would never be conveyed in a signal.

One ever-present risk was that the landing zone for the rendezvous might prove to be in enemy hands. This meant a risk not only of the agents being captured but of the submarine and her war crew of over sixty men being lost. As if this were not enough, in the crucial, last and most dangerous stages of a special operation the submarine had to abandon her tactical advantage of submergence and proceed on the surface. If there should be any doubt as to whether the operation should be abandoned, that decision must be taken by the submarine's captain. The 'Most Secret' classified instructions for mounting Ceylon Submarine Operation, Order No. 10, the operation allotted to *Tally-Ho* on her forthcoming patrol, express this particular point firmly in a sub-heading 'Orders for carrying out Operation Gustavus VI':

Conduct of the operation
  The Commanding Officer HMS *Tally-Ho* is responsible for the safety of the submarine. He is to endeavour to meet the requirements of the leader of the party, but is not, in so doing, to place the submarine in a position of undue risk. He is to have all possible regard for the safety of the party without jeopardising the safety of the submarine.

  The leader of the party is responsible for that part of the operation which takes place away from the submarine. He is responsible for the safety of the party while they are away from the submarine.

  Should, in the opinion of the Commanding Officer HMS *Tally-Ho*, circumstances arise which cause the operation to be attended by undue risk to the submarine, he has the discretion to cancel the operation at any time.

It was no easy position for Bennington, who had full responsibility for the decisions affecting the safety of his boat and crew in a tactical situation which demanded that much of the information about the operation be withheld from the submarine's captain. Such information as he had, he was not permitted to share even with his First Lieutenant. The first group to be carried by *Tally-Ho* for clandestine operations was led by a former planter, Captain Harrison. In the interests of security they were not embarked until immediately prior to sailing.

Once embarked, the Special Forces personnel created few problems. Bennington had already worked out the necessary arrangements, which he never had to vary throughout his dealings with the cloak and dagger brigade. Officers were to be accommodated in the wardroom: this necessitated a 'hot bunks' routine for the wardroom personnel since each bunk now had to serve for two instead of one but Bennington knew no one would complain. Other ranks he would accommodate aft, in the stoker's mess. (On this first trip with Special Forces aboard the group consisted of four officers; there were no other ranks.) He explained to Captain Harrison that while everything would be done to ensure reasonable comfort for his party, it was essential they kept out of the crew's way at all times. The reasons were obvious and there were no arguments; Harrison passed on Bennington's orders and saw they were obeyed.

The special stores, however, did create problems. The collapsible kayaks called 'folboats' had to be stored so that they could readily be disembarked. Although they folded into a flat shape rather like a flattened pea pod, their length remained unchanged when rigged for launching. They were put aboard through the inclined torpedo loading hatch for'ard, and it was obvious that they must be carried in the torpedo tube space. Joe Brighton and his torpedo team groaned inwardly. As well as serving as living space for most of the seaman members of the crew — and, of course, the place where they kept their possessions — its main purpose was to house six re-load torpedoes and the bulk of the food for the patrol; it was also the torpedo team's sole workshop.

The torpedo team had heard it all before but it had never been quite as bad. They were used to confined working conditions that always made their work difficult. This would make it bloody near impossible, thought Joe; he was a patient tolerant man and made it his normal rule to avoid swear words; even so, 'bloody near impossible' expressed precisely what he thought. Jackie Warner as Torpedo and Gunnery Officer discussed the problems with him. After about ten minutes Joe reckoned it *could* be done. 'Good,' said Jackie, 'and before I forget there's a list of stowage requirements for storing folboats — apparently if you tread on them too much they leak!' At this point he noticed Joe's sandy, right eyebrow raised in weary tolerance. 'Oh Hell,' he added, 'we must try not to do it too often! After all they won't be going miles in them — I hope. . . .'

The special stores did not consist only of folboats; there were also heavy items such as radios, armaments and everything that a party of four might need over a matter of months in a hostile jungle. As well as the problem of stowing the heavier items where they would not impede essential mechanisms they added considerably to the First Lieutenant's problem of working out the trim. Steady passed backwards and forwards marking up, altering and re-altering the trim with breezy confidence. It was essential to get the answer as near perfect as possible. While minor inequalities of weight distribution could be 'held' on the hydroplanes, that might impair efficiency to manoeuvre when the vessel was submerged. Steadman knew that Bennington would accept nothing less than an efficient fighting machine.

In the circumstances it was almost a relief when at 1200, 3 December 1943, *Tally-Ho* sailed from Colombo for her second war patrol in the Indian Ocean. As she cleared the harbour entrance and followed her escort, the motor launch *Maid Marion*, Bennington reckoned that in about an hour and a half he'd be in a good place for the initial trim dive. Some forty minutes before then he would call up his Special Forces passengers so that they could breathe some fresh air before their first experience of diving. Sweltering in the noonday sun he reflected that 'outside air' was possibly a more appropriate term.

Once *Maid Marion* had taken her leave and *Tally-Ho* was committed to the four-day passage to her operational zone, he had the Special Forces party brought up to the bridge. He explained briefly that in the sub's present position the risk of enemy intruders was minimal. He had already concluded that the torpedo alert in this area on the first patrol had almost certainly been caused by the sight of a large fish's movement near the surface. Large fish were a familiar feature of the Malacca Strait and Indian Ocean. He also explained that he would probably not be repeating the invitation in the future. 'If it becomes necessary to submerge, I shall pass the order down the voice-pipe: "Press the diving hooter." Below in the control room the klaxon will sound twice; and the crew will go to diving stations. There's ample time to clear the bridge but not to hang about while we're doing it.' His explanation was appreciated: he didn't bother to explain that he himself never hurried. The captain always went below last if he were on the bridge. It looked impressive, perhaps, but Bennington did it because he liked to check things personally; after eight years in 'boats' he could gauge with precision how long it was before the bridge became awash.

His homily did its work and when he suggested to the 'passengers', as he called them, that they might like to go below now, they all disappeared with alacrity. The bridge was left to the captain, the officers of the watch and the look-outs. 'Press the diving hooter,' he ordered. As its strident blare shattered the peace of the control room, the first two look-outs were through the hatch. Finally Bennington passed down through the conning tower, closing first the upper hatch, one clip on, both clips on, one pin in, both pins in; he then repeated the procedure on the lower hatch. The routine was never varied.

He made periscope observations, explained to his passengers that this dive would be only a short one to check trim. As he did so he made a quick personal check that all was well and the depth being held without the hydroplane operators having to make excessive movements of their large brass handwheels. Bennington's movements around the control room caused his passengers to squirm out of one another's way to avoid his movements and those of the crew members at diving stations. 'We won't normally allow you in here when dived,' he explained pleasantly, 'there's not really enough room.' After that they cleared the control room without being asked to do so and throughout the patrol he never had to raise any of these points again. His passengers did exactly as required, frequently before being asked. When *Tally-Ho* surfaced

after her trim dive, the miracle of submergence and resurfacing
having once been completed without incident, the passengers
accepted it as a matter of course thereafter. They were all
volunteers for hazardous service so it was perhaps not surprising
they could be persuaded to take submarine routine in their stride.

For the next four days *Tally-Ho* proceeded with despatch. Her
modifications meant that she carried more than enough fuel oil;
and time was of the essence. They would submerge at the
approach of aircraft except at night if really dark. By day
Bennington spent much of the day on the bridge. The captain does
not stand regular watches but will be up 'topsides' as often as his
duties will permit. When the weather was good and the sea smooth
with little swell, Bennington had the habit of sitting on the edge of
the for'ard part of the bridge cab. Seated comfortably on the ledge
just inside the wind deflector's profile, he would smoke cigarette
after cigarette, gently swinging his legs, an elegant silver cigarette
case open beside him. Alone with his thoughts, not speaking, his
gaze running confidently around the grey smudgy horizon, he was
completely happy. Not so his look-outs — they could not smoke
while on duty. Smoking tended to have an immediate effect on a
man's vision; unaccountably it didn't effect Bennington's. Against
all logic he continued to see as well or better than any of his
look-outs: even Ginger Facer and Ken Lockyer, the surfacing
look-outs in whose vigilance Bennington placed great confidence.

By 0530 on the morning of 7 December 1943, *Tally-Ho* was
already some 1,065 statute miles from base. At that hour, at first
light, she was travelling on the surface. Bennington leaned forward
and spoke quietly into the voicepipe, 'Take her down to periscope
depth'. He had no need to add that the klaxon was not to be
sounded: his crew were already accustomed to his considerate
practice of diving the vessel quietly at daybreak. This meant that
'patrol routine' could simply be replaced by 'watch diving'
without having wakened the two thirds of the ship's company, at
present turned in and asleep.

Had *Tally-Ho* been diving for an emergency, 'diving stations'
would have been called by sounding the klaxon. Not only the crew
appreciated the captain's forbearance, the passengers too were glad
to be saved the ear-shattering, heart-stopping, double klaxon

blasts; and Bennington knew that the arrangement made for more efficient running of the ship. That, after all, was why he had instituted it.

Way aft, in the engine room, Chief Engine Room Artificer John Metcalf Powell gave the order 'Out clutches, secure for diving'. Chiefy Powell supervised the carrying out of the order. With her diesel engines clutched up and electric motors engaged, *Tally-Ho* continued to make progress, at a slightly reduced rate, thirty feet beneath the surface. At this moment in time had Powell, or Bennington been asked if all was well in *Tally-Ho* each would unhesitatingly have replied that to the best of his knowledge and belief all was indeed well.

Bennington ordered the big search periscope to be raised. With a slight squeal of the wires around their sheaves it arose from its well and its gleaming length rose slowly before him. As it cut the murky water overhead, Bennington unfolded the training handles and bent to put his eyes to its twin lenses. He did this not doubting for a moment that the water then streaming down the outside lenses would clear and the image become sharply defined. Even with long experience he had not previously considered what action would be necessary if that did not happen. It was so vital that one could not easily imagine anything different.

He rotated the periscope through 360° for an all round look and handed over to the officer of the watch. Then after a brief comprehensive glance at the chart he retired to his cabin to rest.

He did not rest for long. The quiet call 'Captain in the control room' had him on his feet and instantly awake. 'The search periscope is flooding,' reported the officer of the watch. Bennington took the periscope: one glance was enough to confirm his officer's report. 'Carry on and report if the condition grows worse,' he ordered, already convinced that it could not do otherwise. He still had his attack periscope but for an effectual, offensive patrol the search periscope was vital.

Like all 'T'-class boats, *Tally-Ho* had two periscopes. Both were heavy bronze tubes. They had to be bronze or their vast size would effect 'Faithful Fred' the submarine's magnetic compass. When lowered, the malleable bronze tubes were encased within huge twin sheath-like barrels that supported them when raised.

The larger search periscope was bifocal so that it could be used for range-finding purposes. Two images of the enemy vessel under observation would carefully be adjusted till the fainter, phantom ship appeared on top of the other, that is with her waterline exactly on top of a portion of the other of which the height was known, usually masthead or top of funnel. The captain would then announce, 'My range is *that!*' On the word 'that', a man standing behind him would read off the angle subtended by the difference in inclination of the lenses of the periscope's top lens combination in degrees and minutes. A slide rule calculation would give the range of the enemy vessel. (In the Mediterranean, with a bit of 'lop' on the water, it might be necessary to have 5 ft, or so, of periscope projecting above the surface to complete this evolution. But that wasn't likely to here.) If the captain then said, 'The bearing is *that!*' that, too, could be read from a scale on the periscope and the enemy's precise position relevant to the submarine's own position at that moment plotted. The search periscope was also used for taking land fixes to check navigation, and could be used for sky searches. It could also be adjusted for high and low power use.

The monocular, unifocal attack periscope was only used during the final stages of an attack. At its topmost point it was perilously small and therefore hard for an enemy to observe. However, to try to mount a patrol and navigate by it alone would normally be classed the height of folly. Bennington had a difficult decision to make. He had already brought a fully equipped submarine more than one thousand miles for the purpose of carrying out a special operation and afterwards attacking shipping in the Penang area. It was obvious that the periscope was at present useless, its condition worsening rapidly, whilst it would be hazardous to carry out even the special operation with his periscope in this condition, he was not prepared to abandon the patrol and run for port.

The last sight, taken just before diving, had placed *Tally-Ho* fifty miles south of the Great Nicobar; from there she had proceeded into the Malacca Strait. Bennington now proposed to take her further north, to a region where she would be out of sight of land and relatively undisturbed by passing coastal traffic. Here Bennington brought *Tally-Ho* to the surface, and Scott-Maxwell with Chiefy Powell began their inspection of the defective periscope.

The staunching window was the obvious place to suspect leaks: it was the aperture used for periodic cleaning of the lens prisms with jewellers' rouge. Since there was every sign that it was securely fixed, the trouble was clearly of a much more serious nature, requiring the resources of the depot ship. The lengthy and complicated examination needed, plus any hope of making improvement, would require time and the manufacture of a special spanner. The spanner was made and throughout the day, unprotected on the bridge from the fierce heat of the sun, Lieutenant (E) Scott-Maxwell and Chief ERA Powell laboured at their task while the officer of the watch and the look-outs stayed alert for any enemy approach. When the daylight faded the two men worked by the light of shaded torches until it became impossible to continue. At first light they resumed their task.

Eventually Bennington informed Scott-Maxwell that by the end of the day he must proceed southwards towards the rendezvous for the special operation.

Despite their efforts — and remarkable patience in disassembling the many components of the periscope — they met with disappointment each time they made an assessment of their repairs.

Determined not to be beaten, Scott-Maxwell exercised extraordinary ingenuity in the brilliance of his improvisations. But he was continually frustrated by the inevitable limitations imposed by their circumstances. In the words of Bennington's patrol report, '... improvement was so slight that it was still not possible to see through the periscope'.

Finally, Scott-Maxwell displaying a knowledge of chemistry and physics in addition to his engineering talent, devised a form of desiccator to dry out the water in the periscope. Yet even this failed. Bennington reported: 'At the end of 36 hours of continuous pumping there was no improvement of any kind. In all probability the periscope contained too much water to allow for complete and effective desiccation.'

The rendezvous was to be eight miles south of Pulau Jerak, a tiny island which had its own enclosing reef. It was forty-two miles from the mainland and at least thirty from the Sembilan

Islands and Pulau Rumbia which formed the nearest group. Here *Tally-Ho* was to meet a junk. On completion of the special operation *Tally-Ho* would move away temporarily in the direction of the Sumatran mainland. In this way, after the statutory time limit had elapsed, she could patrol off Penang 120 miles further northwards with nothing to suggest she had come from the scene of the special operation.

Bennington had a last run through the Operation Order, of which there was a single copy. Instructions demanded that it be destroyed by fire when no longer required, lest there be any risk of its falling into enemy hands. The orders listed details of how the junk at the rendezvous was to be recognised. From 1200 onwards a shirt would be hung by its arms from the for'ard shrouds. Two men would meet in the bows for periods of five minutes at intervals of one hour. The leader of the Gustavus party would approach the junk by canoe after dark and establish friendly relations prior to any transfer of personnel or stores. There was a note that if discussions should last for a period of hours the captain of *Tally-Ho* might at his discretion retire to charge batteries. 'Not a word here about flooded periscopes,' said Bennington with feeling.

Tally-Ho found the junk without much difficulty and remained within two miles or so of it awaiting nightfall. It was necessary once to shift position slightly to avoid another junk. By 1810 on Saturday, 11 December the moment of truth had arrived. Bennington gave the order to surface. He was in no doubt that the junk in question was the right junk, but it was perfectly possible it could be in Japanese hands. Two minutes later *Tally-Ho* was surfaced, trimmed low in the water and closing the junk silently under electric motors half ahead, grouped down. The fore hatch was unclipped and opened and the folboats passed up through it. The landing party was quietly away within three minutes of the hatch being unclipped. From the bridge Bennington observed carefully as the canoe approached the junk.

The Vickers gun had been brought to the bridge in case of any trouble, but it seemed wisest to avoid the noise of manning the 4-in gun unless the enemy showed up in strength. An hour and a quarter later the landing party were back. There was to be no transfer of men or stores. Bennington did not ask why: it wasn't his affair. The party were silently embarked, their folboats were quietly sunk.

Complete with her passengers, *Tally-Ho* attempted a patrol close in shore *en route* to Penang. But with only the attack periscope serviceable, conditions were so unfavourable it had to be abandoned. As Bennington put it in his report:

> Normally the unifocal periscope is only used in the final stages of an attack. It has no magnification and is of little value for (range) estimating purposes unless the target is very close. Also, it would have been of little value searching inshore towards the high, green and brown wooded shore of Penang.

In places the mangrove roots grew in confusing profusion, right down to water level, along the shore. Bennington's report continued:

> Even a surface patrol offered no reasonable hope of success. The main Japanese route keeps close to the ten fathom line. A surface patrol along this route would be compromised almost at once. The submarine would almost certainly be sighted from the shore and possibly reported by fishing boats which infest the shallow water.
>
> Further afield a surface patrol would have been a complete waste of time. In fact, it would simply have amounted to lasting out the required number of days at sea.
>
> In these circumstances it was decided to return to harbour with all speed and ship a new periscope.

That virtually was the end of the second war patrol by *Tally-Ho* in the Far East. The return journey was devoid of interest save for the sighting of one vessel fifty miles south west of Great Nicobar, not far from the area where the first flooding of the periscope had occurred. Her masts were first sighted at 1336 on 13 December 1944. At first sight through the attack periscope she had looked like a yacht of about 200 tons. Bennington had been interested enough to approach close to her in case she were an escort waiting to accompany a U-boat. Close inspection, however, revealed her to be a fishing vessel.

Tally-Ho moved off and three days later on 16 December, entered Trincomalee harbour. A valediction to her abortive patrol was provided by Captain H.M.C. Ionides, who, in a minute addressed to the C-in-C Far Eastern Fleet, stated:

It is considered the Commanding Officer acted perfectly correctly in abandoning the patrol in the circumstances. A high power periscope is essential for any prospect of success in this area.

CHAPTER THREE

A Long Wait

Tally-Ho was back in port on 16 December 1943 after her second Malacca Strait patrol; this time she secured alongside the depot ship *Adamant* at Trincomalee. As she entered the big natural habour of Trinco, her officers on the bridge, 'harbour stations' party lining her casing, Bennington was experiencing a pang of frustration. *Tally-Ho* was not returning in the manner he would have preferred, with her 'Jolly Roger' at the head of an improvised flag-staff lashed to her periscope standards to indicate a sinking. Instead his patrol seemed to have achieved virtually nothing.

In his view the major purpose, in fact the only purpose, for operating submarine patrols in the Malacca Strait was to sink enemy shipping — be it warships or merchant ships carrying essential war supplies. It could not be other than a bitter blow for him to return early from an abandoned patrol with gun and torpedo tubes unfired. That it might be no fault of his had probably not occurred to him. Nor was he mollified by the fact that *Tally-Ho* had carried out a special operation — albeit abortively, again due to no fault of his. To Bennington, special operations could never be more than a disagreeable chore — admittedly requiring skill and involving risk. In carrying out such a task he would give every consideration to the individual service personnel involved. None the less, he would always dislike this type of duty because it detracted from what he considered his real duty.

In the past thirteen days *Tally-Ho* had travelled almost 3,000 miles, and all that had resulted had been a conference of one hour and five minutes in the rendezvous junk. To make matters worse he was faced with the unpleasant job of explaining in writing his reasons for abandoning the patrol. He was satisfied that it would have been useless to have continued the patrol unproductively, merely to have lasted out the requisite number of days away from harbour. However, the defect that had caused his premature return was one that occurred so seldom that to report it was tantamount to inviting criticism, perhaps even disbelief.

Not everyone on board *Tally-Ho* thought as did her captain. For Stokers Henry Judge ('Gudge', whose ready humour enlivened the stokers mess) and Bill Illsley the immediate prospect was relief at being back in port for Christmas. For Able Seaman Lockyer, who'd had his twenty-fourth birthday on their first patrol, it meant that his beard would have to come off; thirteen days was hardly long enough to grow a proper one. Everyone aboard would have preferred to have made a sinking. Undeniably it could be argued that many of the crew had to put in just as much effort on any patrol, whether successful or not. None the less, the boredom of an uneventful patrol was harder to take than the excitement of an eventful one.

Bennington, however, kept the worst of his disappointment to himself. Nor did he take out his frustration on the Special Forces personnel. He gladly accepted an offer of a drink from Harrison who had led the party. As regards the written explanation of the patrol's abandonment, that was already virtually complete, in draft. His patrol report omitted nothing; he had been at some pains to make clear the precise reasons for his decisions at every stage of the patrol's development, particularly his reasons for finally abandoning the inshore patrol. He did not restrict his comments to describing his own participation, as the following extract makes clear:

> Altogether five days were spent on the various endeavours to repair the periscope. Apart from the actual pumping, all the work was carried out by the Engineer Officer, Lieutenant (E) P.D. Scott-Maxwell DSC, RN, and Chief ERA J. Metford Powell DSM, RN, D/MX 53617. It is considered their determination and the resource with which they tackled this unfamiliar optical work is extremely meritorious.

Bennington had been fair and deliberately unstinting in his praise of Jack Powell and Peter Scott-Maxwell; in no degree could responsibility attach to them for the patrol's having failed. When they had finally stopped work on the periscope, it had been in the certain knowledge that nothing further could then be done. Bennington was determined that their efforts should not go unremarked. Demanding, as he did, absolute loyalty from his officers and men, he never failed to give them equal loyalty in return.

It was not the first time that Scott-Maxwell and Jack Powell had jointly faced mechanical troubles. They had served together in *Proteus* for over twenty-five months in the Mediterranean, at the time when submarine losses had been at their highest. *Proteus* was an ancient submarine (built in 1929) and the state of her machinery was so decrepit that Scott-Maxwell had applied for and obtained extra staff for maintenance duties. Her oil consumption had risen so fantastically that it had taken all his mathematical ability to predict how long she could possibly 'steam' before it became necessary to run for port. In spite of such disadvantages, their captain, Lieutenant-Commander Philip Stewart Francis DSO, RN, once described as 'one of the most patient men that ever lived', had sunk a total of 39,430 tons of merchant shipping. *Proteus* also survived a ramming before a complete refit could no longer be deferred.

Tally-Ho returned to port still carrying defective torpedoes. One still showed the marks of bad depot-ship preparation, on others there were modifications still to be undertaken. As certain of these torpedoes had been carried by *Tally-Ho* on passage and on her two patrols, it was decided to disembark them and on the next patrol carry only those which had been prepared on *Adamant*. A new periscope was shipped and approved. A post mortem on the flooded periscope established that engine vibration had caused an insufficiently tightened joint to open with resultant leakage. By this time Scott-Maxwell and Joe Brighton found themselves wondering if they were not well on the way to becoming permanently unpopular with the depot-ship personnel.

Before the next patrol could be undertaken, Christmas provided a welcome distraction. In *Adamant*, early on Christmas morning, a signal was received which showed humane feelings and common sense in high places.

From Flag Officer Eastern Fleet — General

0831/24/1943. EVERYONE WISHES EVERYBODY ELSE
A VERY HAPPY CHRISTMAS AND NEW YEAR. NO
FURTHER SIGNALS ARE TO BE MADE. THINK OF THE
SIGNALMEN AND THE PAPER SHORTAGE.[1]

Christmas was celebrated as traditionally as possible. Other
ranks' messes were decorated with bunting and toilet-paper
streamers. The youngest rating made 'captain's rounds' wearing
the captain's uniform. The officers presented bottles of beer to the
seamen and, in turn, visited the seamens' messes to be regaled with
'sippers' of rum. It was all part of a tradition that could exist only
in so British an institution as the Royal Navy.

On board *Adamant*, the Christmas festivities did not prevent the
typing and signing by 'Tinsides' Ionides of a memorandum (dated
Christmas Day) on two forthcoming special operations. They were
code named Gustavus VI and Mud. Both were to be undertaken
in the course of a single normal patrol by HMS *Tally-Ho*.
Bennington was apprised and told that *Tally-Ho* would be sailing
on 27 December. The unwelcome news of the special operations
tended to counteract for him the good news of the early sailing.

Gustavus VI and Mud posed some considerable problems. This
time *Tally-Ho* would carry not four but ten passengers: two
officers and eight other ranks, to be landed in Japanese-held areas.
Special stores for this operation included wireless telegraphy
equipment, three collapsible folboats, three reconnaissance boats
and a number of twenty-eight-pound sinkers to dispose of the
craft after they had outlived their usefulness. The whole transaction was entitled Ceylon Submarine Order No. 13. Bennington
was briefed that the primary object of his patrol was to carry out
this operation and thereafter to attack enemy shipping.

The fact that a rendezvous junk had no modern navigational
aids complicated the detailed arrangements for such operations.
Whilst *Tally-Ho* could accurately find any pinpoint expressed in
coordinates of latitude and longitude, to be acceptable to the junk

---

[1] *Make a Signal!* by Captain Jack Broome DSC, RN, published by Putnam 1955.

the same rendezvous needed to be ascertainable in terms of visible geographic features. At the same time it was vital that *Tally-Ho* was not endangered by her captain agreeing to operate in insufficient depth of water.

The bulk of the stores, as ever, were stowed in the torpedo stowage space, so Joe Brighton and his fore-ends team had a job to avoid their essential torpedo equipment being obstructed or made inaccessible. In particular Joe always strove to make sure the dip-rod aperture to the torpedo operating tank was not covered. Two years before, in *Porpoise*, on a stores run from Alexandria to Malta, he'd found a stowaway in just that spot. The stowaway, a Maltese youth, was seeking to escape the rigours of the beseiged island where everything was scarce and people paid as much as two shillings for a single cigarette. In that critical year fifteen British submarines had been lost in the Mediterranean. Joe was permitting no impediment to instant availability of his vital equipment — and no more stowaways, at least in his department.

The Special Forces party were not the only new faces to appear in *Tally-Ho* for her third patrol. Thurlow was in the sick bay with a poisoned elbow. In his place they embarked Lieutenant P.D. Bennett RN, who was spare crew for submarine duty in *Adamant*. 'Wiggy' Bennett (all Bennetts in the Royal Navy are so called) had had an interesting previous posting in HMS *Graph*, originally commissioned as U. 570 in quite a different navy — the *Kriegsmarine*. On 27 August 1941, she had surfaced in a seaway between Ireland and Iceland to find herself almost directly beneath a Lockheed Hudson of Coastal Command. By all accounts the German skipper, Korvetten Kapitän Rahmlow, was inexperienced and the pilot of the aircraft, Squadron Leader J.H. Thompson RAF, most experienced. The first attack crippled the U-boat to an extent that it dared not dive. Miserably impotent, taking on water from a large number of small leaks, she had hoisted the captain's dress shirt as a white flag and surrendered.

The surrender of U. 570 made history: she was the first submarine ever to surrender to an aircraft. Once towed to port none of her leaks were found to be serious and she was recommissioned to serve in the Royal Navy as HMS *Graph*. Sub-Lieutenant Peter Bennett has been posted to her as his first 'boat' on completing the submarine course. An unenviable prospect since any air or surface craft sighting a U-boat might sink her without flashing a challenge or looking to see what ensign she was flying. Despite this *Graph* had done well; later, commanded by Lieutenant. P.D. 'Sam' Marriott RN, she even sank a U-boat.

When Bennett met Bennington in *Adamant*, he had been greatly impressed by him and as a result had practically talked himself into being taken along on patrol. The smoothness of the submarine's organisation impressed him. No one argued or questioned anything that was required to be done. If ever the possibility arose it was immediately resolved by someone saying quietly, 'The *Captain* likes it *this way.*'

Bennett was embarked only a short while before the Special Forces personnel were taken on. The other ranks were Chinese and Malays. One of the Chinese had brought his own provisions in the shape of dried fish, the smell of which seemed likely to compromise any secret enterprise he might attempt. Once he was accommodated in the stern with the stokers, the smell of the diesel engines, 'the old fish fryers' as Jackie Warner called them, mercifully blanketed the dried fish's presence – though not entirely from the stokers.

The two officers from Force 136, Major Jim Hannah and Claude Fenner, were introduced to Bennington. Hannah, the eldest in the party, was just over forty, Claude Fenner was twenty-eight years old. Both men had worked for some time in Malaya before the war, Hannah as a journalist for many years. Fenner was dressed as an Assistant Superintendent of the Federation of the Malay States Police. Both passengers would be sharing the wardroom with the officers and both were to prove likeable characters.

Fenner at first seemed totally unsuited for life in a submarine. Over six feet tall and well built in proportion, he seemed about to burst out of his khaki shorts and shirt. Bennington was relieved to find Fenner's size did not prevent him passing through hatches and up and down ladders with commendable promptitude. Submarines, he confided, were nothing new to him. He had already made a couple of trips on similar missions in Dutch submarines. The first being the 0. 24.

Conditions in *Tally-Ho* after sailing were vastly different, Fenner found, to those in Dutch submarines. The British boat had a regular complement of four officers plus one under training. This meant that in the wardroom visitors could at best hope for a shake-down on the table or in a 'hot bunk' when one of the officers went on watch. Dutch submarines, on the other hand, had been short of officers so there had been no problem about bunks. The Dutch officers were all men commissioned in peace time and consequently older and more serious-minded than their counterparts in the *Tally-Ho* wardroom. Broome and Fenner being adaptable and in spirit akin to the *Tally-Ho*'s officers, they got on well with them. Many agreeable hours were spent playing liar dice cribbage in the wardroom. The easy companionship went far to relieve monotony and mitigate boredom.

After *Tally-Ho* had sailed, it was readily agreed that Hannah and Fenner might periodically spend time on the bridge; the success of the mission before them might well depend on their fitness; and fitness could depend on their getting fresh air. If while they were on the bridge an emergency developed, the officer of the watch would summon Bennington, calling down the voice pipe, 'Captain, on the bridge'. When this happened, as one of them later put it, Bennington would 'erupt' from the hatchway within seconds of the officer of the watch having spoken. Hannah and Fenner were always careful to keep out of his way and to get below quickly. Fenner's hips were on the wide side for negotiating hatches but he made light of the injuries he sustained in the process.

At times when the passengers were not permitted on the bridge during the first three days of the patrol whilst *Tally-Ho* was travelling on the surface, they would sit beneath the open conning-tower hatch in the control room. There was sometimes competition for this place, but being passengers and without duties they stood a better chance than most of securing it. The most comfortable perch of all was on a leather-covered locker. On an earlier mission, Richard Broome had said to Fenner as they sat there: 'You know they must think of us as Mr Keith and Mr Prowse'. (Keith Prowse, the theatre ticket agency, claimed that they had the best seats.) Snoopy the cat also liked the fresh air and would sit, head on one side, savouring the breeze.

In the easy relationship that existed between the two Special
Forces officers and *Tally-Ho* officers it was usual to make light of
the dangers associated with their own particular jobs. It was
obvious that the submariners believed anyone connected with
Special Operations Executive to be mad and vice versa. The duties
of both branches of the Services called for an élite corps. It was
abundantly clear to the passengers that Bennington possessed a
unique quality. He was worshipped by his men, and manifestly
believed his prime obligation was to sink enemy ships. He seldom
appeared in the wardroom, preferring his own cabin for his leisure.
His observance of the rule of 'one apiece all round' at midday
when submerged and his enjoyment – as thorough as that of any
of his crew – in the single cigarette seemed to Fenner to be at the
heart of the man and of his phenomenal success. At sea
Bennington was unquestionably a 'tiger' (Fenner's own word for
him), but despite this he still retained his human touches. The
midday cigarette and innumerable cups of tea were essential to his
well-being. So long as he could have them he remained the fittest
man on board. His crew, of course, were determined to see that he
was supplied with these small necessities. Occasionally Bennington
would unbend and indulge in good-humoured banter with Fenner.
'How are you going to hide yourself?' he would ask. 'Or pretend
that you're a Malay or Chinese? You're twice the size of any of
them, and you look exactly like an Englishman.' However, Fenner
was highly successful in performing secret work on special
operations for the rest of the war.

Fenner concealed the fact that he dreaded and hated submarines. Before the war he'd taken passage in a submarine from
Hong Kong to Amoy. During a submerged exercise – his first
experience of submerging in a submarine – an uncontrollable
condition had developed and the submarine had resurfaced only
with difficulty. She had been ordered back to Hong Kong for
examination and Fenner had had no option but to travel with her
and subsequently to proceed unwillingly to sea in her once more
for her trial dive. This experience once over, he'd decided not
unreasonably that wild horses would never induce him willingly to
set foot in another ruddy submarine.

Small wonder he found the foetid atmosphere of the submarine submerged was distasteful to him and lingered in his nostrils for days after going ashore. Nor could he approve the presence of Snoopy the cat. It seemed a consummate error to have included a cat in the ship's company. Whilst Snoopy had a sandbox (kept in the 'heads') which he had been trained to use, Fenner felt, even so, that a smell of cat pervaded the atmosphere. But he did realise that Snoopy's presence had a talismanic importance for the crew, and he was impressed by the submariners' tolerance. If one of the crew wanted a cat aboard they would all put up with having one — even if it were against all reason. So Fenner tolerated Snoopy.

On 30 December 1943, when *Tally-Ho* was in a position due south of Great Nicobar, a signal was received from Captain (S). This signal, No. 310956 Z, was of great importance as it contained detailed instructions for a patrol off Sabang, seventy-five miles to the south-east. The last sentence — by far the most important one — proved impossible to decipher. Scott-Maxwell applied himself as though to a mathematical problem; after an hour's methodical juggling he was still no nearer a correct solution. Bennington decided to risk asking for that part of the signal to be repeated: it was a considerable risk and one not normally undertaken. Whilst submerged *Tally-Ho* could receive transmissions; a whole batch might come through at a time; they would be received by every submarine operational in that area. Individually applicable messages were prefixed by each submarine's number so that the cipher officer need only decode what he knew to be addressed to his own boat. To make a signal requesting a repeat would require *Tally-Ho* to surface and risk an enemy radio plot on her position. Determined not to be forced to abandon a second patrol that month, Bennington decided to take the calculated risk.

After dark, having proceeded northwards, *Tally-Ho* made the requisite signal and obtained four repeats of the corrupt portion of the signal; all were identical. Consequently Bennington was faced with a further difficult decision. The object of the patrol off Sabang was not known, he had a special operation pending and no means of assessing what risks were justified. He weighed the prospects in his mind. The last portion of the signal from Captain

(S) might be a reconnaissance report or a rider concerning risk. The water in his present position, between Pulau Rondo and Sabang was deep and currents and eddies were plentiful. No one could remain here unidentified. His decision was that he'd attack any target sighted.

He had his own theories, based on Scott-Maxwell's findings, as to what had caused the final sentence of the signal to be corrupt. When time permitted, he entered these words in his report:

> It is considered insufficient care was taken over the ciphering of this message and it could not have been properly checked. . . .

The night passed slowly without any sightings, but, at 0424 on 1 January 1944 two objects were sighted to the west of Pulau Rondo. The alert that immediately followed awakened the wardroom passengers. Steadman gave them the news that a target could be in the offing, finishing his news with a cheerful 'Happy New Year!' Thirteen minutes later the already shaky composure of the officer passengers was shattered by two klaxon blasts as Bennington decided to go to periscope depth in mid-channel. Fenner and Hannah found themselves wiching they could share Steadman's enthusiasm for action.

Daylight was now coming up fast and before long Steadman was back abjectly deflated. 'Those two objects must have been junks or distant hilltops,' he said sadly. 'Happy New Year!' chorused the two passengers mercillesly. There was little enough for them to be funny about: an early submergence meant an even longer day submerged; and having no duties, their day was long enough. All they could do was lounge around, try not to scratch in the sweaty heat and also try not to contemplate the nearness of the impending special operation. They were probably now less than 200 miles away from the rendezvous zone.

That evening they surfaced in the cool of the evening. Cigarettes could be lighted, meals prepared and the wardroom radio turned on for the Forces Sweetheart. Her two most popular numbers at that time were, 'We'll meet again . . . don't know where don't know when . . .' and 'I'll pray for you . . . wherever you are . . .'.

Small wonder both Hannah and Fenner assumed glum expressions. For Fenner, with his young wife back in Trincomalee and his thoughts on the forthcoming operation, the pangs of homesickness were peculiarly poignant. Still one must not become sentimental.

The thought of sentimentality reminded him of his trips in Dutch submarines. The kindly, mature Dutch officers, all of whom had prewar service behind them, had sometimes shown sentimentality. Clearly they believed the British Special Forces parties were off to certain death. One, Hans Reitsmaar, had insisted on exchanging his own 9-mm. Luger Parabellum pistol for Claude Fenner's Colt automatic. Although pleased with the swop Fenner had been more touched by the motives that prompted it.

The worldly Steadman enthusiastically applauded the voice of Vera Lynn, but had to admit that despite a wide acquaintance in the world of show business he had not as yet met the popular singing star.

Jackie Warner, in his turn, related how the whole ship's company had already benefited from the well-connected Steadman's contacts on their passage out to the Far East. Whilst in harbour at Gibraltar it had been discovered that Steadman's brother-in-law was an army officer with a unit stationed there. As a result the officers had been regular guests in the officers mess, and Petty Officers in the sergeants' mess. 'Snoopy' (the feline version) had suffered an operation at the hands of an army vet; *he* had been quietly put to sleep and *it* had awakened neutered.

As the passengers had no duties on board they were permitted a single drink. Custom demanded that they pass it round the mess for 'sippers' after their own modest first sip. Traditionally, naval custom requires that one barely wets one's lips when accepting 'sippers', so there was no question of the *Tally-Ho* off-duty officers being led astray. The second day of January 1944 drew to a close without incident after this ritual.

The following day Bennington initiated the first phase of Ceylon Operation Order No. 13. This began with a periscope reconnaissance of the Malay coast just north of the Sembilian Islands. He followed his instructions to the letter, going right in to the ten-fathom line. This represented the limit of practicable periscope-depth navigation. He explained that the most practical site for a future submarine rendezvous with a junk was ten miles from the mouth of the Dindings River. The passengers would have preferred a site further north but this the depth available would not permit.

Next day a similar reconnaissance was completed south of the Sembilian Islands. Whilst Bennington openly admitted disliking special operations, there was no question as to his thoroughness in carrying them out. Now he had to agree a rendezvous position for a forthcoming operation, code-named Remarkable, in Kuala Bernam, the mouth of the Bernam River. The passengers approved this southermost site and that completed the day's business.

On the morrow the real business of Gustavus VI began. Bennington had sailed knowing that the rendezvous site to be used would be one of three previously notified to him. The method of informing the agents in the field was rather more interesting. They were instructed to listen to All India Radio, and to note especially the way in which the news was introduced; depending on which of the following alternatives was used, they would know which rendezvous had been chosen:

a. You are listening to a News Bulletin from All India Radio.
b. This bulletin comes to you from All India Radio.
c. This bulletin comes to you from the Central News Room of All India Radio.

It was ingenious. Departmental secrecy demanded that that not even the captain of *Tally-Ho* be aware of the secret. Despite this, and because of perfect coordination, *Tally-Ho* and a junk met at the appointed place, eight miles south of Pulau Jarak. Through the periscope it was perfectly possible to identify individual personnel on board the junk; but identification did not rule out the possibility that the rendezvous might be being kept under duress, with a Japanese prize crew concealed and ready to spring the trap. Accordingly it was necessary to wait until nightfall before making contact and in so doing follow set procedures.

At 1829, in darkness, *Tally-Ho* surfaced near the junk. A reconnaissance boat was passed up on to the casing and quietly launched. Fenner emerged from the torpedo loading hatch into a silence in which his own heavy breathing and heart-beats seemed unbearably loud.

There was a whispered, 'Can you see the junk?'

'No,' Fenner replied, 'Just point me in the right direction.'

Coming immediately from the fore-ends of *Tally-Ho*, which of necessity had to be illuminated, he found he was nearly blind. It didn't matter, he'd keep straight by steering on a star and in a matter of minutes his eyes should accommodate. Three minutes later he still couldn't see the junk. On board *Tally-Ho* no one worried, the observer on the bridge whose keen eyesight was accustomed to the dark could see not only the junk but the reconnaissance boat as well. Fenner half turned and looked over his left shoulder; to his horror, now even *Tally-Ho* had disappeared. He was alone and totally lost, wearing only a pair of swimming trunks, in the midst of the Malacca Strait. He gritted his teeth and continued paddling towards the rendezvous junk that he couldn't see.

His persistence was rewarded for the junk appeared in precisely the right spot. Now came the recognition signal — a password in English with a counter-sign — which began plausibly enough with formal question and answer, then degenerated to rugger-club level of humour:

Question: What's your name?

Answer: Something that clings to the wall.

Question: What's that? Shit?

Reply: No. Ivy.

When he heard the final word Fenner eased his boat alongside the junk. His relief was complete when, on looking back, he was able to see the submarine. The junk had been identified by a scarlet blanket slung, apparently negligently, over her port quarter. This was standard practice in the field and was considered potentially less incriminating than the 'full dress' procedure laid down in the memorandum enigmatically entitled N.E.X.T./3 and prepared in *Adamant*.

Recognition Procedure. From NOON local time on each or both of the above dates, the junk belonging to the EMER-GENCY GUSTAVUS VI party and REMARKABLE I is to be at the arranged rendezvous position, where it will carry out the following procedure, commencing at NOON exactly.

Lower its sail or if two-masted its mainsail for 15 minutes while the crew congregate aft, and then repeat the performance every 2 hours until dark. Two hours before sunset the junk is to endeavour to draw clear of any other junk in the vicinity but, when using the rendezvous position off the coast of MALAYA, is not to close the coast in so doing for fear of leading the submarine into shallow water. After dark the junk is to lower her sail or sails and await canoe from submarine.

The advantage in the field practice was that once the blanket was in position, the junk crew were free to go about their normal business and need not act suspiciously, and in the course of their daily routine they kept an eye peeled for the rendezvous submarine's periscope. The risk of another junk appearing with a red blanket draped over her gunwale was considered well worth taking.

Fenner was helped aboard the junk and a brief conference took place. The object of the rendezvous had been to bring out Broome and Davis and to land the Gustavus VI party. Unfortunately, increased Japanese activity in the area had forced Captain Davis and Major 'Freddy' Chapman[1] to stay away from the rendezvous. The situation was such that any chance of a European attending was completely precluded.

On board the junk, Fenner found Chen Ping, Foreign Minister of the MCP in Malaya, whom Fenner had met before, and Ying, one of the officers whom Freddy Chapman had deputed to attend the rendezvous on his behalf. Fenner with plenty of experience of this type of operation, did not spend long in an exchange of courtesies or in discussions; equally he knew that such matters did require attention. Speaking fluent Chinese, Malay and Urdu he could cope with all such situations. Before long he was on his way back to *Tally-Ho*. He quickly came aboard once more and passed below with a single muttered sentence: 'Don't get the folboats up yet, we may not need them.' Joe Brighton hoped sincerely that that would not be the case.

In his rapid progress through the torpedo loading hatch, up

[1] The late Colonel Frederick Spencer Chapman DSO, author of *The Jungle Is Neutral*, whose suicide on 8 August 1971 shocked the world.

for'ard, down into the bowels of the submarine as far as the wardroom, Fenner was again quite blind. Speed was now vital. He seated himself at the wardroom table and flung on to it a toothpaste tube he'd been clutching in his left fist. Then he set to work. The *Tally-Ho* officers watched in amazement as he opened the tube from the bottom and began squeezing toothpaste on to table without bothering to unscrew the cap. He separated one largish lump from the rest of the mess and appeared to be trying to dissect it, occasionally pausing to wipe his toothpaste-smeared hands on his torso. Inside the tube in a French letter had been concealed a very small piece of paper with upon it a message in cipher and valuable situation reports. The rubber contraceptive sheath which protected the message had been so well concealed that its presence would have been undetected even had the tube been squeezed flat.

Claude Fenner then swiftly deciphered the message. There was to be no transfer of personnel: the strategic situation was far too dangerous. By now his vast frame was coated with perspiration as well as toothpaste. A reply was rapidly composed and borne back to the junk for onward transmission. It would be carried, concealed in the brain cavity of a dried fish, along lonely Sakai tracks, through the equatorial forest, up into the hills where the scattered kampongs were rare to the secret hideout of Blantan Camp, some eighty miles distant as the crow flies and 2,500 feet above sea level. The malodorous hiding place was just as safe as the sophisticated modern cache of the collapsible aluminium foil tube. In addition dried fish was a perfectly natural commodity for anyone passing through the jungle to be carrying.

As soon as Fenner was back the reconnaissance boat was discreetly sunk and *Tally-Ho*, at a speed of twelve knots, moved out of the area north-westwards towards Diamond Point. Procedure for special operations forbade any attack during the next forty-eight hours, and common sense demanded that she make herself scarce and move to another area. At such times the Special Forces personnel could not be unaware of the submariners' disapproval. There was nothing personal in it. The crews of the boats knew that their patrols were intended to sink shipping; they also knew that special operations curtailed their effectiveness to carry out this most important duty. Moreover, the extreme secrecy that attended special operations was a further irritant. Patrol reports of operational submarines were classified SECRET. Those of boats on special operations were MOST SECRET and must be kept separate from the patrol with which they were associated. It was inevitable that no captain and crew of a submarine could appreciate a strategic situation involving special operations.

On 8 December 1941 the Japs had begun their onslaught on the Malay Peninsula with a landing at Kota Bharu and by bombing Singapore. As it became apparent that the Japanese advance was both rapid and impossible to check, the Malayan Communist Party renewed their earlier proposal that they be armed by the British to form a Chinese fighting force to oppose the Japanese. At first this proposal was not favoured in high places, but Federated Malay States police officers and others continued to keep contact as liaison officers with the MCP.

At the same time stay-behind parties were being organised by 101 STS (Special Training School) hastily forming groups to include not only Malays, Chinese and Indians but also such expatriate Europeans as planters and policemen. The Malayan Country Section was formed by Basil Goodfellow with Broome and Davis as his advisers in July the following year. In October 1942, a Chinese escaped out of Singapore to Penang, from there he trekked overland through Siam to China. Careful interrogation of him revealed that a very strong feeling of resistance existed in the Malay Peninsula. So strong was it that even the Japanese massacres and atrocities had failed to crush it. The Malays themselves had also become determined to oust the Japanese invaders.

Chinese morale had remained high and the people supported the guerilla forces. It seemed precisely the time when Europeans with knowledge of the language should be used to direct the resistance. The Chinese, of course, could more easily collect information than could the Europeans but this would form a useful side effect to an operation. One of the first agents was Lim Bo Seng, a Straits-born Chinese, educated at Hong Kong University and trained in India. (Sadly, he was killed before the war ended.) Davis and Broome were keen to get into the field. Transport at this time was by Dutch submarines: the only ones operational in that area. Broome, Davis and Claude Fenner had all been involved in the early Gustavus operations, begun as trips in which Europeans and Chinese were transferred to junks for landings on the coast between Penang and Port Swettenham.

The patrol off Diamond Point was a somewhat dismal one. With an absolute prohibition on all attacks still in force, there was virtually nothing of value that could be undertaken apart from observing enemy shipping movements in the hope of being able to report something of importance. Communications difficulties manifested themselves and there was some concern lest anxiety be felt in Ceylon if the single code indicating the completion of the special operation were not sent. As no shipping movements could be observed off Diamond Point, Bennington decided to shift from the Sumatra side of the Strait across to the Malay Peninsula side. On the following day, once the attack prohibition had elapsed, *Tally-Ho* would be in good position to move southwards and patrol in the profitable Penang area.

However, a whole day was spent patrolling between Butang and Pulau Langkawi. The previous patrol had indicated that this should be on the principal route south, even so nothing whatsoever was sighted; and, at the end of the day, *Tally-Ho* under cover of darkness moved south. During the night passage she was swept north by a tidal movement, and on taking the morning star shot before diving, Lieutenant Bennett established that they had been affected by a powerful tidal set. The day passed without incident. At night *Tally-Ho* proceeded seawards to charge batteries and then set course 130° for the north-west corner of Pulau Penang.

At 0900 on 9 January 1944, still closing Penang Island, the officer of the watch reported sighting mastheads. Inevitably Bennington appeared in the control room promptly after the request for 'Captain, in the control room'. In the early morning light it was difficult to see clearly, and automatically he began mentally to list what he might discover. After seven minutes, two or possibly three funnels could be discerned, a large bow wave — so the vessel was moving fast — and altering course on a zig. The zig-zag movement put her in a position where her extreme

F

length — at least 400 ft, perhaps 500 ft — was apparent. It was also revealed that she had three funnels with no perceptible backward rake. There was no longer any doubt in his mind: he had identified her.

Bennington spoke sharply, 'Cruiser — probably *Kuma* class — look it up in Janes'. The briefest of comparisons between the printed page and the view through the periscope was enough to confirm the diagnosis he'd already formulated. 'No doubt about it: down periscope, steer 230°, full ahead together, group up.' With the grouper switch up and the electric motors armatures in parallel *Tally-Ho* forged ahead on both motors at nine knots, her fastest submerged speed. During the brief respite before Bennington's next periscope observation Steadman passed on the news to the passengers in the wardroom. 'I should watch this,' he said rubbing his hands, 'it could be well worth watching'. With that he was gone. For once Bennington in his haste had attended the control room with only a towel round his waist. Suddenly he nearly lost it. Both passengers grinned at one another in view of Steadman's recent advice.

Leaning out of the wardroom entrance Fenner could just hear Bennington's comments as he made the next periscope observation. 'Cruiser turning sharply to port — away from us.' The rating keeping the control room log scribbled it down eagerly and pencilled the time 0915 alongside it. 'Cruiser's done a complete circle — could be exercising man overboard — I think she's increasing speed: course almost due west — we've lost her.' Regretfully Bennington folded the periscope, training handles inwards, and ordered it to be lowered. His last words before leaving the control room did not reach the passengers just outside it.

Bennington strode swiftly past them into his cabin, doubtless anxious to be more substantially dressed for the next emergency. Steadman reported Bennington's last pronouncement, 'He's certain she's based on Penang, has gone to sea for exercises and must be returning eventually. We'll hang on here: we've got nowhere to go, anyway. What a targer, if she does return!' he ended. Hannah and Fenner both wondered at his serenity; when he spoke of the cruiser returning he seemed radiantly happy. They wished they could experience something other than apprehension about such matters. Their feelings were understandable; they'd been keyed up for the special operation, called back at the last moment, and now had to tag along on an offensive patrol for a whole fortnight.

The atmosphere was beginning to thicken already: duties of some sort would have been a welcome distraction. Hannah reached for the cribbage board that at least could occupy them for a bit. But just what to do after that? Perhaps the cruiser wouldn't be long, he reflected, realising as he did that the very thought of it produced a sinking feeling in the stomach.

Bennington had already established his own forecast of future developments. In all probability the cruiser would use a standard area for her day's exercises. The restricted access to Penang Harbour meant that she'd almost certainly navigate the same course to return as she used on her outward passage. It was certainly worth remaining close to that route even if it took time.

The time that it took was not wasted. Bennington wanted all eight bow torpedo tubes serviceable and on the top line. Jackie Warner reported: 'One torpedo unserviceable when pulled back.' Bennington decided that seven would suffice. A *Kuma*-class cruiser was a plum target and he'd certainly be justified in expending a salvo of seven torpedoes. He regretted it wasn't eight.

The cruiser was next sighted at 1800 hours at a distance of 5 miles again steering a zig-zag and escorted by a smaller ship, probably a destroyer. Bennington decreased speed momentarily to steady *Tally-Ho* and give the Asdic operator the best possible chance by decreasing revs. George Backman reported that the echo he was picking up was being swamped, or blanketed by inshore water noises. Bennington noted this fact with interest as well as chagrin. He was in an awkward position; it was certainly too light to surface: the submarine would have been silhouetted against the eastern sky. At the same time it was not yet light enough for a periscope-depth attack. Their was no point in wasting torpedoes. 'Break off the attack,' he said simply. As he left the periscope his observant glance fell on the control room log and he couldn't repress a wry grin: one of the messengers had filled in the day's date as '9 January 1944 – GLOOMY SUNDAY!' His own contribution to the patrol report later that night, with the cruiser snug in Penang Harbour was more optimistic.

If the cruiser left harbour for further exercises or for another destination, it seemed likely that the route employed would not differ much from that previously employed. It was resolved to sit tight on this route and endeavour to improve the enemy's destination should he appear.

The best strategy would be to close Penang just before dawn and sit on the cruise; route until she did appear. Two days later at 0815, whilst keeping a methodical watch, Jackie Warner, the officer of the watch, reported a float plane apparently following the cruiser route at low altitude. In Bennington's words:

It was felt that this heralded the approach of the cruiser.

Jackie Warner was still at the periscope. For perhaps the hundredth time he focussed on the harbour entrance. Then, without further suspense, what he was imagining was before him in reality. 'Masts of the cruiser in sight,' he reported. Bennington clapped him briefly on the shoulder. 'Good man.' Then to Steadman, 'Close up the attack team Number One.' Jackie reluctantly left the control room to do his own job in the fore-ends.

Bennington tried to focus on the approaching cruiser. The masts had first appeared fine and clear but then followed a period of confusing mirage conditions when the cruiser split itself into three images. Once this had settled down it was clear the cruiser was fine on the port bow on a nearly opposing course to *Tally-Ho*. Therefore Bennington had only the bow wave on which to gauge the enemy's speed. When first seen the range had been over four miles. Bennington adjusted the double images of the search periscope until one was exactly over the other, the phantom *Kuma*-class cruiser riding serenely on the funnel tops of the real one. 'My range is *that*,' he pronounced. Underhill, the Electrical Artificer, standing behind him read off the angle in degrees and minutes from the scale on the periscope. Bennett did a slide rule calculation and announced 6,000 yards.

Bennington spoke again, 'The bearing is *that*'. Underhill read off the mark on the annular scale around the periscope, 'Red Five

Zero'. Scott-Maxwell marked the first target position on the plotting chart. He now knew the target was 6,000 yards away and 20° on the port bow. With three or more such plotted positions, each with its time against it, he'd be able to estimate the target's speed and if necessary predict its future positions. Unlike any other device available at that time the simple plot was a complete historical record with a memory. To exploit it required exact mathematical science.

The duties of *Tally-Ho*'s crew with the attack team closed up were exact. Coxswain 'Ginger' Ridley on the after 'planes, Second Coxswain Arthur ('Simmo') Simpson was on the fore 'planes. Thus Bennington had the best possible controllers of depth and direction at their posts. The First Lieutenant was watching the trim and the indicator lights on the blowing and venting panel. Scott-Maxwell presided over the attack team proper personally marking up the plot; it was not usual yet again Scott-Maxwell had become interested in the job and demonstrated that he did it well. Bennington now liked him to oversee and coordinate all those who contributed to attack efficiency.

The navigating officer worked the Submarine Torpedo Director ('fruit machine' as it was nicknamed). Once the dials of this machine, an early form of computer, had been set to show own course, speed and direction and that of the enemy it would predict a 'director angle', or degree of aim-off necessary to secure a hit. Like any other computer it was only as accurate as its input. If the data, particularly the captain's periscope observations and especially his *interpretation* of what he could see, were at fault the fruit machine had no magic powers to produce the right answer. Scott-Maxwell reckoned he could tell just as much from the plot. This was almost certainly true but it required exceptional skill and practice. By looking after matters of detail with the rest of the attack team Scott-Maxwell left Bennington free to concentrate on his periscope observations.

Bennington's first range and bearing observations were timed at 0906 hours. Over the next five minutes further observations came up thick and fast. 5,200 yards, 3,600 yards, 3,200 yards. To the passengers by the wardroom doorway one thing was apparent: they were getting pretty close. To Scott-Maxwell the plot showed that the cruiser had been going straight for almost three miles: this seemed too good to hope for: there had been only one alteration of course, shortly after the first range and bearing observation. Sure enough, just then Bennington reported, 'She's turning starboard — towards us — about 15° off her previous course. What does that make her course?'

He didn't have to wait long for his answer: '265°,' he was told.

'Director angle for a 95° track angle?' he requested seconds later.

'29° red,' came the reply.

During this period Bennington had not been able to take leisurely periscope observations with the instrument constantly above the surface. It had been essential to raise it only for brief periods and when travelling slowly. To raise the periscope when travelling fast would produce a conspicuous white 'feather' or wake. To do so now would invite sudden retribution. On board the *Kuma*-class cruiser there were certainly look-outs paid to spot periscopes. Whether they'd be drawing next week's pay was problematical.

Bennington now stepped up to the for'ard end of the control room and raised the attack periscope. Fenner knew very well the significance of this move: the attack periscope is only used in the final stages of attack — to take aim. The end couldn't be long delayed now. Then, regardless of whether the torpedoes fired reached their target or not, all hell would be let loose. From what he'd already heard Fenner knew that the cruiser had a destroyer escort in attendance; he also knew very well that destroyers carried depth-charges.

Bennington now spoke clearly and incisively and without emotion. 'Open bow caps 2, 3, 4, 5, 6, 7 and 8.' A pause followed before, 'Put me on my director angle.' Underhill reached up and placed his hands on the periscope handles over those of his captain; he then gently rotated the periscope and Bennington; as he did so Underhill carefully watched the degrees on the annular scale over Bennington's head. 'On director angle,' he said quietly as he stopped.

In the control room now no one moved and the silence seemed unbearable. To Fenner, Bennington still seemed untired and unruffled and did not even look particularly hot. All at once action replaced inactivity. 'Stand by No. 2, 3, 4, 5, 6, 7 and 8 torpedo tubes, prepare to fire on seven-second intervals . . . Fire! Carry on firing on the stopwatch.'

This complicated order meant that seven torpedoes would be fired over three ship's lengths. As a result the first would be discharged a whole length ahead of the cruiser, the last a whole length behind it. Provided the torpedoes ran true, theoretically Bennington could not fail to hit the target. If it remained at its present speed the middle torpedoes of the salvo must hit it. If the cruiser saw the torpedo tracks she could do one of two things: she could go full ahead in the hope they would pass astern, in which case she'd catch up with the first of the torpedoes fired; if alternatively she went full astern she'd lose way and the last of the salvo would get her. At a speed of 20 knots the cruiser would not stand a chance of turning towards *Tally-Ho* fast enough to avoid her torpedoes by 'combing their tracks'.

After the firing of the first torpedo Bennington lowered the periscope and firing of the remainder continued by timed intervals. In the fore-ends, Joe Brighton had removed the safety pins from the small operating levers on the firing panel. Joe did not have Bennington's icy calm — frankly he was sweating like a bull. Beside him Jackie Warner held a stopwatch; he knew the success of the whole attack now depended on the precision with which he passed on Bennington's instructions to Joe. Methodically they worked through the whole salvo, Joe pulling down the levers each time Jackie said 'Fire!'

To Fenner still standing by the wardroom, the interplay of relayed orders was no longer clearly audible. All he could hear was the whump and surging gurgle as each successive torpedo was discharged. Just at the moment his insides appeared to be virtually duplicating those noises and he winced as he felt each torpedo leave its tube. After the last one was fired Bennington spoke calmly, 'Steer 070°, flood "Q", 80 feet'. As the quick-diving tank, 'Q' tank, filled with a noise like steam blowing off under pressure, the needles tilted on the depth gauges and *Tally-Ho* sank below periscope depth.

Bennington was looking quizzically at his watch. The range had

11 January 1944 05°34′N 100°03′

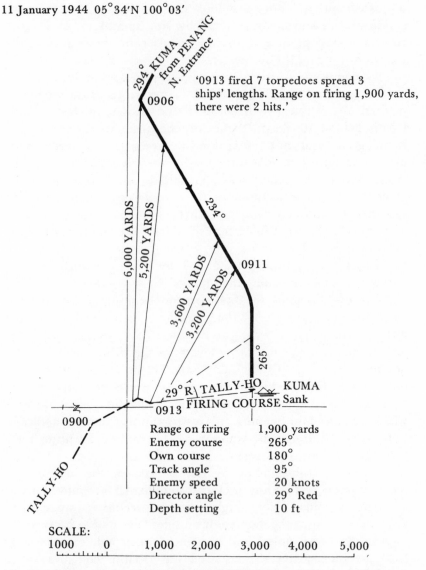

294° KUMA from PENANG N. Entrance

0906

'0913 fired 7 torpedoes spread 3 ships' lengths. Range on firing 1,900 yards, there were 2 hits.'

6,000 YARDS

5,200 YARDS

234°

0911

3,600 YARDS

3,200 YARDS

265°

29° R TALLY-HO   KUMA
0913 FIRING COURSE Sank

0900

TALLY-HO

Range on firing	1,900 yards
Enemy course	265°
Own course	180°
Track angle	95°
Enemy speed	20 knots
Director angle	29° Red
Depth setting	10 ft

SCALE:
1000   0   1,000   2,000   3,000   4,000   5,000

'On completion of the attack, HMS *Tally-Ho* increased depth to 80 ft and proceeded towards Penang North Entrance.

The destroyer counter attacked with 18 depth charges. These were three patterns of 4 and the remainder were single charges. The first two patterns rattled the rigging a bit.

At 1015 periscope observation revealed no sign of the cruiser. Later in the day, a lot of thick black smoke, which lasted 5 hours and suggested burning oil was seen in the vicinity of the position of the attack.'

L.W.A. Bennington
patrol report

been 1,900 yards: no more than 2 minutes running for a torpedo
They must hear something now. Two enormous explosions
followed in rapid succession like violent reverberating, metallic,
hammer blows. 'All right No. 1, make a general announcement,'
Bennington ordered.

Steadman had been waiting for this moment. Unhurriedly he
took hold of the tannoy's microphone and spoke with the incisive,
slow eloquence of a born showman: 'We have just scored two hits
on an enemy cruiser. Shut off for depth-charging. . . . Prepare for
depth-charging.'

The passengers moved into the wardroom and shakily picked up
the cribbage board and cards, each man wishing he had some duty
with which to occupy himself. Still, there was cribbage . . . but for
how long?

Bennington's patrol report has something of the quality of
Steadman's announcement,

> The destroyer counter attacked with 18 depth-charges there
> were 3 patterns of 4 and the rest were single charges. The
> first 2 rattled the rigging a bit.

The party in the wardroom couldn't help taking things rather
more personally. When the first charge exploded, Snoopy shot
from under the wardroom table with a piercing squeal. The cat
was last seen travelling in a straight line, only changing direction
when it struck something solid. It didn't reappear for three days.

The second bursting charge put the lights out with a brilliant
flash from the switchboard in the wardroom. To Fenner, the flash
had no electrical significance: it represented the flash of an
explosion: probably several tons of water would follow it. When
the lights came on again he picked up the cards and went on
dealing. He went on dealing for a long while: it did not occur to
him that another player should deal occasionally.

Steady looked in before long, quite unabashed to give them a
progress report. He was carrying a piece of chalk and explained
that he'd been checking up and marking small leaks wherever he
could find them. He was particularly matter-of-fact about it. 'Oh,'
he said, 'I almost forgot Ben's taking us close inshore. The Japs

will never think of that. Isn't it a good idea?'

He was unable to elicit unqualified support for the stratagem from the passengers. They felt too shaken and ill at ease to be completely convinced by this glib explanation. Minutes earlier they had been plunged into utter darkness and, as Fenner later put it, 'there is nowhere more dark than a submarine when the lights are put out'. To Hannah and Fenner it seemed, frankly, all too simple a ruse and the chances of its success problematical in the extreme.

CHAPTER FOUR

The Hunter Hunted

The Japanese cruiser *Kuma* cost some £1,000,000 to construct. Her construction took two years – all but three days – from the laying down of the keel to her completion on 31 August 1920. On 11 January 1944, her life was ended by two of the torpedoes of the 'hose-pipe salvo' fired from *Tally-Ho* on Bennington's orders.

Kuma had been the first of her class, a new class of 5,500-ton cruisers developed from the *Tenryu* class. Five in all were built and the not inconsiderable armament of each included seven 5.5-in. guns. *Kuma*'s defensive equipment was augmented in 1927 by the addition of a catapult to take a spotter float plane. That float plane was airborne over the Malacca Strait at the time of the attack and so witnessed the end of the cruiser's not too distinguished career. It was a career that had begun shrouded in mystery: no official data had been published on her trials; but it is believed that she achieved 64,500 h.p. and a speed of 33 knots. The high spot of her career came in June 1935 when she was the flagship of the Fifth Fleet.

Anonymity accompanied her demise. No one on board *Tally-Ho* knew for certain that she was the *Kuma*, though it was recognised what class she was when she was sunk in only fifteen fathoms, a mere twelve miles from the north-eastern point of Pulau Penang. Her crew numbered 436 in contrast to the sixty or so aboard *Tally-Ho*.

In the circumstances it seemed hardly likely that the enemy would take the loss of *Kuma* with equanimity. Bennington had spent an entire forty-eight hours after first sighting her, lying in wait outside harbour and finally stalking and sinking her. So it was extremely probable that the enemy would be just as keen to catch up with *Tally-Ho*. This was obvious to Bennington who was also well aware, from intelligence reports, that the enemy would almost certainly mobilise every available aircraft and surface vessel to search for *Kuma*'s attacker. Inevitably, an escorting destroyer was first to the attack.

In common with the vast majority of destroyers and escort vessels operated by all nations at that time, she had depth-charge chutes on her stern and depth-charge-throwers mounted to fire to port and starboard. Thus by dropping a single charge over the stern, then simultaneously firing charges to port and starboard and following up by a further charge from the stern chute, a pattern of four charges in the outline of a diamond shape could be produced. This could be repeated as long as the stock of depth-charges lasted. As one destroyer ran out of 'ash cans', as the charges were popularly called, it could be relieved by another and the attacks could be continued until the submarine's destruction was certain. That was the theory.

Whilst Steadman's explanation of Bennington's strategy may have sounded glib, Bennington's approach to the situation he found himself in was far from superficial. He had already evaluated his enemy: his experience, on the first patrol, had been enough to convince him that he was up against a less cunning foe than he had faced in the Mediterranean or the Bay of Biscay; also one that was not so well equipped. The antics of the submarine chaser, off Penang, on his first patrol had indicated to him that Japanese listening devices were crude and ineffective. It had been only too obvious that the Japanese submarine chaser could only hear with clarity when stopped. The previous night his own Asdic, with a first-class operator on the set, had been rendered ineffective by water noise inshore.

Therefore when he decided to go close inshore, he did so, having decided, first that his opponents would not anticipate this course of action, and second that their sound-location devices would not be good enough to track *Tally-Ho* to her hiding place. It needed skill, it needed technical expertise; both these qualities *Tally-Ho*'s crew can be said to have possessed in good measure. It also needed a certain amount of luck. The submarine stood a far greater chance of being spotted inshore, especially from the air.

In such a situation silence was essential; everyone on board *Tally-Ho* was maintaining silence to an agonising degree. Even the wardroom passengers shuffled their cards silently. Fenner, incidentally, was still dealing and morbidly certain that the Japanese could not fail to see through Bennington's ruse. At about the time he realised that he had been dealing far longer than was usual it became apparent to the passengers that perhaps, after all, Bennington's idea had succeeded. Certainly everyone aboard was going about his duties as though that were a foregone conclusion.

By mid-morning the situation had become agreeably placid. No explosions had been heard for some time and the last had seemed very distant. Needless to say 'silent routine' was still being maintained, and in consequence the quietly spoken orders – the only orders given since the attack – were clearly audible in the wardroom. Just before 1130, Bennington, who had been examining the chart, ordered 'Periscope depth'. 'Oh, no,' groaned two equally quiet voices from the wardroom. Now that things had settled down, surely he couldn't want to start it all over again.

Bennington made a quick and extremely thorough. reconnaissance through the eye-pieces and did not speak until the periscope was again being lowered. 'No sign of the destroyer; a couple or so aircraft flying about the scene of the attack.' Then, almost as an afterthought, he added: 'Thick black smoke over fires on the water in that region, too.'

Steadman was in the wardroom in seconds, beaming gleefully. 'Okay,' said the nearest passenger, 'we heard. What else?'

'We're going down to 60 feet,' replied Steadman and his listeners felt this really was good news.

Elsewhere on board, people were going about their duties as though nothing had happened. Anyone who had served with Ben had faith in him. Most of the crew knew what to listen for in depth-charge attacks. Explosions above the submerged boat were regarded as no more than unpleasant noise. Those at her actual depth were the ones that caused pressure damage. To a layman, being hunted by a destroyer dropping depth-charges seemed a hopeless situation with but one outcome: how long till they got you? In practice, with skill and experience at one's disposal, there was a lot the quarry could do to avoid her hunter. One trick was to change direction when the enemy was actually lining up overhead to drop his charges and, of course, listening for the sound of your propellers. It needed timing of the most precise nature and an icy calm.

With luck you might even persuade the enemy to follow your wake instead of yourself. In the Mediterranean it had been possible to 'layer ride', by remaining in a condition of 'stopped trim' just on the top of a salty layer. As a result the dense saline layer would deflect the attacking vessel's detecting Asdic beam. However, whilst prejudiced in favour of their captain's tactics, the bulk of *Tally-Ho*'s crew were far too busy to brood on the successful outcome or otherwise of the hunt that was going on above them. There was much to be done to repair shattered electrics, to clear away broken glass and the remnants of smashed crockery as well as to navigate the submerged vessel.

In the fore-ends, Joe Brighton was completing an entry in the Torpedo Log. It was necessary to record the serial numbers of all torpedoes fired, that they had been fired at periscope depth and on a 10-feet depth setting. Being a very human person 'Joe' also liked to note any other small point that seemed to him to be of moment. He has never forgotten the entry he made that day:

Sank 5,000-ton cruiser of the *Kuma* class. Gave her the works and waited for the rebate. Got eighteen depth-charges from destroyer escort but none uncomfortably close.

This, of course, was simply Joe's own view. The passengers, for example, would have been hard put to it to agree with him about the nearness of depth-charges. The figure of eighteen was Joe's own. During the *Kuma* engagement Bennington counted up to 600 explosions of depth-charges and/or bombs. After that he gave up counting. But, typically, he did not talk about that. Few of the crew knew Bennington's precise views on the probabilities of survival in the Submarine Branch. All knew that the escape hatches were securely fixed from the outside. Once, on the bottom of the Malacca Strait during an attack, Bennington did confide in Scott-Maxwell that he'd rather stay down below if it came to it in the end. He would not attempt escape by DSEA or any other way if it meant surrendering to the Japanese: he knew too much about them to attempt that.

From the orders that could be heard in the wardroom, it was apparent that *Tally-Ho* was at last edging away from Pulau Penang and the approaches to Penang Harbour, North Entrance. Discreet periscope observations were kept on the scene of the attack. Bennington made precise, professional notes on what could be seen for his patrol report.

Thick puffs of black smoke continued in the same place till 1745. Sometimes there were heavy clouds of smoke and sometimes it dwindled to slight wisps. It had the appearance of an oil fire and it is considered that it was burning fuel from the cruiser. When the smoke was last seen *Tally-Ho* was over 20 miles from scene of the attack. During the early part of the afternoon a number of small explosions were heard. Previous experience suggests that these might have been exploding depth-charges or drums of combustibles exploding.

It is submitted that the cruiser sank.

He didn't add that, in his opinion, it would have been a miracle if she hadn't sunk. Considerable care was necessary whilst making the periscope observations. Aircraft were continually in sight overhead, and periodically the Asdic operator picked up sounds of surface patrol activity. By 1830 Bennington deemed it safe to consider surfacing.

More than usual care was necessary: seven torpedoes having been fired, a pressure had built up inside the boat. Whilst this pressure was not particularly high, the size of the contained volume was considerable; sudden injudicious release of the pressure had buckled hatches in other submarines. Consequently a tackle was rigged so as to get a purchase on the lower 'lid' and effect the release of pressure as gradually as possible. Reaction to the strain of the attack, depletion of the oxygen content in the air by the day's long submersion, and the nausea induced by the sudden influx of air by opening the hatches caused many of the ship's company to feel sick and unwell.

Trim changes due to the loss of the seven torpedoes' weight had to be catered for, and some sudden rapid trim changes were necessary after surfacing to be sure that *Tally-Ho* could make a rapid submersion if she had to. Ginger Ridley checked the rum jars and reported one cracked by the depth-charge explosions. Bennington ordered a supplementary rum issue: it was much appreciated, especially by Joe since it was Johnny's birthday and Johnny made Joe a present of his tot. Joe was so touched that he drew a small sketch of a rum tot measure in his torpedo log. ERA John Stewart Heath and Joe had known one another quite a long time. Even so, the gift of a tot was a very generous gesture. 'Sippers' was not uncommon: 'gulpers', even, not unknown but a whole tot was something to be reserved for special occasions.*

Thoughtfully turning the pages of his log, Joe carefully unfolded his bookmark; it was very precious to him and he still has it today. It was in his daughter's handwriting and had been inside one of the last letters he received from home from his wife.

> 'Dear DaDDy
> When will you come home a gane. I would like to no. Please.
> I am goig to sunday Sgool the South Doon.
> Love from Pat X X X X'
> (There were also three hug symbols: on the reverse side was a picture of a yacht, a boat with two funnels, and a brightly shining sun.)

The bookmark was already beginning to smell of the shale oil torpedo fuel of which the log already smelt. Thinking about his family, Joe wished he did know when he'd be home 'a gane'.

Just before midnight, whilst charging batteries, almost 100 miles south-west of the scene of the attack, one of the look-outs sighted an object astern which very soon assumed the shape of a submarine chaser. It was sighted on the port quarter and *Tally-Ho* altered course away from it. Within seconds of losing sight of the submarine chaser another was sighted to starboard. Again *Tally-Ho* made a 20° alteration of course and also put on speed. Although she succeeded in evading discovery, Bennington decided it would be prudent to submerge and go to 100 feet. Not long afterwards six depth-charges rained down and Bennington considered it likely that the submarine chasers would be lying in wait, listening or searching at very slow speed. Either way he decided to remain down till first light.

* After publication the author learned that 'Johnny' was, in fact, 'Ivy' Watts I × V = Watts) whose first name was Stanley, fore ends torpedoman. He would like to apologise to all concerned, especially since tot-bottling and rum consumption on patrol were strictly prohibited!

By now Steadman had discontinued his periodic progress reports to the passengers who seemed too glum to comprehend. During the night *Tally-Ho* received another troublesome signal; its contents were quite clear except for where precisely she should be mounting her patrol. Despite four transmissions received of the same signal, the all-important code names were impossible to decode. Nor could Scott-Maxwell's ingenuity avail them here. Whilst the location might be Car Nicobar, it could equally be Tillanchong Island or that of Batti Malv — and there was quite a difference.

Since midnight *Tally-Ho* had been proceeding on a reciprocal course back towards mid-strait and away from Sumatra. At 0410 she made a signal. Less than an hour after her signal it was necessary to submerge promptly when an aircraft was spotted. As Bennington put it:

An enemy float plane appeared, flying straight out of the sun and straight at the submarine. The aircraft dropped two bombs which were close enough to shatter the navigation side lights.

The two bursting bombs had roughly the same effect on the nerves of the passengers. With a job to perform the strain would have been less. They wished they could be like the Stoker who simply remarked, 'Them Japanese have got a bloody nerve!' Bennington, for once, felt bitter.

It is possible *Tally-Ho*'s signal had been D/F'd [used for radio direction-finding purposes] by the enemy and the aircraft guided to the position. This signal should not have been necessary. The Code and Decode were new books issued to the submarine the day before the patrol. They were reported as correct and up to date.

In fact Bennington was to be proved correct on this point. The reason why *Tally-Ho* had been unable to decode the place names was because the signals were made in a code issued after *Tally-Ho* had proceeded to sea. By 1241, out of sight of the Malay and

G

Sumatran shores, *Tally-Ho* set course for Car Nicobar, proceeding on the surface at full speed on diesels. An hour later she had to submerge for an aircraft. One of the passengers quipped: 'Them Japanese is bloody persistent!'

The same day came a more welcome signal confirming that they had sunk the cruiser and that it was the *Kuma.*

Almost sixteen hours of passage northwards up the strait followed, with *Tally-Ho* out of sight of land during the first eight hours. The time passed with dreary slowness and without incident. At 0420 on the morning of Friday, 14 January 1944, the bridge look-out reported Car Nicobar in sight and the submarine closed towards the island's northern side.

The island of Car Nicobar guards the Ten Degree Channel which stretches some 100 miles beyond its northern shores. Measuring a bare twenty miles from north to south the island is very nearly as broad as it is long. The greater part is flat but in its central area a single sharp peak rises to a height of almost 300 feet. On its south-eastern extremity is an airfield almost at sea level. In early 1944 this lent considerable importance to the island. The sole harbour of any moment is the ragged, semi-circular inlet of Sawi Bay which looks as though it was formed by some sea monster having taken a bite out of Car Nicobar.

It was off Sawi Bay that Bennington decided to patrol. His plan had its advantages: he was not more than 700 miles from Trincomalee in a straight line; he could afford to spend at least a day here before proceeding home. There was also quite a good chance of sinking shipping. Just before 0610 he gave the order to submerge and made a periscope-depth patrol across Sawi Bay. Nothing seemed to be stirring and *Tally-Ho* remained in the area mounting a periscope-depth patrol throughout that day.

Shortly before tea-time Bennington was at the periscope following the familiar call of 'Captain in the control room'. His enthusiasm at the news that smoke had been sighted was not shared by the passengers. To Fenner, in the wardroom suffering his usual queasiness from butterflies in the stomach, it was something of a tragedy. He had been counting the hours to surfacing time: now it was anyone's guess when they would next see the light of day. Bennington reported from the periscope, 'One

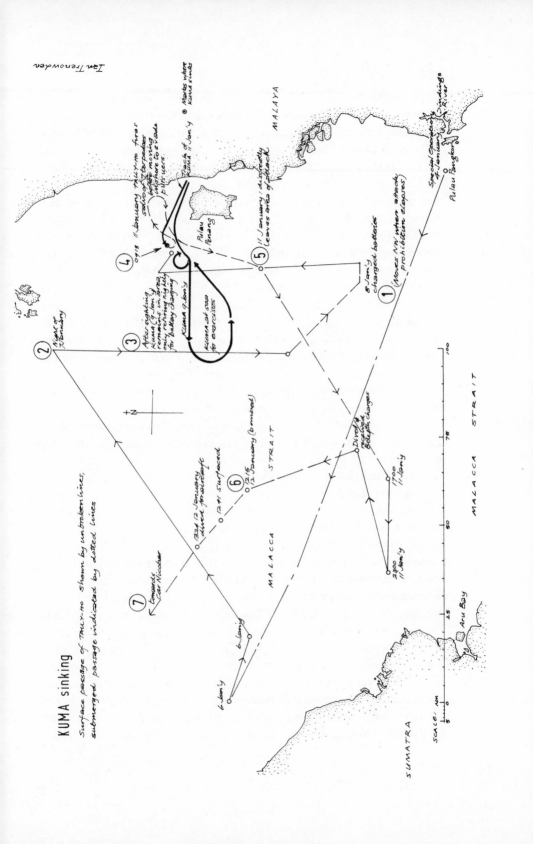

KUMA sinking

Surface passage of TALLY-HO shown by unbroken lines,
submerged passage indicated by dotted lines

Ian Trenowden

MALAYA

MALACCA   STRAIT

MALACCA   STRAIT

SUMATRA

SCALE: NM
0   5   25   50   75   100

Aru Bay

Special Operations
24 January, landings
Jurdick River

Palau Rangton

① (Moves NW when attack prohibition expires)

8 Jan'y
charged batteries

1700
11 Jan'y

2300
11 Jan'y

Dived &
resumed depth charger

② Night of
11 January

③ After sighting
Kuma (9 Jan'y)
remains in area
only retiring nightly
for battery charging

Kuma 9 Jan'y

Kuma at sea
for exercises

④ 0913 11 January TALLY-HO fires
salvo of torpedos
before moving
inshore to evade
pursuers

Track of
Kuma 11 Jan'y

⊙ Marks where
Kuma sinks

Pulau
Penang

⑤ 11 January; destroyer
leaves area of attack

⑥ 1215
12 January (bottomed)

0332 12 January
direct, microcraft

1241 surfaced

⑦ towards
Car Nicobar

6 Jan'y

6 Jan'y

N

medium-sized cargo vessel, probably burning coal. Also one escort vessel'. One of the passengers groaned and said, 'Here we go again!'

Bennington did not hear these comments. He spoke again with infinite sadness. 'He's coming in from the north-east: we're too far to the west . . . and out of torpedo range.' He decided to attempt an interception, giving the order to increase depth to fifty feet and put on full speed to cross the bay across their quarry's bows well ahead of torpedo range.

The enemy did not anchor in the bay. This did not surprise Bennington: there was a fairly rough, short sea running. His suspicion that she was coal burning was confirmed by closer observation. The vessel appeared in all respects to be the *Johore Maru* (6,000 tons) that they had seen on an earlier patrol. Her destination, he guessed, was Port Blair 120 miles to the north beyond Little Andaman Island. It was just dark enough for pursuit on the surface. Bennington followed for nearly four hours, at the end of which time he had apparently lost her. Then, at 2030, smoke was sighted almost dead ahead. Bennington instantly gave the order to slow from full speed ahead to 12 knots.

The radar, for once, was in use; usually Bennington put little faith in it and distrusted it. The first attempts to use it in the early days of the first patrol had been catastrophic. It had kept picking up cloud 'echoes' so that the alarm constantly had to be given for targets which did not materialise: it was so unsatisfactory that he had ordered the set to be switched off. Now, to everybody's surprise the operator reported a firm contact at 10,000 yards range.

Scott-Maxwell placed greater faith in radar than did Bennington. In the Mediterranean, in 1941, in *Proteus*, they had had the sole set in use in that theatre. On the evening of 9 November they had picked up a convoy on the screen. It had been one of the earliest forms of this sighting. *Proteus* had profited by this historic, scientific event to finish the night by sinking the Italian merchant vessel *Ithaka* (1,773 tons). Perhaps tonight's events would convert Ben to thinking that radar had its uses in submarines. At least he did order a range plot to be started.

Half an hour later, *Tally-Ho* was still steering a course of 010° to present the narrowest possible outline to the merchant vessel and escort. The radar plot gave their speed as 8-10 knots: it looked as if *Tally-Ho* might have her work cut out to catch them. The moonlight was brilliant enough for an early visual contact. A quarter of an hour later white cloud was obscuring the moon so Bennington decided to try and put himself on a parallel course with the merchant ship. *Tally-Ho* then ran flat out for ten minutes at full speed in an effort to get ahead of the two quarries. The chase on the surface had started at 1810 and it was now almost midnight.

If the tension was telling on the crew they did not show it, but in the wardroom the passengers were dealing cribbage cards again. Bennington decided to turn inwards towards the bows of his target and submerge in order to get close in before firing. There was no reason to suspect he had been spotted and he could use an ideal director angle of 90°. Even so, by moonlight it was a tricky shot on a medium speed target. It was, none the less, obliging of the enemy to have steered for six hours on a dead straight course. At 0031 *Tally-Ho* was dived quietly, without use of the klaxon, and taken down to periscope depth with the usual practised efficiency. A range of 5,000-6,000 yards was about the extreme: Bennington decided on a full salvo from the internal torpedo tubes. They should all now be working and on the top line. However, since it was possible *Tally-Ho* could have sustained external damage from her earlier bombing, he would fire all six.

After twenty minutes submerged, full ahead together grouped up, *Tally-Ho* was in position and Bennington fired all six torpedoes over two and a half ships' lengths. On firing, *Tally-Ho* increased depth to 300 feet and turned back towards Car Nicobar. As she did so the sound of a single hit brought Steadman to the wardroom rubbing his hands. Three and a half minutes later he was even more pleased; there was a loud explosion that sounded too loud and prolonged to be either a depth-charge or torpedo. A little later there were two more explosions that almost certainly were depth-charges or torpedoes. *Tally-Ho* made a further alteration of course and proceeded northwards towards Little Andaman Island. Five miles offshore, to the west, she surfaced at 0225 and made careful observations in the direction where the attack had taken place. As Bennington put it:

Nothing could be seen. Had the enemy been still afloat, it is considered almost certain that she would not have been outside visibility range.

It is believed the enemy sank.[1] The chase (on the surface and at periscope depth) and the attack lasted altogether just over nine hours. *Tally-Ho* was in no state to conduct a further search.

In short, the batteries were in serious need of charging. She promptly proceeded south, to a position where she could maintain a static patrol between Car Nicobar and Little Andaman Island. At first light, that is at 0607 on the morning of 15 January 1944, she dived. Her crew felt she had not done a bad day's work already. The day's patrol proved uneventful and at the end of it *Tally-Ho* received a signal ordering her to return to base.

Steadman passed on this intelligence to the passengers and explained sadly, 'We've not even seen a fishing boat here. In the Malacca Strait itself we often couldn't move for fear of hitting the bloody things'. He rather relished the shock that his second statement produced in the passengers.

The return journey took the usual three days of surface passage. Steadman stood some of his watches wearing a straw hat on the bridge. The entry to Trincomalee Harbour was made in late afternoon with the Jolly Roger fluttering limply from her periscope standards to record the kills.

Plainly it was a time for rejoicing for some. Fenner for one was glad to step shakily ashore and breathe something other than the rank atmosphere of the submarine's interior. The other passengers shared this view.

Bennington in one of the later comments of his patrol report summed up what he had felt about a patrol with ten passengers on board. Whilst it is extremely frank, the second comment illustrates his fairness of mind.

    (a) Weather conditions were generally pleasant and the health of the crew continued to be good. The presence of 10

---

[1] No one on board knew the name of the vessel they had attacked that day but, in fact, she was the *Ryuko Maru* (2,962 tons). And she had sunk.

passengers caused unpleasant overcrowding and shortage of
water.

(b) The behaviour of the passengers during the depth-charging
and bombing was admirable.

Bennington's recommendations regarding Scott-Maxwell and
John Metford Powell had produced results. A message from the
C-in-C Far Eastern Fleet to the Captain (S) of the Fourth
Submarine Flotilla contained the following extract:

> With reference to No. SO2/1140 of 27 December 1943, the
> ingenious and sustained efforts of Lieutenant (E) Scott-
> Maxwell and Chief ERA Powell to repair the high power
> periscope are noted with satisfaction. It is requested you will
> instruct the Commanding Officer of HMS *Tally-Ho* to inform
> these officers accordingly.

Naturally such tributes were gratifying. Nor did the bouquets
end there. In due course Captain (S) 4 wrote to the C-in-C on the
subject of the last patrol *Tally-Ho* had completed when she sank
the *Kuma*. He wrote:

> This was a most heartening patrol, carried out with exemp-
> lary skill and determination. The CO's appreciation of the
> situation was entirely right and his skill and determination
> received their just reward of two sinkings.
>
> The whole flotilla will benefit from these well earned
> successes, which will do much to take the taste out of one's
> mouth of so many patrols devoted to special operations.
>
> Not the least satisfactory aspect is the fact that all
> torpedoes ran correctly and no faults developed during the
> patrol. The additional tests carried out and the fact that the
> torpedo staff have worked hard and gained experience are
> responsible for this.

Bennington would certainly have agreed with the last comment.
Torpedo routines, checking, test running, pulling back and
reloading had all been carried out with a rigorous regularity that
ignored the heat, discomfort and cramped conditions of the

fore-ends. Nor did the praises end there. In due course a copy of the *Tally-Ho* patrol report was submitted to Rear Admiral C.B. Barry DSO, Flag Officer of Submarines. After reading it he added the following words in pencil in his own hand on one of the accompanying documents:

First rate. Type 291 (torpedo) seems to have achieved the best successes so far on this patrol. Request SO (Staff Officer) Radar and FLC will comment.

Will Secretary please ensure I see this again when Staff Officers have commented.

C. B. B. 29.3 (1944)

His second sentence put the successes of the patrol in their proper perspective. It had been a triumph of concerted team effort. Without a first-rate crew, well maintained machinery and equipment the successes could not have been achieved. Inevitably they were celebrated ashore by all ranks. Snoopy the cat celebrated his home-coming in his usual fashion and had to be fished out of Trincomalee Harbour. Bennington's own feelings about the whole episode were summed up very simply in his patrol report and, as before, they provide a very good note on which to finish.

The patrol off Penang and that off Car Nicobar were most enjoyable.

CHAPTER FIVE

Rammed !

A fortnight's respite was all that was necessary before *Tally-Ho* and her crew were ready for their next patrol. It also provided sufficient time for investigation and resolution of the matter of corrupt signals. Investigation revealed that no discredit attached to *Tally-Ho*. The parts of signals adjudged as corrupt had been encoded using code procedures promulgated after she had left harbour. There was therefore no means whereby they could have been made comprehensible. Although explanation in retrospect afforded some slight satisfaction, there seemed little point in dwelling on what was now part history. After a patrol one tended to be thinking of the next patrol to be undertaken.

Naturally the *Kuma* sinking had been celebrated by all ranks: after all, it had been the concerted efforts of all ranks that had achieved it. For Petty Officers and ratings this presented difficulties: beer was strictly rationed — it could only be obtained on presentation of a beer ticket — and only then in most modest amounts. In harbour this could be irksome: the 'senior rates', who were older than the general run of crew members, sometimes found themselves wishing they could bring back a bottle or two to enjoy on board. A few days before sailing Bennington found himself faced by what he considered his two most unlikely defaulters ever. Coxswain Ginger Ridley, as petty officer responsible for discipline, marched in the first offender: Joe Brighton, accused of having tried to smuggle a bottle of beer on board. Joe found himself outside again within seconds, having admitted the offence and been admonished. To Bennington's surprise, less than a minute later both men were back in front of him again. This time it was Joe who was in charge and Ridley who was accused. Joe briefly stated that Ridley had been found attempting to smuggle a bottle of beer on board. With a wry look at both men the captain repeated the formula of admonishment and dismissed them. Obviously it was high time they were at sea again. Bennington had no wish to have all his best NCO's turning up as defaulters.

Before *Tally-Ho* sailed again Bennington did make one request, on behalf of submarine commanding officers, with respect to special operations. Characteristically he made it formally in writing as an addendum to his patrol report:

> It is considered that reports of special operations should be written as appendices to patrol reports and not submitted separately. Only in this way can a patrol be examined in its entirety. Great value can be derived from the study of a CO's patrol reports if they are complete. A possible objection to the adoption of the suggestion lies in the fact that, at present, special operation reports are graded MOST SECRET whereas a patrol report is SECRET.

The points he raised were considered by staff officers back in Britain, but the questions of the varying gradings of secrecy were considered impossible to resolve and his suggestion was not adopted. Even so, with memories of the abortive, flooded-periscope patrol still vivid in his mind and his recent experience of ten passengers on a patrol Bennington could not help feeling strongly that a patrol could only be judged in entirety. This was impossible as long as reports of a special operation were kept completely separate.

At 1800 on 3 February 1944, *Tally-Ho* sailed from Trincomalee. The patrol began with gunnery and Asdic exercises which were completed before nightfall on the first day. The passage across the Bay of Bengal seemed to take even longer than usual. On the third day, whilst the submarine was travelling on the surface an alert look-out sighted an aircraft astern of them. Although it was flying high, there was no point in taking chances, so *Tally-Ho* submerged and stayed down for some hours. Inevitably this slowed her progress.

Even so, by the early hours of 7 February she was abeam of Pulau Rondo. Yet again *Tally-Ho* was entrusted with a special operation to be carried out around the middle of the month. To this end she was carrying Peter Young, a pre-war employee of the Hong Kong China Bank, who was to be landed with a Chinese wireless operator. Most of those on board were aware that he had already escaped once from Japanese captivity and had suffered terrible privations, although he didn't speak of those experiences. He and his wireless operator were rather less ebullient than had been the passengers on the previous patrol.

Bennington's intention was to work his way down the Strait as far as Malacca prior to carrying out the special operation. This would mean passing through the shallows around One Fathom Bank Lighthouse, which were notoriously difficult to navigate. Bennington was prepared to accept the difficulty because he had been led to believe that beyond it was a good area for picking up tanker traffic from Aru Bay. To this end a periscope-depth patrol was mounted for some days between Aroa Island and One Fathom Bank. By night *Tally-Ho* retired a short distance northwards up the strait to charge batteries. At first light on 17 February, she had to dive to avoid a twin-engined aircraft. Periscope observation revealed the aircraft circling over the original position where *Tally-Ho* had been spotted.

With a special operation in the near future Bennington was obliged to abandon his plan to proceed as far south as Malacca: any attempt to remain in, or pass through, the present area could well have compromised the special operation. His efforts to date on this patrol had been unrewarded and his disappointment can be discerned from his patrol report:

This was the fifth day in the One Fathom Bank Channel and no shipping had been sighted. It was not an easy patrol to maintain. The current had varied from day to day. The Aroa group is low and hard to find. In addition visibility had been consistently poor. By night there had been heavy continuous rains, by day a shimmering haze on a glossy sea had frequently limited periscope observations.

The approximate position of the submarine had now been disclosed to the enemy and, as a result, it appeared unlikely that shipping would attempt to use the passage of this channel in daylight. Coupled with this, the uncertain visibility and the difficulty of maintaining an accurate fix after dark whittled down the prospects of a successful night encounter to practically nothing.

In these circumstances, it was decided to shift patrol to the north-west and examine Aru Bay. A patrol in the neighbourhood of the Sembilian Islands might have been more profitable, but it was thought advisable to keep clear of this area until the special operation had been completed.

Tally-Ho therefore altered course north north-west, and proceeded up the strait. By mid-morning on the same day she was in sight of Pulau Jarak. A patrol was mounted between Pulau Jarak and Aru Bay but not a single target was seen despite a whole day's vigilance. On the night of 14-15 February, *Tally-Ho* having retired to mid-strait to charge batteries, it was decided to move close in towards the Malay coast on the far side of the strait in the hope of encountering coastal traffic. At 0515 the submarine was proceeding on the surface, almost due east towards the mouth of the River Dindings, when Lieutenant Michael Clark RN, the officer of the watch, reported sighting a surfaced U-boat. Bennington was on the bridge when the sighting was made. The U-boat was fine on the starboard bow almost dead ahead and proceeding at approximately 14 knots. A fast surface attack was essential; it could be the easiest thing in the world to miss the target.

At least there was no doubt it was hostile: no other Allied boats were due in that area. The enemy's course was almost due north so Bennington altered course to 090° to put himself on a 90° track angle. As *Tally-Ho* began to answer the helm, the U-boat was lost in an isolated patch of mist. In a surface attack, torpedoes are not aimed by periscope sighting, but by using the Torpedo Deflection Sights fixed to the bridge. Bennington crouched over the sight. His next alteration of course would probably be the last he'd have time to give before firing; accordingly his gaze was fixed on the spot where the U-boat had vanished. He had already ordered the fore-ends team to stand by for firing orders. Less than five minutes had elapsed since the first sighting.

'Steer 060°,' ordered Bennington aligning the sight. He would fire three torpedoes on a 120° track angle. It was now only a matter of waiting for the director angle to come on. It could only be a matter of seconds to firing. Throughout the attack the look-outs had never for a moment relaxed their vigilance. In a surface attack a submarine is in a most vulnerable position whilst her captain is aiming.

'Captain, sir, another U-boat, broad on the port bow.'

Bennington raised his head slightly in the direction indicated. Mentally he registered that as he couldn't see the boat it couldn't be close. He lowered his eyes once more to the bar of the sight just as the director angle came on. Hastily he issued his firing orders, hoping he hadn't missed his quarry. After the three torpedoes had been fired Bennington gave the order to submerge. Seconds before they went below Clark reported that the second U-boat was, in fact, a junk. Bennington didn't recriminate or complain: if he'd missed he didn't need others to excuse himself. Lighting conditions in the early dawn could be very tricky and Clark had particularly good eyesight: Bennington would not blame him.

He ordered *Tally-Ho* to be taken down to eighty feet together with an alteration of course 90° northwards. As he did so he glanced at his watch; the torpedoes seemed to have been running for a hell of a long time. Had the first one missed? However, his aim had not been at fault.

There was a torpedo explosion two minutes and twenty seconds after the firing time for the third torpedo. HE (hydrophone effect) stopped immediately. A few minutes later periscope observation showed nothing in sight. It is considered the U-boat was hit and that it sank.*

The U-boat which *Tally-Ho* attacked thirty miles north north-east of Pulau Jarak and thirty-two miles offshore had indeed been sunk. It was quite a rare specimen: the UIT 23, originally launched on 3 December 1939 under the name *Reginaldo Giuliani*. She had been one of three Italian submarines — the others were the *Capellini*, and *Torelli* -- captured at Singapore when Italy fell. The Japanese had no use for them, considering them too large and ungainly for tactical purposes, so they remained unproductively in

* *UIT 23* (Oberlt zur See Johannes W. Striegler) was hit near her stern by one of *Tally-Ho's* torpedoes and sunk in 10 seconds. There were fourteen survivors, including her captain, all of whom eventually reached Penang.

harbour for some time. On 8 February 1943, Hitler held his first conference as C-in-C of the German Navy: there Grossadmiral Dönitz suggested the Italian boats could be used for cargo-carrying to and from the Far East with German crews.

Accordingly the three boats had their machinery refitted, and radar and radio direction-finding equipment installed. It was a monumental labour, especially carried out as it was in Port Swettenham. The German crews who were to operate the boats were not over-impressed. One of them is quoted as commenting that in 1943, having regard to Allied submarine hunting and detecting devices, they belonged 'not to the sea but the scrap-heap'.

None the less, the three boats already mentioned, plus the *Bagnolini* and one other, were given the numbers UIT 21-25 and code named 'Merkator' boats — no doubt after Gerhard Kremer (Gerhardus Mercator) who lived from 1512-1594, and who produced the first chart on which meridians and parallels were represented as straight lines intersecting at right angles. The big advantage of Mercator's projection is that, on such a chart, if two places are joined by a straight line and its angle measured, the angle will represent the true bearing.

The allusion to Mercator navigation was appropriate for boats that were intended to navigate half-way across the globe: the reality proved not as intended. The *Reginaldo Giuliani*, with a cargo of Malay tin (a commodity of which the Third Reich was falling desperately short), did not get further than the first 140 miles of a journey that would probably have run to 10,000 miles. Not one of the 'Merkator' boats succeeded in bringing even a ton of cargo back safely to Germany. *Reginaldo Giuliani* was quite large; she carried a crew of about sixty and displaced over 1,000 tons on the surface. Her builders had been Tosi of Taranto.

Bennington was not aware of her precise identity when he attacked her. He recorded in his patrol report that she was a large U-boat, probably Japanese. With her massive superstructure she was like nothing German he had ever seen. *Tally-Ho* proceeded away from the area at four knots submerged. At midday she returned to the scene of the attack but there was nothing visible. There had been no attempts at counter-attack. This time the passengers had had comparatively little to put up with by comparison with the previous patrol.

The following day no targets could be seen and *Tally-Ho* moved further south towards the Sembilian Islands for the third phase of special operation *Remarkable.* This proved gallingly frustrating: it was possible neither to contact the agents on shore nor land the party.

Bennington wrote in his patrol report:

17-18-19 February 1944

Carried out Ceylon Operation Order No. 20. HMS *Tally-Ho* has now completed 3 phases of this operation. Altogether nine days have been spent on the operation, in addition considerable restrictions have been imposed on the submarine, both before and after the actual operation. It is felt that only an operation of major importance, that can be guaranteed an excellent chance of success, can justifiably keep a submarine off the fighting strength for such long periods.

Tally-Ho had been obliged to try for three days to make rendezvous with a junk off the Sembilian Islands, and Bennington was irked by the 48-hour prohibition of attacks both before and after the operation. Sinking a U-boat had whetted his appetite and he was keen to seek fresh targets. Towards the end of the third day of the special operation an incident occurred which particularly upset Bennington. At 1345 a medium-sized merchant ship was sighted, coast-crawling, tracking up the strait just outside the ten-fathom line escorted by a single trawler. It would have been child's play to have kippered it, escort or not. Bennington watched it sadly through the periscope lens as it passed slowly at a mere 10 knots. The merchant ship was close enough for him to observe that she was coal burning. He was clearly heard expressing himself in no uncertain terms on the habits of all pongoes in general and those engaged in special operations in particular.

Worse was to come. About half an hour later a larger ship was sighted, following the same course at about the same speed. As it approached it was seen to be high in the water, with a single funnel and square-shaped superstructure amidships. Just abaft of the superstructure two float planes, carried as deck cargo, were visible. Bennington identified it without difficulty. 'The seaplane carrier *Kamikawa Maru*,' he reported. She, too, was travelling north, probably to Car Nicobar where there was an airfield. She was an ex-mercantile vessel, as the suffix *Maru* in her name indicated, and she had been converted for use as an aircraft transport. Her gross tonnage was a full 6,853. To Bennington she seemed to idle past with deliberate, exasperating slowness.

Since both ships passed through his patrol positions, he noted their route in his patrol report. His frustration is evident in the comments he wrote:

> During the third day of the operation (19 February 1944) two excellent targets passed within close range of *Tally-Ho*.
> The orders for special operations precluded *Tally-Ho* from attacking these ships. . . .

The following day was Sunday, 20 February 1944, and Bennington's thirty-second birthday. *Tally-Ho* was dived at dawn south-east of the Sembilian Islands and the day was spent patrolling along the Malay coast — or, to be more precise, the stretch between Pulau Rumbia and Kuala Bernam. Bennington's birthday passed unremarked.

> Nothing of interest was observed and towards dusk *Tally-Ho* surfaced and proceeded towards Pulau Jarak to charge batteries.

So ran Bennington's patrol report. And for the following day it continues:

> 21 February 1944
> Closed to Sembilian Islands at first light and carried out a patrol at periscope depth between the same positions as the previous day.

The routine was dangerously near to becoming monotonous.

Monday forenoon passed without any sightings and was memorable only for the fact that with it passed the 48-hour prohibition on attacks. Patrols at periscope depth on a shipping route with all attacks strictly forbidden were a form of exquisite torture for a submarine captain with offensive spirit. Now at last it was possible to mount an attack should a target appear.

Tally-Ho was in a position fifty miles west of Bernam River estuary at 1410 when a merchant ship was sighted approaching from the south-east. Bennington was summoned to the control room: he came running. The officer of the watch held the periscope focussed on the approaching target. Bennington ducked nimbly in front of him and took over. The vessel, close inshore and a little hard to see against the profuse, rank mangroves, seemed to Bennington to be about 2,000-2,500 tons. The attack team having been closed up, after a brief glance at the plot Bennington lost no time about giving his orders. 'Full ahead together, group up. Steer 300°.' As near as he could estimate this should put *Tally-Ho* on a parallel course with her quarry.

Tally-Ho then ran at full speed for almost a quarter of an hour in an effort to reach a position where a 90° turn would put her on a simple 90° track angle. By mounting a retiring attack, Bennington felt he stood the best possible chance of placing himself in the most advantageous position. His normal impulse was to close quickly with the enemy in an advancing attack. Today, however, he felt he needed the extra time. From the configuration of the coast he knew there was little chance of the freighter turning suddenly off course and presenting him with an impossible shot. 'Steer 034°,' Bennington ordered.

With *Tally-Ho* turning 'on the swing', he made two observations of range and bearing. Lieutenant Peter Bennett reported that the range had closed to 3,300 yards on the first bearing and to 2,200 yards on the second. Scott-Maxwell came up with a target speed of 7 knots. 'Director angle for a 90° track angle.' Bennington demanded. 'Nine one half green,' was reported back from the fruit machine. 'Range on firing 1,300 yards.' The attack seemed to be proceeding with clockwork precision. What a pity it couldn't be the *Kamikawa Maru*! Bennington was put on his director angle and fired within seconds of this being done.

H

Five torpedoes were fired over one and a half ships' lengths. This time in a close-range attack there was barely time for George Backman to report they were all running true before a hit could be heard. Only one, it was true, but in the circumstances one was enough. In the absence of any escort and with no hydrophone effect reported by the Asdic operator, Bennington had the rare pleasure of watching through the periscope the torpedo strike home. The vessel, the *Daigen Maru*, sank within four minutes. Steadman did not give his customary running commentary on the attack but, then, this time the target wasn't a cruiser.

'All right, fall out the attack team. Watch diving. And, Coxswain, check the rum,' Bennington ordered. He always remembered that any successful attack was the product of the combined efforts of the entire crew: with the attack team closed up, every man on board had a job to do. His recognition of such matters was one of the many things that endeared him to his crew. 'Call me if anything's sighted,' he requested politely and was gone from the control room. A few paces for'ard in his cabin, he wiped the sweat from his forehead with a towel and stretched out on the low camp-bed fitted into his bunk. He would have liked to smoke a cigarette but the time for 'one apiece all round' had long since passed. He had no intention of awarding himself privileges that could not be shared with the whole crew. In any case it was madness to think of smoking four hours from surfacing time.

The sweat forming on his arms and legs where they made contact with the camp-bed was something he could readily have done without. But it reminded him that the health of the crew on this patrol had not been too bad. Things were pretty bad, of course, always. Sweat presented a major problem: it was constantly generated and if one couldn't keep wiping it off the salt would accumulate and cause irritation. Frequent washing would have helped but water had to be rationed. Mervyn Wingfield, the Commanding Officer of *Taurus*, had listed the ailments most likely to be encountered on a Malacca Strait patrol. On his first patrol his crew had had, as he put it: Boils, eczema, otitis, cellulitis, dhobi itch and sweat rash — in fact the *usual* troubles in these waters.

Needless to say the ailments were successfully treated. No

medical officer was carried in a submarine, the crew depending on the captain for diagnosis and on the Coxswain for nursing. In *Tally-Ho* the precedure worked as well as in any boat afloat. One of the least welcome ailments to encounter on a patrol was a suspected appendicitis. Yet somehow the patient always responded to 'treatment'. Treatment in this case consisted of being turned in in a hammock with a hot-water bottle and No. 9 (laxative) pills. It always did the trick. Possibly the reason was that anyone with a mild stomach disorder could think himself into believing he had appendicitis. Bennington himself always managed to keep healthy on patrol, though not particularly comfortable – not that that worried him greatly. He had been in the game long enough not to be over-concerned with creature comfort. However, now he did shut his eyes and try to rest, satisfied that he'd given all necessary instructions; and barring the appearance of another target – which he'd welcome – he could probably remain undisturbed till it was time to surface.

At 1850 *Tally-Ho* surfaced midway between the position where the sinking had been made and Aru Bay. She then proceeded on the surface towards Aru Bay to charge batteries. The remainder of the night was devoted to wild-goose chases. At 1833 *Tally-Ho* was ordered northwards towards Diamond Point; then at 2344, south-east towards One Fathom Bank Lighthouse. Throughout the night nothing of interest was sighted. By first light the following morning, Thursday, 24 February 1944 she was ordered back to the Sembilian Islands. Although this area had been promising from the point of view of target availability, today it was unrewarding.

That night, at 1831 *Tally-Ho* surfaced and proceeded on main engines to a position fifteen miles south of Pulau Jarak. The intention was that she should close the Sembilian Islands in the morning. Meanwhile Bennington decided to spend the night proceeding southwards on a zig-zag course in the general direction of the One Fathom Bank Light. He followed his normal night-time routine. Just before *Tally-Ho* surfaced he made a careful all-round periscope search of the horizon. Not that there was ever much horizon to speak of in these latitudes, for sky and sea seemed to merge in an impenetrable grey blur. After the periscope observation, Bennington accompanied by Facer and Lockyer, the surfacing look-outs, would climb through the lower hatch, up the ladder, into the conning-tower.

The lower hatch would then be shut again and block and tackle rigged to it so that it could be gently raised to allow for gradual release of accumulated pressure inside the hull. After twelve hours of submergence a pressure of some inches water gauge tended to build up. Then the upper hatch would be opened just before or just after surfacing. Consequently Bennington and the look-outs would emerge dripping wet. They didn't complain: the important thing was to get up there quickly and take a good look round: the safety of the whole crew might depend on their promptness.

Having come up from a carefully darkened control room illuminated only by feeble red lights, their eyes would quickly accommodate to the outside darkness. After that, as soon as Bennington was satisfied all was well, he'd call up the officer of the watch and two more look-outs. Only then would he consider turning in for the night and, as he always did, he would sleep on the bridge.

Once the officer of the watch had taken over and the two additional look-outs were closed up, Bennington would settle down in a corner of the bridge to doze or try to doze. He did the same each night. There was barely enough room for six people on the bridge at one time but Bennington knew that the advantage of his being there might well save his ship and the lives of his crew. Before the night was over his foresight would have accomplished those aims.

The night passed slowly and seemed interminable. It became as black as pitch, with stars barely discernible. *Tally-Ho* made her way down the strait in the general direction of One Fathom Bank Lighthouse, zig-zagging continuously. Her position in mid-strait meant that for once she ran little risk of tangling with unlit junks. They tended to cluster in coastal waters along the five-fathom line. From time to time large fish could be seen, either as they broke surface or simply as streaks of phosphorescent wake as they disturbed the plankton on the surface.

Nearly three hours after Bennington had turned in, one of the look-outs sighted two wakes ahead. Lieutenant Peter Bennett RN, the officer of the watch, did not hesitate: he woke Bennington. In these latitudes tidal rips that looked exactly like the wake of an approaching vessel could and did occur. But Bennett knew from experience that Bennington preferred to be wakened for any alarm, even should it prove false.

Bennington, on his feet in seconds, orientated himself automatically and almost instantaneously. *Tally-Ho* was still proceeding southwards, still zig-zagging on a continuous wheel, running on her port engine alone whilst putting a running charge on her batteries from her starboard screw shaft. The night was still too dark for the silhouette of any vessel producing the wakes to be discernible. The bow wake had the appearance of that of an approaching surfaced submarine. 'Steady on 350° . . . Yeoman to the bridge,' ordered Bennington down the voice-pipe.

The other vessel appeared to be only a matter of feet away and travelling at speed. The submarines *Truculent* and *Tactician* were known to be in the area so Bennington had to make certain he was not facing a friendly vessel. However the immediate necessity was an alteration of course to avoid a collision. 'Steer 110°, full ahead both,' he ordered.

The other vessel slid across *Tally-Ho*'s stern from starboard to port.

'Make the challenge,' he ordered. Yeoman Ginger Facer was already standing beside him, Aldis lamp at the ready. No counter-sign or reply was received but, with a sudden flurry of spray, the other vessel made a violent alteration of course and bore down on *Tally-Ho* from the starboard quarter, dropping depth-charges. An immediate alteration of course barely avoided a violent impact.

As the Japanese vessel passed, she loosed off a single shot that went close over *Tally-Ho*'s bridge. The shell screamed overhead to fall way beyond them. Its explosion told the party on the bridge that they were up against an adversary armed with at least a 3-in. gun. Bennington automatically registered the fact that the enemy was firing high because she was too close to bring her guns properly to bear. 'Man the Oerlikon gun,' he snapped to the port for'ard look out: if this was to be a shooting fight he had every intention that *Tally-Ho* should give a good account of herself.

Bennington also ordered the crew to be brought to diving

stations but not dive. He was well aware that *Tally-Ho* was operating in a restricted depth and that, if she attempted to dive, she would present her enemy with a perfect target for ramming or depth-charging. The port for'ard look-out was by now on the circular bandstand and, just abaft of the bridge, wrestling with the housing clip that held the 20-mm. Oerlikon cannon trained fore and aft. When he did manage to release it the weapon jammed at the first attempt to fire. 'Jammed with a round up the spout,' the rating reported dismally.

It was now apparent that the enemy had her helm down and was careering round in the tightest of circles preparatory to a second ramming attempt and trying to cram on more speed. Hunched over the voice-pipe, Bennington strained his eyes against the darkness. He knew that he had no chance of diving till the engagement could be broken off; he knew too that *Tally-Ho* had insufficient speed to leave her adversary standing. The best tactics were to keep turning end on to the enemy, altering course at the last moment should she attempt to ram; always bearing in mind that to alter course too early would be worse than not altering course at all.

Although he still could not see the enemy clearly, he was now certain that he was opposed by either a destroyer or a torpedo boat; also that the other vessel was so close that had *Tally-Ho* attempted a torpedo attack, the torpedo would almost certainly have passed beneath the target. Depth-charges were exploding long after the normally anticipated time interval, indicating that they were being dropped in very shallow water. In which case any torpedo fired might, alternatively, hit the bottom and explode prematurely, damaging *Tally-Ho*.

As the enemy vessel was certainly faster than *Tally-Ho*, there was every chance of her eventually catching the submarine. Only one of the enemy's guns appeared to be firing. Bennington ordered 'collision stations' and passed the word for the 4-in. gun's team to be closed up below the gun tower in case the opportunity arose for them to go into action. Meanwhile the Japanese destroyer or torpedo boat or whatever it was closed in again in a further attempt to ram. She was near enough for those on the bridge to see her wake creaming and foaming, her smoke stack lit up by her efforts to cram on all possible power. Bennington delayed his order for alteration of course till the last possible second.

'Hard a starboard!' he yelled. The party on the bridge held their breath wondering whether this time he had left it too late. It seemed impossible that *Tally-Ho* could avoid being cloven amidships; but, no, she was already swinging in answer to her helm. With any luck both vessels would now pass on parallel opposing courses. Despite the darkness, Able Seaman Ken Lockyer, one of the look-outs on the bridge, could make out not only the towering bulk of the Japanese vessel looming over the submarine but also the frantically, ineffectually swivelling gun-turrets aboard her. He felt the impact as her bow struck and the deck below him tilted as the impact caused *Tally-Ho* to heel away from her attacker.

After that all seemed confusion. Lockyer was momentarily deafened by a deep snarl of machinery noise mingling with excited incomprehensible jabbering of foreign voices and the ringing of engine-room telegraphs. He flinched as the heat of the other vessel's labouring engines struck his face and his nostrils filled with the acrid stench of scorched paintwork on the enemy's smoke stack. It was absurd to be so close without shots being fired. As he later put it: 'If anyone had thrown so much as a potato he'd have got a VC!'

Beside him, Bennington fumed silently. It grieved him not to be able to wipe out the enemy's bridge personnel with his Oerlikon gun. The Japanese vessel's bows were now well past those of *Tally-Ho*. It was a question now of whether her stern would strike the submarine. Inexplicably depth-charges were still being dropped. They *were* going to touch after all. Bennington braced himself for the impact just as the two vessels met. As the warship's stern clawed along the submarine's port side the noise was shattering, ear-splitting, like the rat-a-tat of gigantic machine guns to the grim accompaniment of an unmistakable metallic tearing.

The deck of *Tally-Ho*'s bridge beneath his feet shuddered convulsively like a live thing. Then, with a loud rending of metal, the Japanese vessel was past them and they were rocking in its wake. In the instant of passing Bennington had taken in more than Lockyer did, had glimpsed a tripod mast; gun mounted on the forecastle; one funnel, perhaps two; another gun and superstructure on the quarter deck; and, beyond that, a second tripod mast. For his money this meant a *Hyabusa*-class torpedo boat of almost 600 tons with three 4.7-in. guns — altogether a formidable adversary. As she drew away from *Tally-Ho* the last of the depth-charges dropped exploded and he prayed fervently that the Jap might be near enough for them to damage her own stern. Certainly they appeared much nearer to her than to *Tally-Ho*.

Joe Brighton's impression of the engagement were very different from those of his captain. Down in the fore-ends he had seen nothing. To him there seemed to have been a confusing profusion of orders: first 'diving stations', then 'collision stations' and, finally, 'gun action stations'. Joe had closed up with the other members of the torpedo team: Ianto Griffiths, Fulford and Jerrard. If *Tally-Ho* did submerge they could certainly expect firing orders. At 0220 there had been the sound of an explosion for'ard and Joe had shut the watertight doors to the torpedo tube space. (He hadn't waited for orders: such was the internal organisation in *Tally-Ho* that senior NCOs were expected, indeed relied on, to take initiative.) He had barely done that when there was an immediate feeling of an impact with a floating object: not solid like hitting a rock or jetty. The boat at once took on a marked list to port and assumed a bow down attitude. As far as he could tell, though, she was not sinking: he was surprised at his own detachment.

At that moment, had he known it, the fiercely revolving screws of the Japanese torpedo boat, at full power, were chewing their way along the external ballast tanks of *Tally-Ho*'s port flank. They had first struck in the region of rib No. 49 and they broke clear at about rib No. 107 some ninety-six linear feet away. As the tanks were of thin, mild steel plate, not stressed to stand increased pressure with increasing depth, they yielded. The screws of the torpedo boat, being phosphor bronze, were infinitely harder than mild steel plating and, being fully streamlined, they represented an almost ideal cutting shape. In the process of working their way along, they lost large fragments as they inflicted a regular pattern of cuts.

'Taff' Hughes, Engine Room Artificer, was far aft in the engine room when the vessels tore apart. His immediate comment 'We've 'ad it now!' was a solecism that evoked one or two rueful smiles.

On the sloping bridge 'topsides' there was little to smile about. Bennington was coaxing a maximum of speed from his steeply listing craft. As the torpedo boat did not appear to be following, he headed for deeper waters. No one on the bridge seemed to have been injured. There were no signs of enemy reinforcements or air activity. *Tally-Ho* was still responding to helm changes nor did her list appear to be increasing — in short, she had evidently weathered the encounter pretty well. By now her batteries held a moderate charge and so her best defensive policy was to dive. It was perfectly possible the attacks would be renewed with intensity.

It was still too dark to be able to assess the damage she had sustained but, if she were to survive, she must be far away and submerged by daylight. 'Clear the bridge,' Bennington ordered and then, quietly, as he often did when diving at first light, added, 'Take her down to periscope depth.' Descending the control tower, clipping both hatches and inserting the safety pins in the clips took longer today in view of the 12° list. He'd often practised 'collision stations' in wartime submarine service but had never had to order it in earnest before.

One day off Tobermory, on his first command, the 23-year-old H 28, on 18 January 1941, they'd been exercising with HMS *White Bear* when the surface vessel had considered a collision imminent. Sub-Lieutenant Edward Preston Young RNVR[1], had succinctly recorded the moment in his log book entry:

Saturday 18 January 1941
   1056 Emergency surfacing initiated by escort, considering that our course was dangerous.
   Considered by us quite safe.
   1111 Dived for ASP6. Course 210°.

Compared with the recent encounter, that had been nothing. Nones the less, not long after, Bennington had insisted on the

[1] Later Commander E.P. Young DSO, DSC, RNV(S)R, author of *One of Our Submarines*, published by Rupert Hart-Davis 1952. At the time *Tally-Ho* was rammed he was in command of HM Submarine *Storm* also operating from Ceylon.

entire ship's company practising collision stations.

The actions of the present night were to be described equally succinctly in *Tally-Ho*'s log book by Lieutenant Michael Clark RN on the following day:

Thursday 24 February 1944
    0250 Steady on course 350°, slow port, sighted wakes ahead.
    0253 Hard a starboard, half-speed port.
    0255 Full ahead together. Steady on 110°.
    0256 Hard a port, 8 depth-charges heard. Hard a starboard. Destroyer attempted to ram, cut open all port ballast tanks and port fore'planes out of action. 12° list to port.
    0300 Dived.
    0323 Altered course 090°.
    1825 Surfaced 03° 58′ N 99° 35′ E.

But that is to anticipate somewhat. When *Tally-Ho* submerged it was not possible to know for certain the extent of damage to her ballast tanks. Steadman reported to Bennington that there had been no casualties but that the explosions of the depth-charges and the wild firing of the Japanese had caused some shattering of light bulbs and blowing of fuses. These were already being made good. There were also a number of small leaks in the plates of the pressure hull where rivets had sprung. The most serious of these appeared to be in the torpedo tube space, by now isolated by Joe Brighton's timely action in shutting the watertight doors to the foremost bulkhead.* Bennington looked ruefully at the cracked glasses of the depth gauges.

At once Bennington held a brief conference with his Engineer Officer. Scott-Maxwell reported that the machinery was undamaged. He usually succeeded in taking calmly emergencies in submarines, and his report to Bennington was calm, confident and matter-of-fact. He didn't bother to remind Bennington that he, Scott-Maxwell, was almost certainly the only officer in submarines in the Second World War to have survived two rammings. He did, however, suggest that the for'ard hydroplanes which were jammed in a hard a'rise position had probably caught a glancing blow from

---

* Joe Brighton was assisted by his fore ends' crew, Ianto Griffiths and 'Ivy' Watts, in shutting watertight doors to isolate the major leak to port hydroplane gland.

the Japanese torpedo boat. At the time of the impact both hydroplanes had been extended in the diving position and one was probably seriously bent out of true. This meant that the submarine's performance when dived would be drastically curtailed. After a brief look at the chart, Bennington ordered both a change of course and an increase in depth to 120 feet.

For some time the hydrophone operator reported intermittent hydrophone effects, suggesting that the Japanese vessel was still circling in the area of the original attack. An hour after the engagement there was the distant sound of the torpedo boat dropping two final depth-charges. For the next three hours of darkness *Tally-Ho* remained submerged making cautious progress, without using the damaged for'ard hydroplanes, in a northerly direction up strait. In her damaged condition, to maintain a constant depth was particularly difficult and trying. At 0630 on 24 February 1944, when the first light of dawn was streaking the sky, Bennington had her brought to periscope depth.

A quick periscope observation revealed that a destroyer or torpedo boat was searching some four miles away on the starboard quarter. He promptly ordered depth to be increased to eighty feet. Although the enemy hydrophone effect could still be heard for one and a half hours, the shadower was never particularly close. *Tally-Ho* remained submerged throughout the next twelve hours. At the end of that time it was dark enough to risk surfacing. Bennington made a laconic note in his patrol report:

1825 Surfaced 03°58′N 99°39′E, having polished off the first 36 miles of the 1,200 miles homeward journey.

During the day there had been a slight increase in list and on surfacing it was 15°. In the meanwhile *Tally-Ho*'s destruction had been reported by the enemy and in Colombo this report was believed. Since *Tally-Ho* when submerged could only receive wireless signals, and in her patrol area was committed to total radio silence, it was small wonder that she was reported overdue. In fact, conditions had become no worse in the submarine – a careful watch had been kept on the leaks throughout the day.

Once surfaced, Bennington and Scott-Maxwell made an examination of the damage from the bridge whilst four look-outs kept watch. The sea was less calm than it had been the previous night, and as the boat rolled slightly Scott-Maxwell could see signs of grave damage to the port ballast tanks. They were all open almost to the top and beyond practical use. It was not surprising that he had heard ominous creakings from them during the day. . . . The water of the Malacca Strait being pretty murky, it was difficult, in what daylight remained, to assess fully the damage sustained. Both Bennington and Scott-Maxwell found themselves sharing the same thought: 'We're bloody lucky not to have rolled over.'

With her port ballast tanks useless to take pressure, the blow put on the starboard tanks in surfacing would have created an eccentric moment that could well have turned the craft over. Had *Tally-Ho* not still been deep in enemy waters, an underwater inspection, using DSEA as shallow diving dress, would have been possible — always assuming the diver was weighted to overcome positive buoyancy. There were four sets of DSEA on board for just such an eventuality. It was clear, however, that here the relative opacity of the water rendered a diver's examination useless even had it been safe to attempt one.

Tally-Ho remained on the surface till 0615 the following morning. Even so, without equal buoyancy on either side, she was plainly in considerable danger since little could be done to correct her list. Scott-Maxwell pondered the problem of reducing the list. From his experience of being rammed in *Proteus* he knew that, provided the machinery remained in working order, *Tally-Ho* had a fair chance of making port. *Proteus* had lost an entire hydroplane when she was rammed. He decided that it was worth experimenting by changing the weight distribution inside the hull to see whether this could reduce the list. One thing, with over 1,000 miles still to go, they were not short of time for experiment.

Once *Tally-Ho* was on the surface with the conning-tower hatch open, Scott-Maxwell was able to smoke his pipe as he considered possibilities. His initial suggestion to trim down to minimise the effect of the list had already been put in hand. As it seemed relatively satisfactory he decided to leave well alone for a further twenty-four hours.

The following day his theoretical calculations were put into practice in the fore-ends. First, No. 2 and No. 6 torpedo tubes were drained down and their twin 1½-ton torpedoes pulled back. Then the torpedoes were stowed further aft in No. 1 and No. 3 reload racks in order to transfer some of the weight to the starboard side. So far, so good. Scott-Maxwell was pleased because this did lessen the list slightly. After discussion with Joe Brighton, No. 3 tube was drained down to lighten the bow still further; so too was the WRT (water round torpedoes) tank. After that Joe, sweating profusely, swarmed out from the tube space and joined Scott-Maxwell in the fore-ends and the watertight doors in the foremost bulkhead were closed. They measured the inclination and were delighted to find it had been reduced to 4°. Filthy and exhausted, the party from the fore-ends gasped their relief shortly afterwards as life-giving fresh air flooded in as the hatches were opened on surfacing.

However, the trials and tribulations of the fourth patrol were by no means over. The submarine was still three days from port. A day or so later, crossing the Bay of Bengal, she encountered the south-west monsoon. In such conditions — greater buoyancy being essential — it would be folly to remain trimmed down: there was no option but to trim up as high as possible. As a result, in the most open part of the bay, the boat rolled from 0° to 30° and some of the most experienced crew members were sea-sick. It was a relief to all when they were clear of the area.

And then, when almost home, she again encountered worsening weather. By blowing the compensating water from her midship fuel oil tanks, she was enabled to ride higher. It was a desperate measure. It is normal procedure to take on compensating water as fuel is expended. Without the weight of the compensating water *Tally-Ho* was deprived of her ability to dive in a hurry. The look-outs were warned to be doubly vigilant lest they encounter a marauding Japanese U-boat close to home. Mercifully, this did not happen.

The last stages of her home passage came dangerously near to degenerating into low comedy. In bad visibility she missed her escort outside Trincomalee Harbour and suddenly found herself in the midst of Admiral Sir James Somerville's battle fleet at exercises. Still, she was cheered as she entered the boom at Trinco on 29 February 1944. After a few days in harbour all torpedoes were unloaded and she moved to Colombo. In dry dock at Colombo it was possible to examine the full extent of her damage. Observers were amazed.

* * *

What of *Tally-Ho*'s adversary? As far as Bennington was able to discover her steering had been damaged by the explosions of her own depth-charges. That accounted for her circling movements after the engagements, her screw blades shaved down to the bare shaft bosses. No wonder her movements had seemed ill coordinated! One of *Tally-Ho*'s for'ard hydroplane blades had pierced her hull, though not below the water line. She was subsequently beached and is believed not to have put to sea again while the war lasted.

However, in making his evaluation of the patrol Captain H.M.C. Ionides, Captain (S) of the 4th Submarine Flotilla concentrated on other aspects:

> This was a most useful patrol, resulting in the sinking of one U-boat and one 2,500-ton merchant ship. It terminated in what might have been a fatal encounter with the enemy. In fact, I think, the comparatively happy issue was entirely due to the CO's practice of sleeping on the bridge. This is an entirely uncomfortable procedure and its adoption demonstrates devotion to duty of the highest order and a very tough constitution.

CHAPTER SIX

Repairs and Magnetic Mines

'Just like a ruddy toast rack . . .!' was Claude Fenner's view when he first saw the scarred flank of *Tally-Ho* in dry dock. As an afterthought he added 'Thank Christ I wasn't in her! You were lucky to get her back, Ben.' Certainly, there was some truth in the last remark. Over the five days of the return passage the damaged plating of her saddle tanks had made ominous groaning noises which had dismayed even the stoics like Scott-Maxwell. Bennington had been obliged to talk about the incident probably more than he cared, and once the damage had been accepted as a *fait accompli*, he was mainly concerned with how long repairs might take before *Tally-Ho* could become operational again. Yet even he had been surprised when the dry dock had been pumped out.

The general view, even of experts, was that the damage had to be seen to be believed; in places, amidships and far aft, the metal plating of the external ballast tanks had almost disappeared, whilst further for'ard the regular gashes inflicted by the Japanese torpedo boat's screw were indeed reminiscent of a toast rack. Scott-Maxwell was able to view such things with the dispassionate detachment of a professional marine engineer, and he was already weighing up the pros and cons of repairs by welding and by rivetting. He had also rationalised a theory on the probable risks when surfaced submarines encountered surface vessels as *Tally-Ho* had done. Years later he summed it up by saying:

To the best of my knowledge, the *Proteus* and *Tally-Ho* were the only two submarines (Royal Navy) to survive, albeit battered, from personal encounter with enemy destroyers. In both cases I believe the warships ultimately sank. Given their rather frail structure compared to that of the submarine, the answer would appear to be: be bold and resolute, do not dive, and endeavour to keep on the same or opposing courses. On both occasions our survival must be attributed to the cool and calculated counter-action by the respective COs.

True to his view that a patrol could only be judged in entirety, Bennington produced a patrol report in which the ramming incident featured as only a single incident. The encounter would put *Tally-Ho* out of action for perhaps two months, but on the same patrol she had sunk not only a U-boat but a merchant vessel as well. The whole tone of his 'remarks' section in the patrol report reflected his preoccupation with strategic aspects of patrolling the Malacca Strait.

Remarks.
(a) This was the fourth successive patrol in the Malacca Strait. The general visibility even during the full moon period was poor particularly near the One Fathom Bank Area.
(b) Hopes were high that One Fathom Bank Channel would prove a happy hunting ground. It was disappointing to find nothing and even more so to watch valuable targets go sailing by on the afternoon of 19 February 1944 without being able to serve out more of HMS *Adamant*'s *carefully prepared* torpedoes.

After the first two patrols the torpedo question had been carefully resolved and, now that the troubles were over, he was the first to give credit where he felt it was due. He was also unstinting in his praise of the conduct of all officers and men during and after the attack. It can be seen, however, that missing the chance to attack the *Kamikawa Maru* and an unnamed merchant vessel still rankled.

The fate of the damaged *Tally-Ho* was of course a military secret: the Japanese would no doubt have been interested — and disappointed — to know that she had made port safely; contemporary photographs of her were overprinted 'Secret'. This prohibition did not prevent her being seen by officers as spare crew from the depot ship HMS *Adamant.* One of the latter was Lieutenant

HMS *Tally-Ho,* the hunting submarine.

Tally-Ho during working-up trials.

Bennington at the periscope.

Yeoman 'Ginger' Facer holds the *Porpoise* Carrier Service flag recording the number of 'Stores runs' made to besieged Malta. Bennington commanded *Porpoise* in 1942, and 'Stan' Hawkey, 'Buck' Ryan, French and Barker in this group were among those *Porpoise* crew members who joined *Tally-Ho*:

Coxswain 'Ginger' Ridley holds a model submarine made by him, and still in Bennington's possession, while Bennington, Steadman and Thurlow look on.

The whole ship's complement of *Tally-Ho* at time of the *Kuma* sinking. Bennington is holding 'Snoopy' the ship's cat.

Tally-Ho crossing the Great Bitter Lake on passage through the Suez Canal.

lly-Ho returns to port after
king the Japanese cruiser
ma. The Force 136 officers
her bridge can be picked
by their khaki uniforms;
ner is the tall figure to the
of the forward periscope
dard.

Japanese light cruiser
ma sunk by *Tally-Ho* on
January 1944.

The party decorated for the *Kuma* sinking. (*Left to right*) Lieut-Comdr. L. W. A. Bennington DSO*, DSC, Lieut. J. M. Steadman DSC, RNR, Lieut. S. A. Warner DSC, CPO C. H. Ridley DSM, Chief ERA J. M. Powell DSM*, EA R. H. Underhill DSM, Able Seaman E. E. Fulford DSM, Leading Stoker G. W. French DSM.

Admiral Somerville (accompanied by Bennington) inspects members of the *Tally-Ho* crew. (*Left to right*) Chief ERA J. M. Powell DSM, AB Kenneth Lockyer, L/Seaman Albert Sutton L/Stoker Betts, AB D. A. Harvey, L/Seaman Stanley Hawkey DSM, Stoker W. Illsley, L/Stoker G. French, AB C. S. Love, Stoker H. Barker. (*Back row, extreme right*), Stoker J. H. Gale.

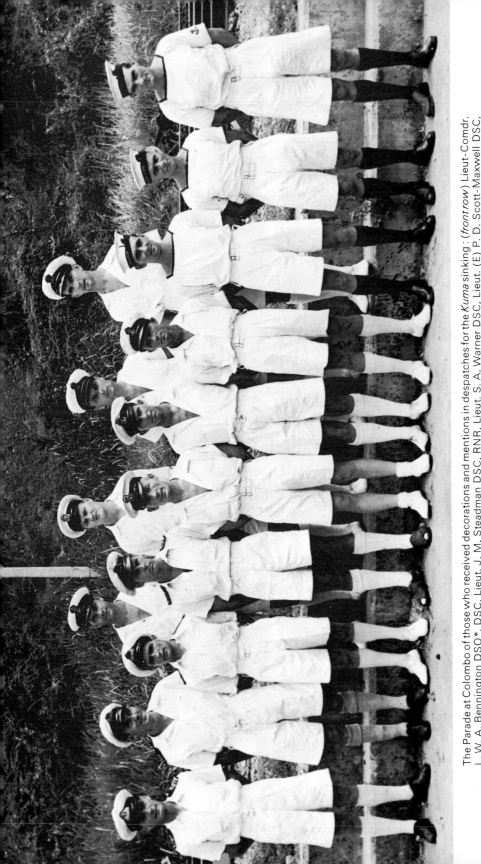

The Parade at Colombo of those who received decorations and mentions in despatches for the *Kuma* sinking: *(front row)* Lieut.-Comdr. L. W. A. Bennington DSO*, DSC, Lieut. J. M. Steadman DSC, RNR, Lieut. S. A. Warner DSC, Lieut. (E) P. D. Scott-Maxwell DSC, CPO C. H. Ridley DSM, Chief ERA J. M. Powell DSM*, Stoker PO J. J. Wheeler (mentioned in despatches), AB E. E. Fulford (mentioned in despatches), Leading Stoker G. W. French DSM, Leading Seaman H. J. Barker (mentioned in despatches). *(Back row):* PO (LTO) S. F. Fensome (mentioned in despatches), ERA Arthur Bulless (mentioned in despatches), PO J. C. Brighton DSM (mentioned in despatches), EA R. H. Underhill DSM.

Lieutenant (E) P. D. Scott-Maxwell DSC*.

Chief Engine Room Artificer J. M. Powell DSM*

Lieutenant C. T. M. Thurlow DSC, RNR.

Lieutenant S. A. Warner DSC.

The ballast tanks of *Tally-Ho* sliced 'like crackling on pork' by the screw of the Japanese Torpedo boats.

Tally-Ho rammed ! After her return to port the full extent of her damage becomes apparent as the dry dock is drained down.

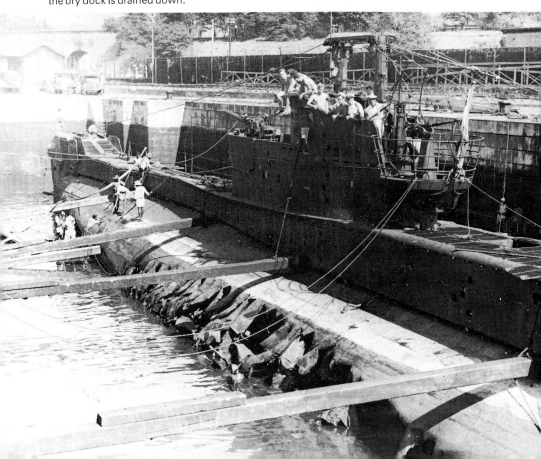

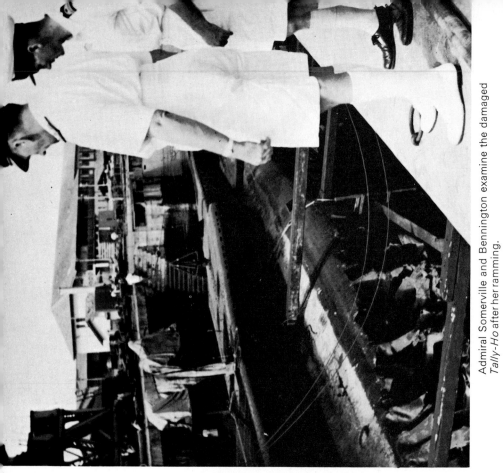

Admiral Somerville and Bennington examine the damaged *Tally-Ho* after her ramming.

Bennington holding a fragment of the phosphor-bronze screw of the Japanese torpedo-boat that rammed *Tally-Ho*; the fragment was extracted from the submarine's ballast tanks.

'It was like this . . .' Bennington explains the ramming to Admiral Somerville.

Admiral Somerville congratulates Leading Seaman Stanley Hawkey, DSM, on the Long Service and Good Conduct Medal. (Hawkey had served eighteen years in the Royal Navy, ten of them in submarines.)

Cuts in the *Tally-Ho* ballast tank plating — some of the first cuts that were inflicted — made by the screw of the attacking torpedo-boat.

Tally-Ho in dry dock at Colombo; the repair patches on her ballast tanks can clearly be seen.

Tally-Ho officers photographed on the bridge on their return from the Far East. (*Left to right*): Lieut. S. A. Warner DSC, Cmdr. L. W. A. Bennington DSO* DSC*. Lieut (E) P. D. Scott-Maxwell DSC*. Lieut. P. J. Rouse, Lieut. L. D. Hamlyn, Lieut. C. T. M. Thurlow DSC, RNR.

Captain G. P. Claridge welcomir
Bennington home after his arriva
at Blyth.

Tally-Ho, berthed alongside harbour jetty at Blyth, with her crew mustered on the bridge and casing. Note the seaman holding 'Snoopy', the ship's cat, in the front row.

Tally-Ho officers at play.

(*Top*) 'Jackie' Warner and 'Snoopy' Thurlow ragging in the snow. (*Below*) attempting to spit-roast the 'bag' on a rough shoot in Ceylon.

Photograph taken 20 July 1945 in the forecourt of Buckingham Palace. (*Left to right*) CPO J. C. Brighton DSM*, CPO C. H. Ridley DSM, Chief ERA J. S. Heath DSM, Chief ERA A. West DSM, Lieut. (E) P. D. Scott-Maxwell DSC*, EA R. H. Underhill DSM, Cmdr. L. W. A. Bennington DSO*, DSC**, Lieut. S. A. Warner DSC, Leading Seaman H. J. Barker DSM, Lieut. C. T. M. Thurlow DSC, RNR, Leading Seaman A. Sutton DSM, Leading Seaman S. Hawkey DSM*, Leading Telegraphist V. G. Backman DSM*, Leading Stoker G. W. French DSM, and Leading Stoker J. E. Neale DSM.

Bennington's last posting in the Royal Navy was to HMS *Daedalus*. Here he commanded the Fleet Air Arm Field Gun Team, and under his command they never lost.

Laurence Douglas Hamlyn RN. Later that year 'Jimmy' Hamlyn, as he was generally known, was appointed First Lieutenant in *Tally-Ho*. His impressions of the extent of the damage were much as Fenner's had been. Eyeing the shredded, crinkled edges of the light green, camouflaged plating he remarked: 'It's like a lot of lettuce.' Here and there the metal was rust-tainted: clearly the chopped lettuce had been standing in the sun too long.

Not least of those interested in examining the damage were the crew of *Tally-Ho*. Joe Brighton lost no time in making a personal search of the ballast tanks and was delighted to discover what he had suspected must be there: phosphor bronze fragments of Japanese screw blades. Joe selected the largest he could find to keep as a souvenir. However AB Dave Whitehead cast envious eyes on it and persuaded Joe to swop it for a bottle of best Navy Rum. Joe has always regretted this transaction: by any standards that fragment was worth at least two bottles! Others managed to obtain fragments, too, Jackie Warner among them.

Nor was *Tally-Ho* permitted to blush unseen by those in high places. Admiral Sir James Somerville, C-in-C Far Eastern Fleet inspected the submarine and all her ship's company. For this event ratings wore carefully scrubbed white singlets and shorts, their navy blue socks serving to distinguish them from officers who wore white stockings. Officers were supposed to wear white buckskin shoes. Scott-Maxwell obstinately refused to do so. Sandals, he considered, were infinitely more healthy, and as ever he had scientific facts available to support his view. In the event Admiral Somerville was not critical of the smartness of the *Tally-Ho* officer and crew turnout. His morale-raising inspection was concluded by an official photographer taking a close-up of Bennington holding one of the largest phosphor bronze propeller fragments.

Examining the group photographs afterwards one cannot but be impressed by the seriousness of mien displayed by Jackie Warner. Anyone with knowledge of Jackie's irrepressibility must realise that sooner or later this mask was bound to crack. Very soon after this it did: Snoopy Thurlow was by now out of the sick bay and inevitably he and Jackie got together.

A film show was to be put on aboard the depot ship *Wolfe*.

I

Most of the *Tally-Ho* officers were in attendance, including Jackie and Thurlow. The film was perhaps a shade too decorous — by *Tally-Ho* standards it was frankly a crashing bore — so Jackie and Thurlow decided to liven up the proceedings. Someone, on a similar occasion previously, had connected a smoke generator to the ship's ventilation system: the results had been hilarious. But Jackie was determined on originality. He and Thurlow left before the film ended and had a quick look around the ship. It was Jackie who hit on the best idea.

'Just the thing!' he exclaimed, unhooking a fire hose. Both Thurlow and he had done fire drill and, with a promptness that under different circumstances would have been praiseworthy, they got lengths of hose and nozzles coupled up in time for the end of the show. As the officers who had attended the show were leaving, the hoses were turned on them. Uniform caps flew in all directions and all dignity was lost under the onslaught of powerful jets. Even some of those drenched, were amused, Steadman amongst them. But one thing misfired: there were visiting officers present who did not immediately appreciate or understand the hilarity of 23-year-old submarine officers letting off steam between patrols. In particular there were the Dutch flying-boat pilots who flew the Sunderland flying boats in and out of China Bay. The commander of the Dutch squadron was not amused — nor was Bennington. Jackie and Snoopy received strict instructions to report to the Dutch air base and make their apologies, clad in best bib and tucker. To make sure this duty was not skimped Bennington ordered Scott-Maxwell to accompany the culprits.

The culprits realising they might be heavily outnumbered enlisted Steadman for moral support. The party duly attended the Dutch HQ, in best white uniforms and buckskin shoes — apart from Scott-Maxwell, of course. Apologies were duly tendered. Jackie, whilst doing his level best to appear as sincere as possible, could not help feeling he was not getting through to the Dutchmen. The party were about to leave when Jackie was tapped on the shoulder by an enormous Dutchman. 'Oh, no!' he thought. 'I've said I'm sorry, surely that's enough; he can't insist on my stepping outside so he can pin my ears back.' But the Dutchman, instead, leaned forward and spoke quietly in his ear. 'You like drink?' he asked in a completely expressionless voice.

'Oh, yes,' replied Jackie sheepishly, thinking inwardly, 'Oh Christ! The original Dutch uncle!'

The Dutch officer nodded and said 'Komm,' and beckoning the whole party led them into the ante-room and to the bar. Glasses were put into their hands without further delay. Their conducting officer raised his glass to Jackie and his face split in an enormous grin. 'The other night was bloody beautiful!' he announced.

After that everyone wanted to meet them; they were pressed to stay to dinner and the evening turned into probably the best party Jackie had ever attended. As hosts the Dutchmen could not have been bettered. The party continued until late at night. Finally the *Tally-Ho* contingent took their leave amidst effusive good wishes. Jackie, in particular, felt he could not go without expressing the feelings of them all. 'Thank you all: tonight has been bloddy marvellous!'

He felt a restraining hand behind him and a whispered 'Come on, you BF, don't overdo it'. Somehow, however, he knew that tonight he could do not wrong.

Indeed, Jackie's state of euphoria was shared by their whole group. . . . All the younger members of the party stripped completely and dived over the side and swam to the depot ship. Protocol was not forgotten, however, and they punctiliously saluted the surprised officer of the watch as they boarded the depot ship. Scott-Maxwell followed with more dignity, his appearance still immaculate. He resembled a Scottish gentleman returning after a good evening's entertainment in convivial company; which, after all, was not inappropriate. Still it was quite late − 2345 to be precise − and so to bed. He said his goodnights and retired to his cabin. As he closed the door he could still faintly hear Jackie's voice repeating 'Bloddy . . .'.

Minutes later there was a tap on his door. When he opened it he was confronted by a grim-faced Bennington. 'Nothing to worry about,' Scott-Maxwell, began. 'Good relations established with the Dutch.'

'It's not that,' said Bennington, 'but I must admit I'm worried stiff. I met the paymaster early this evening and he said he'd given me £300 of personal back pay; said he didn't dare hang on to it any longer. What's more, I can't for the life of me remember him doing it and I'm blowed if I can find it. I've spent the whole evening worrying about it.'

'The paymaster got it wrong,' said Scott-Maxwell, 'he didn't give it to you. He gave it to me to give to you.' He reached for a wallet, 'Here it is. I've had it with me all the evening. You should have come with us.'

Bennington's relief was considerable, but he didn't waste time or words. 'Thanks. Goodnight. I'll buy you a drink the moment the bar's open tomorrow.' Had Jackie been present he would undoubtedly have described Bennington's expression as 'bloddy pleased'.

The repairs to *Tally-Ho* took weeks to complete and it was fully two months before she was operational again. In the meanwhile the officers had time on their hands. There were many parties, many 'blacks were put up' or many gaffes perpetrated. Or so it seemed. To avoid undue severity or particularisation in the matter of recriminations and 'bottles' (or 'dressings down') handed out by those in high places, an apologies club was formed. Members of the club were Snoopy Thurlow, Jackie Warner, Scott-Maxwell and John Steadman. They took it in turns to tender an apology when requisite. Strict rotation was adhered to regardless of whether the apology-tenderer had been concerned or not. As Alistair Mars put it:

> The officers had some licence in *Adamant*'s wardroom where
> I can recall some pretty startling scenes usually led by the
> officers from *Tally-Ho*.[1]

During the eight weeks period of recommissioning Scott-Maxwell had the responsibility of attending upon Walker & Sons Ltd, of Colombo and making sure the workmanship was adequate. The naval base staff at Colombo — whose overseer came from a Royal Dockyard — had been called in to assist and decide how the repairs should be made. It was agreed that the repairs should be welded since this seemed the best practical solution available from the Tamil labourers who were to be employed. Scott-Maxwell

[1] *HMS Thule Intercept* by Alistair Mars, published by Elek Press 1956.

produced the 'as fitted' drawings of *Tally-Ho* and before long a blue-print had been produced of the plating patches to be welded into her port flank. Bennington, interested to see how it was to be done, was probably more interested to know how long it would take; but, as ever, he did not interfere with the technical experts. There were problems: the profile of the saddle tanks was a bulbous convex (in two planes) which made the cutting and fitting of a patch more than usually complicated.

In all, eighty feet of new plating went in and the patches stretched from where the screws had entered — on the line of rib No. 49 in No. 2 main ballast tank, all the way through Nos. 3, 4, 5 and 6 main ballast tanks, right up to the line of rib No. 107. It was a mammoth task, as was Scott-Maxwell's in checking the work. Fortunately good relations existed between the Engineer Officer and Walkers right from the start.

Of course tolerance was sometimes necessary and Scott-Maxwell had enough experience to realise that a degree of understanding produced better results than storming at the workers. One morning, instead of the party of welders, he was met by a messenger holding two sheets of pink flimsy on which the following message was inscribèd neatly in pencil:

The Engineer Officer
HM Sub Tally-Ho
Sir
    Beg to inform you that the party on the Casings will not be working today, so many men did not turn up owing to New Year (Hurdu) which is falling tomorrow. I shall try my best to put as many tomorrow and get the job finished up.
    Hope you will excuse me this, and this will be the last occasion I ask an excuse of you please.
Your Obt. Servt.
(signed)
Supervisor 12/4/1944

True to his word the supervisor asked no more excuses of the Engineer Officer as the remainder of the work proceeded.

Sundry other communications arrived for *Tally-Ho*. Not all

were apologies for non-completion of the repairs. On 11 April 1944, a citation for awards for *Tally-Ho*'s captain, officers and crew appeared in the *London Gazette*.[1] Everyone was pleased by the awards: an award to any member of the crew was an award to *Tally-Ho* and that was what mattered. Jackie Warner, used to taking things in his stride, decided to behave as though his award had never happened. Inevitably, though, the occasion called for celebration. . . .

Preparatory to the patrol, Bennington made enquiries whether the field of action of patrols was likely to be extended beyond the Malacca Strait. He was already predicting that targets would run out, that the boats from Ceylon were becoming too well known, that the major traffic from the Sumatra oilfields to Singapore was following routes between the shallows making them almost impossible targets. It was a pity if *Tally-Ho* were not allowed through the Sundra Strait to patrol around Singapore – her additional fuel oil tanks had been adapted with this in view – but the Washington Conference of May 1943, which established a zone of operations for the South East Asian Command, decreed that British submarines would patrol no further than the upper reaches of the Malacca Strait down to One Fathom Bank Lighthouse. No argument was permissible.

Whilst repairs were carried out the *Tally-Ho* officers lived in the Dutch accommodation ship *Plancius*. As Scott-Maxwell put it, 'We did our level best to live up to their high standards'.

One of the features of life in *Plancius* that Jackie Warner particularly enjoyed was Saturday lunch. This was always a Rijstafel, an Indonesian speciality, traditionally consisting of some twenty dishes including pickled cucumber, chutney, ginger, butterfly prawns, fish and spicy meat curries, not to mention coconut and popadams. To Jackie it seemed like 'steak, eggs, chips, sausages and chops – for breakfast'. Another of the consolations of life in *Plancius* was Bols Gin without water. The cordial relationships cemented by the apology party happily continued. Happily, too, the 8,500-ton, coal-burning, auxiliary depot-ship was destined to survive the war.

During the weeks of enforced inactivity, another popular meal

[1] See Appendix (No. 5).

was that which Jackie and Thurlow were able to organise at Passionate Quest. This was the delightful name for a spot near the end of a creek where two Ceylon RNVR officers had a bungalow. Their duties were almost certainly concerned with providing labour for various naval tasks; fortunately their job permitted them sufficient spare time occasionally to entertain parties of officers from *Tally-Ho*. If Snoopy and Jackie went they'd take a couple of ¾lb explosive charges to fish with. Thereafter the cook boy from Passionate Quest would prepare a curry. Jackie and Thurlow would always bring the booze. This sort of exchange arrangement seemed to work perfectly. It was very pleasant to swim from Passionate Quest and even more pleasant if a Wren or two could be persuaded to join the party. (There were few WRNS in Ceylon so choice was limited.) Jackie once commented in his own inimitable way, if you took a Wren out, you practically had to sign an undertaking that you'd return her in the same mint condition as you had accepted her.

For the 'other ranks' things were not quite as exhilarating. True they, too, could swim from the splendid white beaches. But beer was only obtainable against tokens and the ration was two bottles per man. It was powerful Canadian Black Horse Beer but, even so, many sailors regarded it as miserably inadequate for an evening's entertainment. Consequently there was a thriving black market in forged beer-tickets, but for a short time only. Similarly, far too many people found out far too quickly about the only short-sighted bar tender on the island. Or perhaps this was just a rumour – many said he'd issue beer against a bus ticket – it seemed altogether too good to be true.

Very often seamen went ashore in groups: men liked to be with their 'oppos'. At sea Ken Lockyer was a member of a rum 'school', or syndicate, with 'Buck' Ryan and 'Wally' Crole the Oerlikon gunner. Any rum from the daily ration that wasn't immediately consumed they bottled for future consumption on shore. The practice was strictly forbidden but was done discreetly.

One of the places on shore where they used to take the rum was the 'Earls Court', a hostel run by an army captain named Walker. Here they would shift beds together, foot to foot, so that they could spend the evening congenially, rum jars close at hand, swopping yarns until either fatigue or the strong spirit got the better of them.

The petty officers tended to keep their own company. Most had nicknames and habits that were well known. Joe Brighton was 'Grandad', as befitted the oldest inhabitant. The Coxswain, Charlie Ridley, suddenly became 'Tojo'. The Yeoman was 'Ginger' Facer. (Yeomen of Signals were rarely found in submarines.) The NCOs formed a companionable and diverse team, two contrasting personalities of their group being Chiefy Powell, and Foo Fensome who earnestly talked socialism.

The lower deck, although they complained bitterly about the heat and the cramped conditions, were devoted to their captain and officers. In addition to being an efficient and fit crew they were one of the youngest ever manned. Their shortage of years contrasted with the wealth of experience they'd gained in *Proteus* and *Porpoise* — to say nothing of the recent patrols in *Tally-Ho*. The crew of *Porpoise* had included Boy Seamen Medhurst and Henley — 'the only Boys in submarines' — who had done several patrols in *Tally-Ho*.

The entire crew profited from the extra-long rest period before the next patrol and it was noticeable that all looked particularly fit and well. A few more plum targets like those of the past two patrols, they felt, and they *would* show the command they were the best boat in it. Bennington didn't gainsay this: he approved the spirit although he shunned the ostentation of such expressions of feelings. He too was determined, that given the targets, *Tally-Ho* would show her mettle.

By Thursday, 26 April 1944, *Tally-Ho* was ready to be taken from dry dock. And two days later even Scott-Maxwell was satisfied with the performance of the repaired saddle tanks. The submarine was passed over the degaussing coil to give her immunity from magnetic mines. It was usual for this to be done approximately once a year but, in the present instance, it was a timely gesture since on her next patrol *Tally-Ho* was to be carrying magnetic mines. None of her crew, however, apart from Bennington were as yet aware of this fact. On Saturday, 29 April she put to sea and sailed from Colombo for Trincomalee.

The following Saturday she was still in the big, natural harbour at Trincomalee and twelve mines were being embarked. This was strictly Joe Brighton's department. These were mines, magnetic Mark II and could be loaded, two at a time, in each of the internal tubes 1, 2, 3, 4, 5 and 6. They would be expelled from tubes by compressed air. Once released they would plane gently to the bottom guided by a fin like a hydroplane. Their disadvantage lay in the fact that the submarine had to pass over her own mines once they were laid. They were magnetic mines and the newly degaussed boat should therefore be immune from them. But it was impossible to avoid feeling some risk existed. As well as that they had a delayed-action safety device, but one never liked to take chances in these matters.

Degaussing was a way of neutralising a vessel's magnetism. Surface vessels were equipped with a degaussing girdle, a band of wire fastened round the hull and energised by an electric current. At one stage during the war 1,200 miles of wire were being used each week to fit out the fleet and mercantile marine. The name was derived from that of the unit of magnetic flux, called after the German scientist Karl Friedrich Gauss (1777-1855). Submarines did not wear degaussing girdles, instead their hulls were wiped when they were passed over the coil. A senior officer of a minesweeping flotilla, after searching unsuccessfully for a magnetic minefield, is said to have complained that he had been sent on a 'wild Gauss chase'.

Because *Tally-Ho* was carrying magnetic mines she was six torpedoes short. Understandably Bennington was not pleased by this reduction, but he was determined that the six reload torpedoes that she would be carrying, and if possible the five in the external tubes, would be used to the best possible effect. Not that he was any stranger to mines. *Porpoise* had been a mine-layer but her mines had been the spherical, horned, contact type. The method of mine-laying from *Porpoise* had been entirely different to that proposed for *Tally-Ho*. *Porpoise* had had a mine casing, high enough for a man to walk upright inside it. Two mining rails, just like ordinary tramlines, had stretched the length of this casing (the conning-tower was set slantwise to permit them to do so) and on these rails had run a train of some fifty mines. The mine casing had large doors, opened by remote control, at the stern end; when mines were to be laid the train simply trundled over the stern. Once the mines were released they went straight to the bottom. After a safety time-lapse, a soluble plug in the sinker (the lower portion to which the flanged wheels were attached) would release a predetermined length of cable and the mine would be left tethered, fully armed, at exactly the right depth to make contact with passing enemy shipping.

This form of mine-laying also had its disadvantages. The high casing had given the old *Porpoise*, built in 1931-33, an embarrass-ingly high silhouette when surfaced. Also when submerged, air tended to be trapped in the mine casing and a really fast submergence was out of the question.

On Tuesday, 9 May 1944, complete with magnetic mines, *Tally-Ho* sailed from Trincomalee. As usual the first three days of passage to the strait were made on the surface. Thurlow, once more, was on board and doing the navigation. This meant periodic sun or star shots followed by twenty minutes of calculations to establish the submarine's position. Scott-Maxwell performed this task which he enjoyed because in some ways it was like proving a theorem so that one felt like writing QED at the end if the correct answers turned up first time. As *Tally-Ho* streamed a log it was always possible to check the result by one's dead-reckoning predicted position. Thurlow, a precise and experienced navigator, took pride in his task and greatly appreciated Scott-Maxwell's assistance.

Only once did the right answer prove almost completely elusive. The precise time of the observation had to be taken. This was sung down the voice-pipe and written down in the control room. Once an error was made in writing the time of the observation. Scott-Maxwell had laboured at his calculations before suddenly exclaiming, 'The time must be wrong!' Inevitably he was right. When asked if it had been difficult to deduce what had been wrong with the navigation calculations, he replied modestly, 'Och, no. It was the only thing that fitted'. None the less he made it clear that the credit for *Tally-Ho*'s precise navigation lay with Thurlow. Despite this there was a tendency to credit him with almost supernatural powers. Certainly Scott-Maxwell was a versa-tile performer. At times when Joe Brighton had trouble with torpedo equipment, he would do a repair job for him on the small lathe in the engine room far aft and just alongside the watertight door into the stokers' living accommodation.

Scott-Maxwell was rather older than any of the other officers in *Tally-Ho* apart from the captain. His twenty-seven years gave him something of a start even on the First Lieutenant: John Steadman was twenty-five. By now Thurlow and Warner were both rising twenty-four. Scott-Maxwell was not a Royal Navy career officer. He was instead a temporary 'hostilities only' officer and had acquired a Mention in Despatches and a DSC by the time he joined *Tally-Ho*. At times his views of service matters could be unorthodox, but he would have never dreamt of arguing such matters with Bennington and consequently they enjoyed an excellent working relationship.

Scott-Maxwell's entry into the forces had been conventional enough. He had joined the RNVR during the first week of the war for the usual patriotic reasons. Having studied marine engineering and being well versed in the ways of heavy marine diesels, he felt that submarines could well be his métier. Commissioned as a (probationary) temporary Sub-Lieutenant (Engineer) RNVR on 10 September 1939, on completion of his preliminary training — square-bashing and the like — he had volunteered for submarines. As a result he became the first and only RNVR officer to be listed in the Submarine Branch Seniority List produced by the office of Vice Admiral (S) (revised to 1 August 1940).

By Christmas 1940, he was serving in *Proteus* where, throughout two arduous years of service, his Chief Engine Room Artificer had been Jack Chiefy Powell who came with him to *Tally-Ho*.

After their heroic battle to keep the ageing machinery of *Proteus* functioning, Scott-Maxwell and Jack Metford Powell welcomed a transfer to a new 'T'-class boat. Together they made a good team. In addition to his technical expertise Scott-Maxwell maintained a canny, Scots practical sense. He was hard to surprise, even harder to impress and possessed a great sense of humour — far subtler than that demonstrated by the obvious practical jokes perpetrated in the depot ship wardroom and elsewhere between patrols. However, in addition to being older in years than his fellow officers in *Tally-Ho*, he had also more sea-going experience than they and as a result possessed an increased self-confidence. This gave him a degree of tolerance that enabled him to secure not only co-operation but also a happy working relationship with both his fellows and the engine-room staff.

Moreover, in an emergency he contrived to keep remarkably cool and to view events with singular detachment. When he was serving in HMS *Liverpool* in September 1940 with the Mediterranean Fleet, the cruiser was hit by a torpedo from an Italian torpedo-carrying aircraft. Scott-Maxwell, in the wardroom at the moment of the first explosion, was interested to note the snapping of a wine-glass stem through 'bent-beam effect'. Half an hour later the cruiser's aviation spirit store erupted in an inferno of green flame. Scott-Maxwell laboured unflinchingly throughout the night despite heat that buckled the vessel's decks and sides. For the night's work he and three others of the ship's company were awarded Mentions in Despatches.

Bennington had first found him a proficient Engineer Officer. Thereafter, a close personal bond had been established. Scott-Maxwell's engineer's temperament never permitted him to accept anything he was presented with as the best or final solution to any problem. Typically, his personal opinions about *Tally-Ho* were extremely individual. Whilst conceding that her diesels were reliable – never once during her Far Eastern commission was she obliged to return to port or curtail a patrol – he felt, none the less, that in this theatre the 'T'-class boat could never be fully effective.

To be hundred per cent effective while tactically deployed in the Far East war *Tally-Ho* would have required greater range, several knots increased speed and an air-conditioning system. Unquestionably Scott-Maxwell could have given fairly precise specifications on how these improvements could have been secured. Bennington, though well accustomed to making the best possible use of whatever type or condition of ship in which he found himself, in his patrol report put a suggestion how things could be improved on Malacca Strait patrols:

REMARKS
(a) Most of the crew (on this patrol) have suffered from

† · JUST LIKE AN AMERICAN SUB !

heat rash in varying degrees and there have been 10 cases of boils. It is suggested that submarines carry a stock of sulphur tablets, if these are available, to help combat blood disorders.

(b) The food was below the normal standard. It is considered greater variety is needed. Tomato or fruit juices in particular would be most welcome.

(c) The patrol was very dull.

Perhaps by his standards it was dull. Four days of uneventful passage after leaving port, *Tally-Ho* was off Benga Shoal, near the coast of north-east Sumatra, preparing for the mine-lay that was the first objective of her patrol. At 1334 on 14 May, Bennington ran in for a periscope reconnaissance of the area prior to laying the mines. He noted that the red and white conical buoy at the south-eastern limit of the inner shoal had been moved to a similar position off the outer shoal; he formulated a reason which he noted in his patrol report:

The fact that the buoy had been moved suggests that the inshore route is no longer used by north-bound shipping, but, as it can never have been of much service to south-bound traffic, it does not necessarily follow that the route has been completely abandoned. In any case, it is possible that increased aircraft activity may tempt the enemy to use this channel more frequently. It was decided in these circumstances to adhere to instructions in the mine-laying operation order and lay mines around 03°42'N 99°04'E, (i.e. in the inner channel).

Mine-laying from a 'T'-class submarine is rather like a game of musical chairs. Whilst the mines have to be laid from internal torpedo tubes, it is not politic to use all six internal tubes to carry mines on passage since, if a torpedo target is sighted, there may not be time to pull back the mines and reload torpedoes. Consequently, to gain the best of all possible worlds a certain amount of swopping of torpedoes and mines between tubes and reload racks is essential. Fortunately a rack that takes a single torpedo will accommodate two mines but, even so, the process is by no means easy. By the time the laying was ready to start, Joe Brighton and the fore-ends team had good cause to curse the mines, magnetic Mark II.

The actual lay was commenced at twilight that day at periscope depth. As there were no landmarks of any value — one palm tree tends to look very like another — the position had to be picked up by a line of surroundings using the Asdic short transmission unit. Navigation has to be precise when laying mines: their exact location must be known so that one's own shipping can avoid them; it is also essential that they are in precisely the right spot to trap an unwary enemy. The first four were laid in a depth decreasing from nine to seven and a half fathoms, and they were spaced carefully one cable apart. At this stage *Tally-Ho* withdrew a short distance southwards and bottomed to reload a further four mines.

In order to reload as quickly as possible, it was usual, at that time, not to drain down the tubes before opening the rear doors to load the next mines. Instead, the bow caps were shut and the rear doors then opened; consequently a full 200 gallons of water per tube flooded to the fore-ends. It was difficult, inconvenient and dangerous. The *Thetis* disaster had already shown what could happen were a torpedo tube rear door opened with an open bow cap. However, Joe's watchfulness was a byword and beneath his scrutiny none of the fore-ends team would have dared skimp the safety drills. The task was frankly boring and it had to be completed for each of three successive lays of four mines each.

By the end of the second lay the depth had decreased to as little as six fathoms. *Tally-Ho* had also bottomed two or three times inadvertently. (Accidental bottoming can block inlets and cause other complications.) She therefore surfaced for the final lay. As each mine is expelled by compressed air from the torpedo tube, it bottoms just before the submarine passes over that precise spot. This results in a queasy awareness, as the lay is taking place, that if a mine's safety devices are defective or if for some reason the degaussing is ineffective the exercise could end in irremediable disaster.

In any case, mine-laying was far too inaccurate a method of

sinking enemy ships wholly to recommend itself to Bennington. Accordingly he was keen to move off across the strait and prospect for torpedo targets. The next two days were spent traversing the strait and moving south towards Port Swettenham. On the first day an armed trawler was sighted twice, not far from Aroa Island. It did not appear to be particularly belligerent and Bennington ignored it with that studied indifference he had developed towards Japanese anti-submarine craft. Their listening gear was evidently effective only when they were stopped; as targets they were not worth a torpedo; as a foe, they were, in Bennington's view, beneath contempt. However, it was imprudent to become blasé or careless about them: they could too easily summon air support if by chance they did get a contact.

On 17 May, in the early forenoon, *Tally-Ho* made a reconnaissance at periscope depth of the ten-fathom line between Kuala Selangor and the estuary of the Bernam River. There was no shipping to be seen so she proceeded further south. By 1439, still at periscope depth, she was twenty miles from Kuala Selangor and still forty miles from Port Swettenham when the officer of the watch, at the periscope, reported a float plane flying southwards. Bennington's first thought was that it could be escorting something out of Port Swettenham. He took over the periscope himself and six minutes later sighted a large U-boat also proceeding southwards in a position inshore of *Tally-Ho*. 'Steer course 065°,' he ordered.

Despite the air escort there seemed a good chance of making a classical attack on a 90° track angle. So *Tally-Ho* continued on a near reciprocal course on the off-shore side of her target, ready to turn on to the 90° track angle at the last moment. The fact that the enemy was travelling on a dead straight course, on the surface, without attempting to zig-zag suggested extreme naïvety or an excessive degree of trust. Clearly she could not for one moment be anticipating an attack. She was travelling, as far as could be judged, at a full twelve knots – a fair speed.

Scott-Maxwell reported a range plot of 1,800 yards. The fruit machine gave a director angle of 14° red for a 90° track angle. In a mood of general rising excitement, Bennington ordered tubes 1, 2, 3, 4 and 5 to stand by for firing. At 1449 he fired all five one after the other, aiming them separately. In the control room no one spoke. For the past ten minutes they had listened to Bennington's comments on the impossibility of missing such a target. After firing, Bennington gave orders to alter course to 130° and increase depth to forty-five feet. Two loud explosions were heard four minutes after firing. They proved nothing: they could equally have been bomb or torpedo explosions.

The Asdic operator reported hydrophone effect from a reciprocating engine still continuing. Obviously the U-boat could not have been hit. Bennington brought *Tally-Ho* quickly to periscope depth and made a discreet observation.

'Quick, Chief, take a look at this,' said Bennington, 'You wouldn't credit it. It's unharmed and still on just about the same course. What's more the whole crew are mustered on the casing.'

Scott-Maxwell replaced Bennington at the periscope. 'Every man jack of them lined up on the casing. It's German, all right,' he declared.

Bennington then lowered the periscope and spoke in a tone of weary patience. 'Okay we'll do another attack.'

He still had No. 6 torpedo and the two for'ard external torpedo tubes. An enemy U-boat was a priority target and if it proposed to continue sailing on an unchanged course with a crew of sightseers on board, there could be a fair chance of a successful second attack. Two minutes later Bennington altered course to 100° when he found the enemy had altered course to 135°.

The second attack had to be quick. Three minutes later he fired all three torpedoes on a 145° track angle. He had been obliged to choose a broad track since, although relatively certain of the enemy's speed, he could not be certain of its course. In any case the range was extending and he did not have the speed to chase his target.

'Down periscope,' he ordered a moment later. 'Aircraft is flying down the torpedo tracks and is turning towards us. Flood Q. Take her down to seventy feet.'

No explosions were heard. It did not seem possible that the U-boat could have escaped a second time. She seemed to be enjoying an undeservedly charmed life. Twenty minutes later Bennington brought *Tally-Ho* to periscope depth. Periscope observations revealed nothing in sight — not even the aircraft.[1] Now, for the remainder of her patrol, *Tally-Ho* was restricted to a stern salvo of the three external torpedo tubes, all of which had a depth setting of eight feet. After leaving port the external tubes are inaccessible and there is no question of being able to alter depth settings. Undeterred, Bennington mounted a patrol north-west of Aroa Island and continued it the whole of the next day.

From 18-23 May 1944, *Tally-Ho*, on signalled orders, attempted to cover the exits of the southern port of the strait. The signal indicated that there was a possibility of enemy heavy fleet movements in the area. As a result *Tally-Ho* mounted watch day and night. Unfortunately the assignment that gave promise of interest proved deadly dull — not a thing was seen. Two small incidents alone provided any excitement during this patrol.

18 May, 1326 HMS *Tally-Ho* surfaced for a sun shot and was sighted by an aircraft. The aircraft dropped one bomb some minutes after the submarine had dived. Two hours later a large minesweeper appeared and remained stopped for quite a long time, about two miles from the submarine. With only a stern salvo set of 8 feet HMS *Tally-Ho* lacked the where-withal to close and give this vessel a clout.

The next day two submarine chasers and a trawler appeared, apparently hunting for *Tally-Ho*, but did not come within two miles of her. *Tally-Ho* also patrolled the ten-fathom line in one or two of her previous haunts without result.

After an uneventful passage she was back in Trincomalee on 3 June 1944. The most remarkable aspect of the patrol, Bennington felt, was a marked change in the Japanese deployment of aircraft.

Aircraft sighted were more numerous than on previous patrols. Occasional float planes were observed searching the area. It is believed these were standing patrols. No aircraft were heard or seen at night.

Obviously the Japanese had heard the old aviator's proverb: 'Only fools and birds fly . . . and birds don't fly at night.'

---

[1] The U-boat did survive and was inspected by Scott-Maxwell at Loch Ryan, Galloway, after her surrender. He was interested to find parts of her cast iron keel blocks replaced by ingots of Malay tin.

K

CHAPTER SEVEN

Where is the Enemy?

On Friday, 21 July 1944, *Tally-Ho* was once again secured to *Adamant* at Trincomalee. Once again, too, the prospect of a run ashore loomed happily large in the minds of her crew. For the majority the most popular rest centre was the army camp at Dijatalawa, 4,000 feet up in the mountains, where the air was far cooler than at sea level. Being away from the sea and ships helped to assist the process of relaxation and general revitalisation. As recreational facilities for submarine crews in Trincomalee and Colombo were minimal, all ranks of submarine crews were now permitted to stay there on patrol leaves. Various pastimes were possible at Dijatalawa. Warner, Thurlow and Steadman devised their own — a shoot.

Equipped with various borrowed arms they sailed forth determined to approach the problem scientifically. It proved good fun, though the day's outing resulted in a 'bag' of one minute bird which, after an attempt was made to spit roast it, proved totally inedible.

Dijatalawa boasted a golf course. It had natural hazards. These were leeches. To overcome them, one trick was to wear ladies' stockings which the leeches were not keen to climb. If they did, they were burned off with a lighted cigarette. However, at least half the battle was to acquire the stockings. The best bet was a Wren's cast-off laddered pair: the WRNS might frown on laddered stockings but they discouraged the leeches.

Typically, the team of Warner and Thurlow devised an improvement on Dijatalawa's golf. Their version was taxi golf. Two taxis would be loaded with liquid refreshment. The party would drive off from the first tee, board the taxis and chase the balls. A handicapping system provided that the winner of any hole must sink a beer as soon as he'd sunk his winning putt. Scoring a birdie entailed downing a double spirits; a bogey, a single tot. If a hole was halved, everyone had a drink. Nine-hole matches were rare and eighteen-hole ones unknown.

Added to the fun and the unwinding of tension of that leave was the heart-warming news of a citation in the *London Gazette* of awards for gallantry to twelve of *Tally-Ho*'s personnel. Appropriately, the date of the awards was 6 June 1944 — D-Day.

During this leave period Scott-Maxwell had been attending to matters far from frivolous. Certain mechanical defects which had occurred in *Tally-Ho* had to be remedied before she went to sea again. The responsibilities of an Engineer Officer before a patrol were considerable. During the three-week patrol period *Tally-Ho* would be operating at least 1,200 miles from home, and the full responsibility for defects latent and patent must be his. As soon as *Tally-Ho* was back in port, Bennington would be eager to be off again. But essential repairs and maintenance could not be ignored, and such was the trust and respect existing between Bennington and his Engineer Officer that *Tally-Ho*'s captain could anticipate — and indeed appreciate — any necessity to defer to Scott-Maxwell's judgement.

When on Saturday, 24 June, it was time for *Tally-Ho* to sail on her sixth patrol in the Far East, Bennington had mixed feelings. He already knew that targets were getting scarce (he felt he had searched the Malacca Strait pretty thoroughly over the course of the last patrol) and he couldn't help feeling it was a hell of a long way to go for nothing. If only he could push beyond the normal operating area. . . . Inevitably he was stuck with a special operation again. Whilst he could feel affection for the personnel involved (they were not too much trouble really), he would never be able to like the duty.

Steady would not be accompanying the party on this trip; he had gone sick, suffering from complete physical exhaustion. No one who had seen him on the previous patrol would have suspected that Steady was otherwise than his normal self until suddenly, in port, he had complained of some minor ailment; when he reported sick the doctor had ordered him to bed, absolutely forbidding him to sail on the next patrol. In his place Lieutenant Allan Gordon Tait DSC, RN, was embarking as First

Lieutenant. 'Harry' Tait was no stranger to *Tally-Ho*. He had
travelled in her on passage out to Ceylon, being embarked at
Gibraltar and carried as far as Colombo. Consequently he was well
conversant both with Bennington's ways and what he required of
his officers.

It was generally agreed that Tait, a New Zealander, was a good
chap and a first-class officer. He spoke in a soft voice gently
accented with a New Zealand inflexion. Throughout the patrol he
fitted in well with the regulars.

As *Tally-Ho* slipped and proceeded, Bennington was reminded
of other departures and patrols. When war was declared he was
already at sea, on patrol off the southern coast of Norway. That
patrol had passed without incident. But Bennington, eager for
action, did not have long to wait before becoming intimately
involved in the hazards and violence of war at sea. Seemingly
nothing ruffled the calm of his extraordinary self-control. It was
that absolute command of himself which was a vital key to his
later absolute and respected command of his ship.

On the night of 26 December 1939, the submarine *Triumph*, in
which Bennington was serving, struck a mine. The boat was
forty-five miles beyond the northern limit of the German Declared
Minefield. The mine she struck had certainly broken loose from its
moorings and drifted away. *Triumph* was on the surface, riding
into the swell, in the teeth of an east wind carrying flurries of
snowflakes with it. Only Bennington, who was officer of the
watch, and a single look-out were on duty on the conning-tower.
They had glimpsed the mine riding on the crest of a wave, just
before *Triumph* hit it. Immediately Bennington yelled an alteration of course down the voice-pipe but there hadn't been time for
the boat to answer the helm.

As the spray cleared following the explosion Bennington was
astounded to find himself and the look-out both unharmed. The
first eighteen feet of *Triumph*'s bows had vanished and so too had
the wireless mast that had been just above their heads. There had
been six torpedoes in the for'ard tubes and not one exploded.
Incredibly the blast from the exploding mine had forced the
watertight bulkhead of the tube space back a full half inch. Some
of the torpedoes had vanished – in No. 6 tube only tail-fins

remained — and one warhead had been stove in completely. The pistols, or exploders, in the torpedo warheads were designed to explode on impact *after* firing; the fact that not one exploded was a remarkable testimony to their design and construction.

Bennington was surprised the blast had not seemed more violent. Later, when a Press correspondent asked him to describe the blast, his reply was characteristic of the man. 'It was just medium.'

The incident represented the first of a long line of lucky escapes for Bennington. And *Triumph* in dry dock, like *Tally-Ho* at a later date, astounded all who saw the formidable injuries she had sustained so that they marvelled at her miraculous return to port.

Now, once again, *Tally-Ho* was engaged on a patrol that was proving anything but exciting. Even the special operation (to contact agents on shore) proved a blank. After an uneventful passage, made for the most part on the surface, she had patrolled the fringes of the ten-fathom line south of the Bernam River inlet. Here she encountered nothing larger than junks. Whilst it would have been easy to have sunk one or two, Bennington did not wish to run the risk of being deprived of a larger target by so doing. To declare one's presence by attending to such insignificant targets would, as Bennington put it, 'Have been tantamount to throwing in the sponge as far as the weary search was concerned'.

It was apparent to Bennington that submarine mine-laying operations had forced the enemy to use very narrow searched channels for coast crawling. By night, inshore patrols were to be encountered here; no doubt their primary duty was to prevent further mine-laying, which they believed would be done at night. Although Bennington felt sure nothing above about 500 tons would attempt to traverse the inshore route after dark, he did patrol the ten-fathom line assiduously by day as well as by night. Both exercises proved equally fruitless and he noted in his patrol report that the area of the Malacca Strait south of Pulau Jarak was dead and that this was emphasized by the absence of daylight and surface patrols. He went on:

One cannot help feeling that the activities of HM Submarines during the last six months have spread Alarm, Despondency and a great big 'D' for Defeat among the enemy. It is very likely that the very recent half-hearted endeavours of Japanese night patrols are nothing more than attempts to occupy attention and stave off contemplation through the periscopes of more fruitful areas.

On the moonlight night of 6 July 1944, while surfaced and maintaining a patrol parallel to the coast in the vicinity of the Bernam River, look-outs observed two dark objects inshore. As it was a particularly clear night it was possible not only to identify them as submarine chasers but also to be sure they were alone and not on escort duty. *Tally-Ho* remained quite close to them and observed them periodically exchange signals by signal lamp. Inexplicably they did not seem belligerent, and though *Tally-Ho* was close enough that the signals might be addressed to her, neither vessel made any move to intercept, investigate or challenge *Tally-Ho*. As soon as it was clear that the submarine chasers were steering north or west, *Tally-Ho* avoided them by moving to the south-east.

Twenty minutes later the submarine chasers reappeared, one dead astern and one on the starboard quarter, and made a half-hearted attempt to chase *Tally-Ho*. This lasted for two and a half hours, at the end of which time *Tally-Ho* eluded her pursuers by diving to eighty feet. It was possible to plot the pursuers' movements as they crossed astern of her. Half an hour later they dropped three single depth-charges, not one close enough to matter.

It was all a little perplexing. The enemy's intention was impossible to divine. When first sighted, the submarine chasers appeared to have been either mine-sweeping or on an anti-mine-laying patrol. In this patrol report Bennington recorded:

There may have been an enemy submarine in the area or it is just possible that a U-boat patrol has been established south of Pulau Jarak for the unwary. Both seem unlikely, because once the chase had started no attempt was made to make a recognition signal. Another reason for the chasers' reluctance to give battle may have been that they were waiting for reinforcements. Even this does not seem much of a reason for failing to start the battle.

There was a good chance that the affairs of the night would cause the enemy to suspect *Tally-Ho* of mining the shallow waters between the Sembilians and Bernam River. In view of this it was decided to shift the patrol to the area west of Aroa Island.

Before turning for home, *Tally-Ho* did find a little more excitement. On 10 July, not far from the spot where she had been rammed, she sighted a small ship of about 250 tons approaching from the south-east. When first sighted she appeared to be to the seaward of the line of fishing stakes along the Malay coast. Bennington at once ordered *Tally-Ho* to close in pursuit. As a target such a small vessel was not worth a torpedo, but the patrol was almost over and he had definite ideas about the salutary effect of a successful gun action on his crew's morale.

On 24 November 1942, off Kerkenah Bank, *Porpoise* had sunk the *Giaconda* (739 tons) by gun action and Bennington had written in his patrol report:

> This gun action was the very first of the war for *Porpoise*. Apart from its success, it had a very beneficial effect on the ship's company. For once in a while they were totally concerned in the attack and the gun's crew had had the satisfaction of seeing the results of their actions. A periscope attack on the other hand provides little of interest; there is nothing to be seen and very little that the majority of the ship's company can understand.

Whilst, by naval standards, this might be considered an unorthodox viewpoint, he had no doubt of the effect it would produce on *Tally-Ho*'s crew. In addition, this would be the first gun action of the war for *Tally-Ho*. There is something very democratic about a gun action in a submarine. Only the layer and trainer were regular members of the gun's crew: the full quota would be made up from the rest of the boat's personnel including, for example, the cook.

Twenty minutes after the first sighting, *Tally-Ho* surfaced due west of the Bernam River. Seconds after she broke surface the sodden crew had got the first shell away. Jackie Warner, as Gunnery Officer, was on the conning-tower alongside Bennington watching for the fall of shot: it fell short by some considerable measure. Mirage conditions made range estimation difficult. The estimated range had been 3,500 yards but the actual range seemed nearer 4,500-5,000 yards. Also, contrary to expectations, the enemy was inshore of the fishing stakes. Jackie Warner yelled corrections to the gun crew to try to improve their aim, but by now the submarine was almost on top of the fishing stakes and the water was very shallow. In all, forty rounds were fired in the space of about fourteen minutes and four direct hits were secured.

The enemy ran close inshore and fled out of effective range into the Bernam River estuary. *Tally-Ho* was forced to break off the attack and proceed away on main engines towards the south-west. A careful watch was kept for any enemy reinforcements but no aircraft or surface vessels appeared. Some hours later an unproductive watch was mounted on the northern exit to Klang Strait. Not a single target could be found here and *Tally-Ho* left her patrol area on 13 July 1944. The return passage, like the outward passage, was made on the surface without sighting the enemy.

The most exhilarating event that occurred was the receipt of a signal promoting Bennington to Commander. To say that *Tally-Ho*'s officers and other ranks were pleased would be an understatement. Bennington reciprocated their pleasure by insisting that all the officers take half a glass of sherry in the wardroom — the only occasion on which they ever partook of alcohol on a patrol. He also directed Ginger Ridley to check the rum in storage for any cracked jar . . . the last three half-hearted depth-charges of 6 July had seemed far away, but . . . it would be a pity if it were not possible to squeeze out a small supplement to the crew's evening rum issue. That evening all ranks solemnly drank their captain's health. The news of Bennington's promotion was also notified to Trincomalee. On Friday, 21 July 1944, as *Tally-Ho* entered the harbour boom, a launch stood ready to come smartly alongside and pass up a 'brass hat'.

As a Commander, Bennington was entitled to a single row of

gold oak leaves around the peak of his cap and all in Trincomalee were determined he should enter harbour, on the bridge of *Tally-Ho*, properly attired with the insignia of his newly conferred rank. Bennington already wore three stripes on his shirt shoulder straps. Ginger Ridley had seen to that; by a careful piece of surgery he had transferred extra stripes from the shoulder straps of his captain's 'No. 2 rig'. When Bennington thanked him for his thoughtful gesture Ridley replied that it had been a pleasure — which was no less than the truth.

His crew's pleasure at his promotion was infectious, but for Bennington himself there was the usual regret at returning to port without the Jolly Roger flying to indicate a sinking. However, there was satisfaction in *Tally-Ho* having become the senior submarine of the Flotilla — not many 'boats' were captained by Commanders. And Bennington took some consolation from the thought that *Tally-Ho* would have to complete another two patrols, at least, and there was a chance he could wrest official sanction from Captain (S) to a patrol in which she might range further afield. It could be called a happy homecoming.

Happy it was, but less spectacular than the return to port of *Swordfish* in the second week of the war. In the grey dawn of 14 September 1939, approaching Dundee, Lieutenant Bennington, the officer of the watch, had glimpsed through the spray and early morning mist the outline of another vessel on a closing course. The other's intentions had been only too apparent: she was attacking. Bennington ordered *Swordfish* to dive and alter course. Thus an almost certainly fatal attack was avoided. The other vessel had been *Sturgeon*, commanded by Bennington's friend David Gregory. *Swordfish* coming in from the north-east had had to alter course to avoid a large British convoy. *Sturgeon* had not expected to meet a British submarine on such a course and had, therefore, assumed her to be hostile.

Bennington's prompt action had caused the two torpedoes fired by *Sturgeon* to pass over her and explode in shallow water. *Sturgeon* had observed the torpedo explosions and assumed she had a kill. She at once signalled Dundee to claim a U-boat sunk; that resulted in red faces later on. Bennington bore no ill will for that mistaken and all too realistic attack.

Once *Tally-Ho* was secured to the depot ship, Bennington discovered that plenty of other wardrooms were only too keen to celebrate his promotion. Requests to come aboard 'to wet your third stripe' became very frequent. On such occasions wearing the brass hat was of course *de rigueur*.

One day Bennington asked Underhill, the only man visible on deck, if he would please ask the wardroom steward, Lesley Parker, to bring the cap. Underhill returned in a couple of minutes holding the cap by its peak, with a piece of writing paper folded protectively around it to prevent his fingers spoiling the 'scrambled eggs'. Bennington was touched by the gesture and enquired why Underhill, a skilled technical NCO, had taken it on himself to perform such a menial task.

Underhill explained sheepishly: 'Joe Brighton's got a torpedo stuck in an awkward position in the fore-ends. Everyone's helping him out: even your steward.' Seconds later, he, too, had disappeared below in the direction of the fore-ends. Bennington felt it said a lot for the calibre of his crew.

In fairness to Joe it should be emphasized that snags whilst embarking torpedoes were so rare as to be almost unknown. He rarely had to ask for help; but if he did he knew it would be forthcoming.

Bennington's first days in harbour were not entirely devoted to social events. Items of the patrol report had to be tidied up. There might not have been much action but there were other things to be recorded:

The health of the crew has improved considerably since the fitting of the FREON cooling plant. In addition there has been a noticeable improvement in the food. On medical advice each man has had a daily issue of common salt over and above what he normally uses. This made some people vomit. Its effect on the remainder can only be decided by a skilled apothecary.

At the end of the report Bennington appended his signature, for the first time as: L.W.A. Bennington
                    Commander in Command.

Over the period of rest in port prior to the next patrol the official badge for *Tally-Ho* was received. There was something of a story behind this. Ever since she sailed from Britain, in her wardroom had hung a badge designed by an RAF Squadron Leader who was a friend of Bennington's: everyone liked it and approved of it but it was not the official badge. It showed a rampant seahorse in peaked naval cap crushing a swastika with its tail and surmounting an enemy vessel cleft in twain. The Squadron Leader, a classical scholar, had appended the motto: 'Celeriter in hostem' ('Swiftly among the foe').

Everyone who had seen it was delighted. They deemed it entirely apposite. Bennington had applied through official channels for its adoption, only to be told that it was unacceptable and that an official badge would later be notified. Meanwhile *Tally-Ho*, her original and unofficial badge hanging in her wardroom, had sailed and engaged the enemy. When the official badge arrived and was unwrapped, the initial impression was not good. The official badge featured a fox emerging from a bush. The criticism expressed by the first officer to see it perpetuated the general opinion: 'It looks like a fox with a bush of laurels growing out of its arse. What's more they couldn't even get the motto right.'

The motto on the official badge read: 'Celeriter ad hostem.' Bennington didn't argue the point: his friend was a classical scholar: his version was good enough for the captain of *Tally-Ho*. It seemed a pity to take down something they were all attached to and replace it by something no one liked.

'I think,' said Bennington, 'the best thing would be to send it to Chiang-Kai-shek. I don't like it at all and I'd rather not see it in the wardroom.'

That settled the matter. The new badge was not hung and, space being at a premium, Thurlow decided to act on his captain's request. As Correspondence Officer, anything connected with post was clearly his province. He debated the question whether he should include a simple message of good wishes or, perhaps, the words 'with compliments' typed on a sheet of writing paper headed HMS *Tally-Ho*. It is often said that in the armed services the best policy is 'never complain, never explain, above all never ask questions'. Thurlow decided to suit the action to the words.

The gift should speak for itself. If Chiang-Kai-shek did not like it either, there would be fewer come-backs. Thurlow parcelled the shield in brown paper and inserted it in an official paid envelope. He addressed it clearly and, perhaps, optimistically: 'Chiang-Kai-shek, China.'

Thereafter he dispatched it and forgot about it. It seemed a small thing and of no great importance. If the great man wished to acknowledge the gift he had the name of the ship. Should *Tally-Ho* be sunk on her next patrol, no doubt the badge would increase in value on account of its scarcity.

For Thurlow there were more important matters on hand. His friend Jackie was sick with dengue fever and this would prevent his being on the next patrol. A replacement had to be found for him. Lieutenant Dennis John Adams RN, who was doing spare crew duty in HMS *Adamant* was embarked as Torpedo and Gunnery Officer.

'Fanny' Adams (anyone called Adams is always 'Fanny' in the Royal Navy) was a cheery, freckle-faced, red-haired character who had been on the same training course as 'Jackie' Warner and they had been together in *Medway II* at Haifa. He fitted into the *Tally-Ho* officer crew without difficulty and often used to go down to the fore-ends and chat with his Torpedo Gunners' Mate. Joe found him a congenial conversationalist with marked views on most topics. They got on well together.

As well as a new Torpedo and Gunnery Officer, *Tally-Ho* carried a new First Lieutenant on her next patrol. Lieutenant Frederick Melbourne Piggott RNR, had served under Bennington in *Porpoise* on one patrol in the Mediterranean. As a result he knew Thurlow as well. He found that with well-experienced officers and crew used to working together, taking over *Tally-Ho* presented no great problem. Bennington, he discovered, had not changed with promotion: he still lived only for one thing – to be able to sink the enemy.

Tally-Ho duly sailed on 6 August 1944, passing the boom at Trincomalee at 1700 hours. Bennington was especially pleased because this patrol did not include a special operation. The first three days were spent in surface passage. During this time Thurlow, who did the navigation, had time to reflect on how his war seemed to be passing. At the outbreak he had been a Merchant Navy Apprentice fresh out of the Training Ship *Conway*. At that time although he had a passing interest in reading about submarines, he had no thought or wish to serve in them. One of six volunteers from *Conway* for RNR cadets, he was listed in the Navy List as a (probationary) Midshipman RNR, with seniority from 31 December 1936.

His first posting was to the cruiser *Dunedin* on convoy escort duty in the northern patrol area. His next was to the destroyer *Saladin* which performed distinguished service at Dunkirk.

Before the end of 1940, he decided that service in large ships was not for him and volunteered for the Submarine Branch. At first his captain tried to dissuade him: RN officers could be drafted to the Submarine Branch but the RNR could only volunteer for such service. Thurlow was adamant and on 18 May 1940 began the submarine course. He finished top of the RNR intake and was rewarded with a choice of postings. He chose Alexandria little suspecting he would find a bride there. Arrived in Gibraltar, he took passage in HMS *Tetrarch* through the Strait. (*Tetrarch* was lost on the trip back to Gibraltar from Alexandria.) Next he did one trip as 'spare bod' in HMS *Thunderbolt* (the refloated *Thetis*), which was lost a year later. (The sinking of *Thetis* was responsible for the subsequent fitting of a safety device to all torpedo tube rear doors. It was the safety swing bolt, thereafter called the 'Thetis clip' in the Submarine Branch and perpetuated the memory of the men lost in the 1939 tragedy.)

By now Thurlow had been promoted Sub-Lieutenant and his eventual posting was to *Porpoise* as 'fourth hand'. *Porpoise* was then commanded by Commander E.F. Pizey RN. Bennington took over early in 1942. Thurlow's service under both Pizey and 'Ben' in *Porpoise* provided a good apprenticeship in the Submarine Branch.

It was in Alexandria that he met Ludmilla, the daughter of an aristocratic White Russian *émigré* family living exiled in Egypt, and he courted her between patrols.

A major snag in his life now, while he patrolled in Far Eastern waters, was that Ludmilla was still in Alexandria and passage back to the UK for civilians was practically impossible to obtain. Nor was there excitement to divert Thurlow's mind from his personal problems. The patrol was proving drearily uneventful, to the disappointment of all ranks.

At last on 22 August 1944, at periscope depth, midway between Penang Island and the Langkawi Group, twenty-six miles off-shore, *Tally-Ho* sighted a small coaster, apparently a motor vessel of about 300 tons. The submarine promptly altered course towards the target and closed at full speed. At 1748 Bennington ordered the gun crew to be closed up and gave the signal to surface off the Bunting Isles. The gun crew had a positive field day; during twelve minutes sixty-six rounds were fired at about 2,000 yards range and many hits were secured and, at the end, the enemy's thick wooden hull was on fire. Once it was clear that the enemy was sinking, *Tally-Ho* moved south.

Two days later she sank three junks approximately forty-five miles south west of Penang. The cargoes appeared to be iron ore or bales of some sort. For the remainder of her patrol she could find no other targets and was back in Trincomalee on 30 August 1944 with her crew far from satisfied with the meagre compensation provided by the recent minor successes.

As Captain Ionides put it:

> Although no targets of any size were encountered, one 300-ton merchant vessel and three junks of 50, 70 and 150 tons respectively were sunk by gunfire. This may seem a small return for a 24-day patrol but, in the present desperate situation for enemy shipping, all such sinkings are valuable, not only for the cargoes destroyed but also because it makes the other junks unwilling to sail on account of the danger.

At this stage in the war the Japanese supply lines were stretched to breaking point in order to supply their armies, and the junk traffic, particularly that carrying rice and other food stuffs, was indispensable to them.

CHAPTER EIGHT

Surfaced Action

While still two days out of Trincomalee, *Tally-Ho* received a truly startling signal. The message was decoded without difficulty; it was brief to the point of being epigrammatic but its meaning was totally inexplicable. The text read: HMS SEVERN HOISTS JOLLY ROGER IN HARBOUR.

Bennington had served for almost two years in *Severn* prior to the war. His promotion to Lieutenant had come while he was serving in her. He'd had affection for the old River-class boat which, like the other two of her class, *Clyde* and *Thames*, had leaked oil from her external fuel tanks. She was large and fast — quite a change from L69, his previous boat.

In the circumstances it did not seem politic to ask for a report or an explanation; so, since it was clearly neither an instruction to initiate action nor a caution to change course immediately, Bennington decided to defer questions on the signal until he reached port. Had anyone in *Tally-Ho* happened on the correct explanation and made so bold as to voice it, there is no question but that he would have been disbelieved.

On entering the harbour at Trinco it was observed that the water was besmirched with thick fuel oil. One of the stokers seeing it exclaimed in uncompromising fashion, 'Cor! Look at that. I wonder wot dropped that lot.'

Some days previously, whilst *Severn* had been in harbour her torpedo team had been preparing an 'air shot' from the stern torpedo tube. This was, in itself, nothing strange and involved no possible risk — provided the torpedo tube was empty. On the command 'Fire!' there had been the usual woomph and, contrary to everyone's expectations, a torpedo had streaked straight across the harbour making for a strategically placed tanker. One moment the tanker was lying tranquilly at anchor and the next she was struck amidships by the exploding torpedo, which neatly perforated her hull. In a matter of moments she gently trimmed down and came to rest on the harbour bottom.

It was incredible. It is said that the tanker sank so gently her master refused to believe his ship had been torpedoed. Although the incident happened at breakfast-time, an emergency fire party from HMS *Adamant* was on board the tanker in minutes. Fortunately there was no fire outbreak. Nothing, however, could prevent the escape of a great volume of fuel oil into the harbour. The accident occurred through an inadvertent slip in firing drill. It was providential that an ammunition ship, usually berthed close astern of *Severn*, was absent on this occasion.

The multitude of natural bays and inlets that compose the natural harbour of Trincomalee make it a pretty place. Before the war it was frequented by the wealthy yachting fraternity of Ceylon. It was, even in the summer of 1944, a very pleasant place for small-boat sailing and swimming. Unfortunately the *Severn* incident and resulting jagged rent in the tanker's side put paid to all that.

Arrived in Trincomalee, *Tally-Ho* remained in harbour until 18 September. Just before that date, two new officers joined her: Lieutenants Laurence Douglas Hamlyn RN and Peter James Rouse RN, both regular officers (Hamlyn had been RN Special Entry and Rouse had been a cadet at Dartmouth before the war). Jimmy Hamlyn, who was a classical scholar, joined as First Lieutenant. He had had his first sight of *Tally-Ho* in dry dock at Colombo, when he had observed that the crumpled plates of her ravaged ballast tanks looked like lettuce. He decided she looked a lot better now.

The presence of Hamlyn and Rouse in the Submarine Branch was due to a policy directive that had been introduced by Sir Max Horton while Flag Officer of Submarines. He had secured Admiralty approval to the impressment of all RN officer intake to the Submarine Branch. This ensured an influx of highly trained officers for the boats at a time when numbers of officer crew available had become sorely depleted by the high rate of losses in the Mediterranean.

Hamlyn was far from rejoicing over his drafting to the Submarine Branch. And to make matters worse, it happened at the very weekend that he had arranged to get married. But he had a philosophical outlook and was determined to make the best of things.

Now, two years later, he was married and a father – and he took his responsibilities seriously. His mature outlook was in contrast to the more usual devil-may-care attitude of his contemporaries and tended to make him appear rather older than they. He was, in fact, no older than Thurlow and actually a year younger than Steady.

He had often seen Bennington on board *Adamant* and it was in her wardroom bar that Bennington, glass in hand, met and greeted him after his appointment to *Tally-Ho*. Bennington's first action was to offer his new First Lieutenant a drink. Courteously and patiently Hamlyn explained that he did not drink though this was not on moral grounds; it was simply that as a sportsman (he had played hockey for the Royal Navy) he had never wanted to undo the effects of training. As a result he'd never acquired the taste for drink.

Bennington showed himself perfectly understanding and explained briefly what he expected of his new officer: 'You're the First Lieutenant, you know your job – bloody well do it! If you do I'll keep out of your way. If you don't, I'll be down on you like a ton of bricks.'

Hamlyn didn't see Bennington again until just before they were ready to sail. Very early on he discovered the admirable qualities of Coxswain Ginger Ridley. In fact he later said that he never had an easier job as a First Lieutenant because of *Tally-Ho*'s coxswain.

Rouse was about a year older than Hamlyn. He spoke slowly and deliberately and was painstaking and persevering in the performance of his duties. His individual manner of speech when passing the order to group up the motors when the boat was submerged, led to him being stuck with the nickname 'Group . . . up', initiated by Bennington.

The three or so days of surface passage to a patrol area were especially tedious, but they were lightened by the hope of successful action ahead. An uneventful patrol was therefore not merely unbroken monotony but a keen disappointment.

Playing the gramophone in the wardroom was one way of

L

lessening the tedium. But the repertoire was limited. There were only three records: Rachmaninoff's 'Piano Concerto No. 2 in C Minor', 'Liebestraum' and 'The Road to Mandalay'. The third, much loved by Bennington, was often played on passage because the lower deck had a superstition about it. They professed to believe fervently that its being played would be followed soon by a sinking. That the charm had been known to fail, in no way blunted their faith. The officers, out of consideration for those who believed the legend, pretty much reserved 'Mandalay' for a patrol area.

Hamlyn, a stranger to *Tally-Ho*, coming in as First Lieutenant was impressed especially by two factors: there could be no mistaking either the resolute nature of the crew or their determination to achieve sinkings.

The first four days of passage towards the Malacca Strait were uneventful. But Friday, 22 September was distinguished by an aircraft alert and the receipt of a signal ordering *Tally-Ho* to a position seventy miles north-west of Diamond Point. After two days of tedium, Bennington gave orders to shift the patrol area further south.

On Wednesday 27 September, as dawn was beginning to break over the densely wooded hilltops of the Malay coastline, a look-out reported a coal-burning vessel steering almost due north. The vessel was about 1,000 tons -- certainly worth attacking. Just possibly it could be escorting a U-boat. Bennington estimated that if *Tally-Ho* made a fast surface chase there was a good chance of being able to dive and execute an attack before the vessel reached the Sembilians. At the end of two and a half hours running all-out, when *Tally-Ho* appeared to be gaining on her quarry, an aircraft was sighted to the west. Bennington promptly ordered the boat down to eighty feet.

At 0804 *Tally-Ho* came to periscope depth and a quick all-round look and sky search revealed that two bombers had taken over from the original aircraft; the enemy clearly meant business. Blessing the enemy's inobservance Bennington ordered the submarine down to eighty feet once more. During the forenoon *Tally-Ho* again came to periscope depth and found that two float planes were relieving the bombers. At 1815 *Tally-Ho* surfaced to find the enemy aircraft had finally abandoned the search. The following night, after fruitless search for targets, Bennington gave orders to close the coast of Sumatra once more. At 0536 the look-out reported three columns of smoke approaching from the south east and two bomber aircraft circling overhead in their vicinity.

Bennington was delighted by this report. It not only meant coastal traffic but the presence of escorting aircraft was a fair indication that the enemy was rattled. By 0830 *Tally-Ho* was at periscope depth, with the attack team closed up, and the approaching ships had proved to be three submarine chasers escorting three coasters. The coasters were 'flying light', riding high in the water without cargo. This was a disappointment but, with targets becoming so scarce, Bennington felt beggars could not be choosers. *Tally-Ho* followed on a roughly parallel course to the convoy, keeping inshore of them. This procedure put the submarine in rather shallow water, but it had the advantage that the enemy ships were silhouetted against the available light and would probably not be expecting an attack from the landward side.

The enemy vessels were in line ahead with four cables between each of the coasters, and the submarine chasers about 4,000 yards ahead of the formation. At one stage the formation made an alteration of course towards *Tally-Ho*. Bennington wondered if this could have been because either one of the coasters or the spotter aircraft had seen his periscope. The reason for the alteration was not apparent and, after a very brief interval on that heading, the coasters altered back on to almost their original course. (Later Bennington was to discover the enemy had an anti-torpedo net stretched between the fishing stakes in this area, and had evidently hoped to take refuge behind its barrier.)

With the nearest enemy vessel still 4,100 yards away, the plot gave confirmation of its course and speed. Bennington's plan was to 'kipper' the leading vessel on a 90° track angle at point blank range. The escorts keeping well ahead of the convoy greatly favoured such tactics. At this point Thurlow reported soundings were well below the recorder mark (at 2½ fathoms) mindful that, in a minute or two, there would be very little water – if any — below the submarine's keel. Nothing daunted, Bennington made his attack at 0921 on a 60° track angle and at double the range planned, loosing off a single torpedo set for a depth of six feet, aiming at the centre of the leading vessel. Then he promptly turned to starboard.

One minute and twelve seconds later the torpedo went up, probably on hitting the torpedo net (as then unsuspected), and by then *Tally-Ho* was burrowing into the mud. As there was no enemy opposition, Bennington was unworried by this, although a number of boats had bottomed in muddy conditions and been unable to work free. However, in the Malacca Strait bottoming was not too rare an occurrence and a gradual 'wriggling' technique could usually free the keel. Some people liked to come off stern first; it was a matter of choice. Ben would never have done. 'I don't do things arse-wise.' Captain H.M.C. Ionides took the matter rather more seriously and endorsed Bennington's patrol report as follows:

> HMS *Tally-Ho* eventually got into deeper water after this fine example of 'pressing on' under most adverse circumstances.

Realising that the Sumatra side of the strait must be quite dead now, Bennington took *Tally-Ho* across the strait to patrol south of the Sembilans for the next three days. Here the submarine patrolled along the ten-fathom line towards the mouth of the Bernam River, along the route taken by the vessel sighted on 27 September. The days were monotonous: no wind, no sea, consistently poor visibility and heavy rain storms at night. Certainly unsuitable conditions for a further attempt to explore the Malacca Strait.

On 4 October *Tally-Ho* returned to the coast of Sumatra under cover of darkness, sighting North and South Brothers on the starboard beam before daybreak. At 0526 she dived eight miles from Jumpal Bank. Two aircraft appeared as soon as it was light and shortly after two columns of smoke were sighted fine on the port bow. They were from two ships moving southwards, which had already passed Jumpal Bank. It was galling to have arrived in position just too late. Nothing of interest appeared for the rest of the morning. But at 1215 a small, modern-looking motor vessel of about 200 tons appeared to the west. *Tally-Ho* altered course 190° and attempted to close, tracking along the fishing stakes lining the coast. Two minutes later Bennington called 'Gun action stations!' and *Tally-Ho* surfaced.

Bennington on the bridge, with Adams, as Gunnery Officer, beside him on the small platform that had been made to enable Jackie Warner to see over the top of the bridge cab, saw the motor vessel turn inshore and run aground. This was Adams big moment: as soon as *Tally-Ho* broke surface he ordered the 4-in. gun to open fire. The range was 4,500 yards. Now with a stationary target, she ran in at full speed. An MTB (motor torpedo boat) promptly returned the fire with small-calibre automatic weapons. None of her shells burst within 2,000 yards. Nor was *Tally-Ho* proving too lucky: the target was clearly visible from the bridge but both gun layer and trainer complained they could not see it from the gun sponson. From down there the line of the fishing stakes and the unbroken line of mangrove swamps merged together.

After firing thirty-four rounds very erratically, Bennington told Adams to give the cease fire. 'Cease Fire. Check, Check, Check!' yelled the Gunnery Officer, 'Check, Check, Check!' had been introduced to avoid an order to cease fire being lost in the noise of discharging automatic weapons. 'We were merely wasting ammunition,' said Bennington not unkindly to Adams. A Gunnery Officer's task was considerably hindered by having his gun team firing blind. Lieutenant Adams had done his best but circumstances were against him.

In the course of the action *Tally-Ho* had come close inshore and was now within 100 yards of the nearest line of fishing stakes. Bennington could see that a fence was stretched between them. It protruded a full two feet above sea level and extended from one fishing enclosure to the next. Bennington had never seen anything like it before. He was convinced that not only was this not a fishing adjunct, but that it was an anti-torpedo net. He was also sure that the presence of this anti-torpedo baffle was the reason for the sudden change of course by the coaster attacked on 30 September 1944. Precisely he noted the presence of the baffle for the Intelligence Services back in Ceylon.

'Alter course 070°: full ahead, both,' Bennington ordered, and at twelve knots *Tally-Ho* made for deeper water. At once the MTB, which throughout the action had remained close to the coaster, decided to demonstrate a possible tactical use for the baffle. She turned sharply towards the shore, passed through the gap in the fishing stakes and baffle, ran inshore of the obstruction for a short distance, then turned sharply and, emerging from another gap, appeared to fire a single torpedo at *Tally-Ho*. Certainly a very conspicuous splash was seen near to the bows of the MTB before she turned and raced back to the stranded coaster.

'Starboard 40°,' ordered Bennington: no torpedo track was sighted. He thought contemptuously that he would not have missed at that range. But he was damned if he'd go to any trouble to kipper an MTB. After ten minutes on the same course he decided it was safe for *Tally-Ho* to submerge.

By first light on Friday, 6 October 1944 *Tally-Ho* had attempted to close to Aru Bay. Heavy rain had fallen all night but at dawn it had lifted just a little. A very acute mirage effect was encountered each time periscope observations were attempted. On the shore of Sumatra the mangroves and palms seemed distended in a nightmarish surrealistic fashion. Ben remarked that the trees stood out like cathedral spires.

By seven o'clock in the morning it was becoming even harder to be sure of anything one saw through the periscope. At one point Bennington reported: 'Large object visible, sticking up well above the tree line. Don't close up the gun team yet.' For once he was quite unable to identify what he was seeing. Multiple images were a common feature of mirage effect in these latitudes, but never before had he sighted a stationary object that so completely defied recognition. As *Tally-Ho* closed the object he began a commentary on what he could see.

'It looks just like an English stone bridge with a trickle of water below the arch.'

In the control room men listened in silent disbelief. Bennington spoke again:

'I've got it! I can see more clearly now. It's the Aru Bay Light Vessel, dead ahead. Check soundings against the chart.'

Tally-Ho was quite close to Aru Bay as estimated. Bennington ordered an alteration of course to 340°. At the Asdic set George Backman sat keeping a constant watch and making continued sweeps. One mile after Thurlow had checked the chart position Backman spoke. 'I'm picking up echoes from mines on the starboard bow — about 500 yards.'

'Alter course 320°,' ordered Bennington. 'Range of echoes now?'

'Four hundred yards.'

'Can you be sure they're from mines?'

'Yes, sir, they're always the same, they sort of ripple like.'

Bennington and Thurlow examined the chart. The position gave cause for concern. There was a marked tidal 'set' and *Tally-Ho* appeared to be being drawn not only into very shallow water but towards what was almost certainly a magnetic minefield laid by *Trenchant* a few days earlier. Bennington made a quick periscope observation. Away to the north east, fine on the starboard bow, was an indistinct blur that could be another vessel. It was essential to take quick action. He was far too close inshore and in insufficient depth for further submerged manoeuvres, especially with the lurking menace of magnetic mines close at hand. His best policy would be to take a 'quick squint on the roof'.

Just after 0830 *Tally-Ho* broke surface. From their elevated position on the bridge, it was clear to Bennington and the look-outs that a submarine chaser was about three and a half miles distant. Its hostile nature was not in dispute since it immediately turned towards *Tally-Ho* and opened fire. 'Close up the gun team,' Bennington ordered. 'But wait to go to gun action stations.'

Below, outside the wardroom, directly under the gun tower, the gun team lined up headed by the layer and trainer with sighting telescopes slung around their necks. The magazine was opened and the first shells extracted ready for passing up to the gun team. On the bridge Lieutenant Adams joined Bennington.

'What do you think, Guns?' the captain asked his Gunnery Officer. 'Still a bit far away?'

Bennington had already decided this, but he would not have departed from the established procedure of verifying the matter with the specialist officer. The control room reported that *Tally-Ho* was almost clear of the magnetic minefield and now had just sufficient depth to submerge to periscope depth. The enemy shooting was still far wide of the mark. The chaser was using a semi-automatic gun mounted on the forecastle. At 0840 Bennington gave the order to dive to periscope depth.

At once Asdic searching impulses were picked up. Clearly this meant they were faced by a well-equipped and probably well-armed opponent. In the next hour the search continued and three depth-charges were dropped. This sort of search could last for quite a long time and the enemy might call up reinforcements of air support.

'Enemy abeam, to port: 2,500 yards range,' reported George Backman from the Asdic set. 'Turning towards us, revolutions increasing: range decreasing.'

The enemy was cramming on speed and coming in for the attack.

'Gun action stations. Stand by for surfacing.'

Bennington was aware that he was faced with what could prove a formidable adversary in a surface scrap. On the other hand, he knew he had a first-class gun team and the 4-in. gun was probably a superior weapon to anything the enemy carried. If, however, the chaser succeeded in inflicting damage to the pressure hull, the submarine might be prevented from any further diving on this patrol and, the Japanese having established her position, she would not have the speed to leave attackers behind nor the arms to resist sustained air attack. Bennington considered the calculated risk was worth taking.

He raised the periscope — rain was still teeming — and checked the submarine chaser's latest position. She was still about 2,500 yards distant and practically end on to *Tally-Ho*. He repeated his instructions to the Gunnery Officer: the first shell must be away at the first possible moment after the gun was out of the water. If the first shell went wild it didn't matter: at least it kept the enemy's head down. Directly it had exploded it provided data for correcting for further salvoes. The Gunnery Officer, twenty feet above the gun crew, could see further than they. If he could accurately direct their salvoes, they could keep the salvoes coming as fast as any gun team in 'the trade'. Adams felt perfectly confident. He opened the conning-tower lower hatch, mounted the ladder, and positioned himself just below the upper hatch. In any gun action the Gunnery Officer emerged from the conning-tower just before the captain. Bennington was still at the periscope passing updated range and direction information to the gun crew. He would remain at the periscope till the last possible moment before surfacing. Then, miraculously, he would appear on the bridge hard on the heels of the Gunnery Officer.

Inside the gun tower the gun team were tightly packed on the ladder, just below the upper hatch. The gunlayer, 'Artilleryman' Henry James Barker, weighed the gun lock in his hand with practised ease. He was awaiting the signal that *Tally-Ho* was at twenty feet before removing the first clip of the gun tower hatch. The hatch clips were already unpinned. Down in the control room the First Lieutenant, Jimmy Hamlyn, stood by the blowing main ballast tanks for full buoyancy: the hydroplanes were all that were preventing her going up like a rocket. As First Lieutenant, he was responsible for trim, surfacing and diving movements. Hamlyn kept his eyes fixed on the depth gauge; directly the needle passed the 25 feet mark he would order the hydroplanes to be reversed and *Tally-Ho* would shoot to the surface like a cork.

'Both hydroplanes hard a'rise. Surface!'

At the sound of Lieutenant Hamlyn's voice all hell broke loose. Both hatches were unclipped and flung back. In the conning-tower Adams leapt through the hatch opening and sprang on to the small platform erected on the bridge deck for the Gunnery Officer. The gun tower hatch covers (there are two in a 'T'-class boat) were also slammed open. Leading Seaman Barker fitted the breech lock with wet fingers, gasping at the effort, as sea water cascaded from the gun's open breech. Then he slipped into his seat on the left of the gun; the trainer was already in his seat on the right of the gun. The breech worker, in place behind the trainer, watched as the first shell was rammed home. Above their heads Adams called the range data. 'On,' said Barker decisively. 'Shoot!' Adams yelled.

Adams's first action on emerging had been to check the range. It was spot on — 2,500 yards. From the size of the bow wave, the submarine chaser must be running at full throttle. As the first shell screamed away he caught the acrid reek of cordite. Inside the gun shield the gun bucked in its recoil like a live thing. The metal plating floor perforated with drainage holes trembled beneath the gun crew's feet: the hydraulic damping device of the 'recuperator' could not fully absorb the gun's powerful kick. In the moment of silence following the gun's discharge the breech slid open and the spent cartridge case came out with a metallic clang. An asbestos-gloved hand caught it up and flung it over the side while the next shell was being loaded into the still smoking breech. The ammunition number rammed the shell case home with the back of his clenched fist. He had to do it that way otherwise, with fixed ammunition and a semi-automatic, quick-firing weapon, the automatic closure of the breech block would whip off his fingers. The horizontally sliding breech block slid across, pushing his hand safely out of the way; he touched Barker's shoulder, indicating that the gun was ready to fire again.

Above them, leaning over the bridge cab, Adams saw the fall of the first shot: the line was right, but the range was just over. The water spout of the exploding shell erupted behind the submarine chaser, silhouetting the outline of her forecastle and squarish superstructure. She was one of the latest type, a bare 180 feet long, quite fast — anything up to 24 knots — and displacing just under 300 tons. The light, semi-automatic gun on her forecastle seemed to be unmanned. 'Down one hundred. Shoot!' Adams shouted.

Bennington had reached the bridge in time to see the first fall of shot. Behind him had come Wally Crole, the Oerlikon gunner. Wally had not waited for orders to shoot; in such circumstances his orders were to fire independently. On the exposed 'bandstand', at the after end of the bridge, he dropped the first ammunition pan he was carrying neatly into place on the weapon and traversed on to the submarine chaser, opening fire with his aim on the bridge. After firing two thirds of the first pan the weapon jammed with a round half-way up the barrel.

The Oerlikon gun frankly did not stand up to frequent immersion. It had to be cocked and that weakened its springs. It was necessary to keep it cocked; an elaborate process involving putting a long strop over a projection on the base of the mounting, looping it over the cocking handles and tilting the weapon right back to its highest angle of elevation. There wasn't time for all that when going into action nor was there time to open the watertight ready-use lockers: Wally had to carry ammunition pans up with him. He was pretty deft at changing barrels but that didn't help when the gun jammed in action. The only thing he could do now was go below and leave it — Bennington would never allow him to remain on the exposed 'bandstand' struggling with it.

The next shell fired by the 4-in. gun burst just astern of the submarine chaser: the range was perfect. On the superstructure of the Japanese vessel Adams could see a light flashing, not a signal, probably a machine-gun firing. On either side of *Tally-Ho* the rain-speckled, grey-green water became pock-marked. Bullets drummed against casing and ballast tanks. Holes appeared in the bridge breastwork: large areas of it were brass to avoid interference with the magnetic compass, so it was not bullet proof.

With a slight correction to port, *Tally-Ho*'s next shot should be on target. 'Two (degrees) left. Shoot!' yelled Adams. At the same instant something struck his right side, whirling him round and flinging him on his back. He lay staring at the sky.

In quick succession three shells exploded just aft of the submarine chaser; she must have increased speed since the last correction. 'Adams, you're firing wide. What the hell's up?' Bennington demanded, then saw Adams lying on the deck beside him. The gun crew had not had an order for the last two salvoes, they'd also heard Lieutenant Adams cry out when he was hit. Had the engagement been broken off? Was the bridge party wiped out? For a fraction of a second they hesitated; one of them leaned down the gun tower to shout below.

On the bridge Bennington leaned over the cab to see into the gun mounting. The gun crew surely couldn't be going below? What did they think he could do up here on his own? He didn't ask questions or hesitate; at the top of his voice he roared, 'Come back you *bastards*! No one gave the order to cease fire!'

The gun crew were *not* going below, but they got the message. Bennington gave quick instructions to correct their shooting and they bent to their task with a will. The next five salvoes were all direct hits on the target. As they were fired Bennington gave orders down the voicepipe for Adams to be taken below and placed in the captain's bunk. Barely had this been done before

Bennington's eye caught the movement of a low-flying float plane taking up obviously hostile position astern. This he reported down the voice-pipe, wondering what could be done about it: the 4-in. gun was not an anti-aircraft weapon: the Oerlikon cannon was jammed and unserviceable. Ginger Facer bustled up from below with a stripped-down Lewis machine-gun cradled in his arms.

Ginger Facer was in time to get away two thirds of a pan of .303-in. incendiary ammunition at the float plane as it made its second pass over *Tally-Ho*. As the enormous radial engine swept noisily by, only feet overhead, Bennington took in, professionally, first the fact that Facer was certainly scoring hits and second that the enemy seemed to be hosing the water around *Tally-Ho* and wasting ammunition. The Japanese pilot was probably having difficulty in bringing his fixed forward-firing armament to bear — every pilot knows the hypnotic effects of target fascination can be equally as lethal as the target vessel's return fire.

The aircraft, still at low level, was banked in a steep turn over the submarine chaser as the latter received the last salvo from the 4-in. gun. It must have hit the chaser's depth-charges stowed on deck aft. The submarine chaser instantly blew up, scattering fragments over a wide area. The aircraft that had been above it seemed to stagger in its flight and began to lose height trailing a plume of smoke.

'Cease fire, Check, Check, Check! Press the diving hooter.' Bennington's order to break off the action was followed by the klaxon shrilling twice. The gun was locked, fore and aft, the lock removed and sighting telescopes unshipped. Everyone went below in the shortest possible time. On the way Bennington heard a final distant report. Strange, he thought, there hadn't seemed anything of the submarine chaser left to explode. Hearing Facer's voice he turned his head and noticed that the Yeoman was grinning happily. 'The aircraft crashed, sir. I saw it.'

'Did you by Jove,' said Bennington. It had been quite an action. After ordering depth to be increased to eighty feet and a course to the north-east he went straight to see Adams.

Dennis Adams looked very pale. His wound was severe and it seemed he could be saved only by major surgery. This, certainly, was beyond the resources carried in *Tally-Ho*. Bennington personally administered morphia to him and Ginger Ridley gently laid a soft pad on the open wound. It was apparent that he had been hit by a ricochet off the periscope standards. He was cheerful, lucid and professed to feel no pain. To Joe Brighton he remarked, 'We're in one hell· of a mess.' However, his general demeanour was such that hopes of his recovery rose. Ginger Ridley was called to the fore-ends to deal with ·the only other injury that had been received. Able Seaman Peters had been hurt during the action.

The young Herbert Peters had been inside the gun tower passing ammunition up to the gun crew. At the height of the action a newly ejected shell case had struck him on the thigh, laying open the flesh; it looked like pork. He was handed below and taken to the fore-ends. Ken Lockyer at once took over his duty. At times like these, orders were not necessary; if one hand had to fall out from his duty another jumped in. That was always typical of the *Tally-Ho* crew. The seaman's thigh wound was a fearsome sight but Ridley was used to coping with such situations. A tot of rum for Peters, one for the Coxswain, and Ridley was ready to begin. Briskly he broke open one of the small glass tubes containing a sterilised gut suture already threaded into a curved needle. 'Out!' Ridley curtly told one of the patient's 'oppos' who had stayed to keep up the spirits of his pal but now looked even greener than the injured man.

Ridley didn't consider himself a medical expert – that was the captain's province. Nursing and care of minor ailments were Ridley's task. When he was half-way through sewing up the wound he administered more rum to his patient and gratefully accepted 'sippers'. The job completed, he slapped Peters on the back and ensured that with a bit of help he was hoisted into No. 1 reload rack. As a special concession Peters had been allowed to smoke a cigarette while the operation was carried out. It had gone well and now he needed a long rest. Ridley could not stay with his patient; he went directly to the control room to confer with the captain about Lieutenant Adams.

In the captain's cabin, conveniently close to the control room, Adams lay quietly, still pale, calm and still very cheerful; he seemed almost relaxed. Bennington advised against any attempt to probe his wound. The patient's good spirits could indicate a possibility of recovery but Bennington feared any attempt at treatment might induce too great a shock. Adams asked if he might speak to Thurlow; and they spent some time together. Everything possible was done to fit in with the wounded man's wishes and keep him happy without, if possible, exciting him.

At about three o'clock in the afternoon, with *Tally-Ho* still submerged and moving north-east, Bennington gave Adams more morphia. Half an hour later the morphia began to take effect and Adams relaxed and fell asleep. Bennington was deeply concerned – but he had to think both of Adams and his crew. Periscope observations had revealed the presence of an aircraft searching no doubt for *Tally-Ho*. There could be no question of surfacing before nightfall. The submarine was deep in enemy waters, committed to radio silence as well as having a seriously wounded officer on board.

Adams slept soundly for four hours. After that his breathing became heavy and laboured. More morphia calmed him, but he vomited shortly after its administration; after that he fell into a light slumber. His brow seemed cool despite the sweat-odorous heat of the submarine's interior. Bennington moved quietly into the wardroom; Adams's loyalty might cause him to try to rouse himself if he saw his captain and Bennington wanted to avoid that. He spoke softly with Ginger Ridley: the best thing would be for the Coxswain to keep an eye on Adams. 'Call me if there's any change,' Bennington instructed.

Just before 2050 Ridley appeared and said quietly, 'Captain, sir. It's Lieutenant Adams: he's died.' Bennington came at once. Ridley had closed the young officer's eyes and he looked, in death, calm and peaceful and very young. Bennington immediately gave orders what should be done. He knew what he'd have liked to do: Adams deserved a funeral with full military honours. But Bennington had to take into consideration the tropical heat. Ridley had arrangements put in hand. Adams was sewn up in a hammock – the custom had not changed since Nelson's days. The hammock was weighted with 4-in. shells and at once Bennington ordered *Tally-Ho* to be brought to the surface.

The hammock containing the body of Lieutenant Adams was carefully hauled up the conning-tower and committed to the deep by 'Brum' Sutton. The knowledge that the enemy was still probably hunting *Tally-Ho* prevented any ceremony being held on the bridge. However Bennington ordered Lieutenant Hamlyn to assemble the ship's company in the control room where he personally conducted a memorial service, reading the service for Burial of the Dead. Only the minimum crew needed to work the machinery and keep a look-out were obliged to stay away.

Joe Brighton was present and remembering Adams as he had known him. Two patrols were not a long time in which to get to know anyone. He probably knew Adams as well as any man on board. War was a terrible thing but one must not allow oneself to brood upon it; if one gave way, one could not go on. It was essential to try and conjure a false perspective. He used to enjoy the occasions when Adams visited him in the fore-ends for a chat – a shame he couldn't do that tonight. That was the way to think of it, that he'd been a jolly good shipmate – in *Tally-Ho* officers could be shipmates.

Lieutenant Dennis John Adams was the son of Gordon Mills Adams and Beatrice Ellen Adams of Oxford. Bennington wrote his epitaph in his patrol report with these words:

Lt. Dennis John Adams joined HMS *Tally-Ho* in July 1944 and this was his second patrol. His conduct was exemplary. His death at the early age of twenty-two is greatly regretted.

Bennington had decided that, since the events of the previous night had taken the submarine a great distance from her intended route, there was no question of complying with an earlier signal from Captain (S) received that day. Therefore *Tally-Ho* had best return to base. He would advise this change of plans as soon as it was possible to signal Trincomalee. This was not possible till two days later on 8 October 1944. By then AB Peters was down from his reload rack, walking a shade stiffly but, most certainly, walking. He recovered without complications and Ridley, much later, received a commendation. He got several from Peters of course, and even, a tot. What man can give more? Joe's comment was probably the most apposite – and complimentary. 'You did a damn good job there, Charlie, in the fore-ends with all the filth in the world floating around.'

During the surface return passage, which took till 11 October 1944, it was possible to inspect the damage inflicted on the bridge by the submarine chaser. Many bullets had riddled the bridge casing; several were discovered in the folded radar antennae and they were of 0.5-in. calibre. The one that had struck Lieutenant Adams had already penetrated the bridge fabric and a strengthening brass angle-iron. Most people felt that Bennington had unquestionably had a lucky escape. 'Hell of a do,' was how Ken Lockyer described it. Characteristically, he refused to be drawn conversationally on this point.

Bennington did not comment. In the same way he kept to himself the narrowest escape he'd suffered thus far during the war. Ironically it had been on dry land, but the injury he sustained could well have precluded him from any further service in submarines. During the first air raid on Belfast, in the Victoria Dockyard where firemen and submarine crews were struggling to rescue the injured and control the raging fires, Lieutenant Bennington received an injury to his left eye from a piece of flying concrete. Subsequently the left side of his face became paralysed. Unused to taking personal injuries particularly seriously, he had waited a week before reporting to a doctor.

The doctor took a serious view of his injury and for a month Bennington was kept in hospital lying on a board, movement of his head inhibited. The injury troubles him even today. After two months of sick leave he underwent tests and detailed examination and passed the eye tests at the first attempt.

To have been denied the chance of further service in submarines, particularly at a time when he was about to assume his first operational command, would have been heartbreaking. The fact that he retained above average eyesight was little short of miraculous. But that was not a word in Bennington's personal vocabulary.

CHAPTER NINE

Tally - Ho's Last Patrol

Jackie Warner rejoined *Tally-Ho* soon after her return to Trincomalee. He had been sent up to the hills to convalesce after his bout of dengue fever, and with characteristic single-mindedness had enjoyed himself. His natural ebullience therefore was tempered by the news of Adams's death and the realisation that he had been killed when standing on precisely the spot where Jackie usually stood for gun actions.

Jackie was ready for duty and hoping that *Tally-Ho* would be leaving shortly on another patrol. Unknown to him there existed a points system by which the crews of the boats qualified to return to the UK. *Tally-Ho*, after all her actions, had already acquired sufficient points to justify her return home. Bennington, however, volunteered to make one final patrol: he disliked breaking off something he had started before it was completed. He was convinced that the Malacca Strait area was dead as a source of targets but, if asked to go there again, he would go with pleasure. Had Jackie known, he too would certainly have volunteered.

He was pretty accustomed to taking things as they came. The Royal Navy had been his life — just as it had been Bennington's — since the age of sixteen. Jackie had enlisted as a Boy-Seaman on 10 February 1936. He had chosen the Royal Navy 'because my brother was in it'. When war began he had been serving in the battleship *Ramillies*. Very soon after that he served in 'Q' ships. His sense of humour is very evident in his comment on the subject: 'We were ordinary merchant ships with hidden guns; our aim was to be torpedoed because then we'd stay afloat — being full of timber baulks and empty oil drums for buoyancy. Then, we'd drop our screens and open fire.'

Commissioned, he became an Acting Sub-Lieutenant on 23 August 1942 and was quickly drafted to the Submarine Branch.

M

Having no taste for doing things compulsorily, he rectified the position by volunteering, as did a great many young officers in his position.

Once again *Tally-Ho* was to be entrusted with a special operation on her last patrol. As yet only Bennington knew any details. Just before leaving Ceylon five passengers and a ton of special stores were embarked. Joe Brighton mildly cursed every time he saw the torpedo stowage compartment — already crowded with three weeks' provisions. Of medium height and stockily built he undoubtedly owned the largest waist measurement aboard. But that did not prevent 'Grandad', as he was called, from being as active as any other member of the ship's complement. Nor did Joe forget that space on board *Tally-Ho* was less confined than had been the case when he served in 'H'-boats where his sleeping space had been 4ft 3in. by 1ft 9in. of bare plating: and he had contrived to sleep comfortably.

At 1700 on Sunday, 29 October 1944, *Tally-Ho* sailed from Trincomalee. No one felt a sense of occasion; it might be the last time she would sail for an operational patrol, but it did not pay to attach significance to such matters. It was a patrol, like any other. The four days of passage to the patrol area were spent uneventfully, dropping into the normal patrol routine. Ken Lockyer began to grow a beard; so, too, did George Backman. They had a little ritual which accompanied their abstinence from shaving: at such times they would solemnly address one another as 'Major' and 'Colonel', the higher rank being automatically accorded to the one who spoke first. It was part of the mystique of *Tally-Ho* — like cursing the conditions but having no desire to be elsewhere.

Steadman was no longer with them. Recovered from his illness, he had passed a brief spell of spare-crew duty in the depot ship *Adamant*, and soon received a posting as First Lieutenant in *Severn*.

The daily 'trim dives' were short and uneventful. With *Tally-Ho* making her surface passage on main engines as swiftly as was reasonable, Bennington liked to spend as much time as possible on the bridge. To combat the noonday sun he wore a cloth sun hat. Seeing this one day Ridley quipped: 'Ask him if he wants a deck chair up there.'

Bennington was not perturbed by such reactions: he knew that his crew would follow him anywhere, whatever he wore. Just as they would save up the tinned crayfish for Snoopy the cat when rations were running low. Such things were simply signs that the spirit the crew had displayed on earlier patrols was still vital — as was Jackie's irrepressibility. He could walk into the wardroom and state cheerfully, 'Do you know? This morning I woke up with a moustache of cockroaches. It doesn't pay to sleep with your mouth open'. The relish with which such statements came out helped to amuse the passengers and divert their thoughts from hot bunks, cramped conditions and the dangers that lay ahead of them.

On Wednesday, 1 November 1944 at 0630, the presence of aircraft necessitated a brief dive but caused no excitement. *Tally-Ho* passed through the Sombrero passage and on 3 November made a periscope-depth patrol inshore of the Thailand coast, off Ko Phuket. There was nothing to be seen and the greatest excitement of the day was generally agreed to be the lower deck discussion, in the control room, on how this name should be pronounced. During the night a signal ordered *Tally-Ho* further south to patrol off Pulau Jarak. For once there was no difficulty in receiving the signal, though it was some time before a reply could be satisfactorily transmitted.

Periscope-depth patrols were mounted off Pulau Jarak the following day without result and *Tally-Ho* remained in the area when night fell. To Bennington there seemed little doubt that the area was indeed dead. However, having come all the way from Ceylon, no possibility of finding targets could be spurned. Moreover, anything less than maximum vigilance would dull the edge of his crew's temper and that he would not accept.

Throughout the night an intensive listening watch was maintained. Quiet prevailed. There was no breeze whatever and the surface of the water remained smooth. A moon shone fitfully through wavering mists that would have made the estimation of distances very difficult. Despite the undeniable beauty of nights in these waters the look-outs might not relax their vigilance. They were in the centre of a main thoroughfare for junks and few carried lights. At night, without wind to bear them along, the crews allowed their craft to drift; even to the extent, sometimes, of the entire crew turning in in the tiny cabin for'ard in the poop. Whenever a junk was sighted, it was essential to turn end on to it to minimise the risk of the submarine's being identified. Whilst it would have been quite simple to sink, ram or board the junk and embark her crew, any such activity was liable to compromise chances of finding future targets. There was no alternative but to turn away from the junk and increase the distance between it and *Tally-Ho.*

Tonight there was not even junk traffic to break the monotony of watching. Bennington followed his usual custom and spent the night on the bridge even though he felt convinced that this well-tried precaution had never been less necessary. He could sense his crew's frustration and it added to his own. He could remember other nights better spent.

He was familiar with night's quiet darkness when he would strain eyes and ears for any sign of another vessel. No matter how uninterrupted the serenity, complacency was unthinkable. Surprise could emerge from the darkness at any moment.

On the night of 2-3 September 1940, First Lieutenant Bennington was officer of the watch on the bridge of HM Submarine *Tigris* (commanded by Lieutenant Commander Howard Francis Bone RN, later awarded DSO and DSC) patrolling off Lorient. The submarine took station two to three miles offshore directly in the path of any U-boat leaving Lorient.

At 2330 precisely he was aware of the approach of an unlighted vessel. The sound of her engines was barely audible but the movement of her bow wake indicated she was travelling at a steady pace. Bennington was convinced the vessel was a large German U-boat outward bound. He promptly gave orders for alarm stations and summoned the captain.

Bone decided to mount a surface attack and Bennington went below to supervise the firing of the torpedoes. There was little time to ready *Tigris*, and no margin for error if the attack was to succeed. At 2334 a single torpedo was fired and an explosion was heard almost at once.* *Tigris*, was dived immediately after firing and Bone and Bennington were satisfied their attack had been successful. All the circumstances and conditions attendant on the

* The late Rob Roy McCurrach DSM* was in the fore ends when the torpedo was fired; his unpublished MS, in the Imperial War Museum, makes exciting reading.

attack combined to justify their conclusion. *Tigris* therefore claimed the destruction of an unidentified U-boat off Lorient.

That night's activity was, much later, to bring frustration to Bennington. Since the war the claim has been dis-allowed. It has been asserted that *Tigris*, in fact, sank a French trawler, the *Sancte Michaël* (600 tons) in error.

The Germans claim that during the whole of September 1940 they lost only one U-boat — off Kiel. German sources also indicate that the *Sancte Michaël* was sunk on 2 September 1940 off Brest — 100 miles north of Lorient. Tigris's weekly log book attests to the fact that from 2-7 September she maintained a stationary patrol off Lorient.

Questioned by the author in 1971, Bennington replied without hesitation: 'A trawler? Oh, no. It was definitely a submarine. I saw it and heard the diesels. Had it been a trawler I could have told by the engines.'*

And Bennington's reputation for possessing unusually acute vision was vindicated over and over again on subsequent patrols.

The whole of 5 November was spent vainly patrolling off Pulau Jarak at periscope depth. It was not too difficult to navigate the shallows by following the fishing stakes, which in the Malacca Strait, can sometimes be found even in mid-channel, near platforms to accommodate a fisherman.

On one occasion whilst navigating the fishing stakes, Jackie Warner was at the periscope and observed a single fisherman a short distance ahead in an open boat. As it was daylight, he lowered the periscope to avoid being spotted. The next time he raised the periscope, the fisherman was still visible but, this time, he was in the water. His boat, Jackie is convinced, must have been overturned by the action of raising *Tally-Ho*'s search periscope the second time.

During the night of 6 November *Tally-Ho* received a radio signal to search for a B 29 aircraft dinghy in a position further south in mid-strait. Bennington calculated that it would take four hours to reach the area and gave orders for a course to enable them to arrive at daybreak. An intensive search was maintained in the area from 0530 until 1030. No sign could be seen of the dinghy. At 0830 a distant aircraft was seen flying northwards towards Penang.

* The U-boat attacked by *Tigris* was *U-58* (Oberlt Georg Schonder). Her logbook records an unsuccessful attack by a River-class submarine. *Sancte Michaël* was *mined* off Penmarch Point, on 1 September 1940 — well away from *Tigris'* position.

At 1030 Bennington decided reluctantly that the search must be abandoned and gave orders to proceed back to the vicinity of Pulau Jarak.

He was loath to abandon the area where the dinghy had been sought though the search had been hopeless from the start. None the less, a very few aircraft were successfully rescued in this area; their crew stood a scant chance of survival if they were picked up by the Japanese. This patrol was becoming as dull as the previous one. Bennington, experiencing the excruciating boredom of inactivity, turned in for some rest.

The following day, 7 November 1944, was divided between the Pulau Jarak and Aroa Island areas. At first light one aircraft was seen approaching from the north-west, and almost an hour later another appeared, apparently searching. *Tally-Ho* quickly dived to a depth of eighty feet and thereby avoided discovery. At moments like these, Jackie Warner felt, inactivity was harder to take than action. A long day's submergence, broken only by the midday cigarette, passed with agonising slowness. The danger of detection might be ever present but that did nothing to relieve the tedium of the long weary day.

The routine for officers was a rugged one. Two hours on watch followed by four hours rest. The rest period was taken up with eating, sleeping and resting before going back on watch again, and, in the case of Thurlow, of keeping the log book up to date, doing the navigation and generally attending to confidential books and ships' papers. For Scott-Maxwell there was ciphering as well as his particular responsibilities as Engineer Officer. Bennington personally kept the patrol report up to date — in his own handwriting. No one else ever saw it whilst on patrol.

Thurlow, however, kept a careful 'track record' and this from time to time was passed to the captain. The track record was a careful tracing which could be laid over the chart to show the submarine's precise position at any time. A very few of the positions would be 'dead reckoning' ones, arrived at by pure calculations and readings from the log they streamed. But usually there would be a night stars 'shot' or morning sun 'shot' to act as a check. In addition to these methods one could produce a position by taking periscope sights on objects on shore. Then the submarine's position would appear as the 'intercept' of three bearings. With luck, they should all meet at one point. Sometimes the three bearing lines would form a triangle or 'cocked hat' as they called it. In this case the submarine's position would be taken as the centre of the cocked hat if all things were equal, its apex point nearest to any known hazard if all things were not equal. It was not a bad ritual but one was not sorry when it was broken.

The dry, uninteresting tinned food of the wardroom lunch did little to vary the tedium. The evening meal was more fun. Jackie swore that one of the ship's officers once ate a cockroach with his fried liver. Red-tinted glasses were worn before going up to the bridge on surfacing. They helped to accustom the eyes to the darkness, but they made eating rather a hazard. At diving stations, all the lights in the control room were red and subdued. One had to know one's way around or one walked into valve handles — all conveniently mounted at eye level or forehead height. It could be painful, as the passengers found out from time to time.

Very early on Tuesday, 7 November an Asdic contact of a reciprocating engine was reported. *Tally-Ho* moved to investigate. George Backman was convinced it was a diesel engine and he was not given to mistakes. The alarm was sounded and the crew went to diving stations, but gradually the Asdic echo faded. When first tracked it had been moving slowly, which suggested a submerged U-boat. As it faded Bennington gave orders to move away from Pulau Jarak towards the Aroa Islands. If, as he hoped, it was a submerged U-boat they might pick it up there.

Shortly after lunch *Tally-Ho* picked up supersonic underwater transmission from *Terrapin* and *Trenchant*, which had lately entered her patrol area. Neither had anything of interest to report. After a brief exchange of courtesies *Tally-Ho* eased away from the other two. It was commonsense not to congregate in enemy waters and *Tally-Ho* had a special operation coming up only forty-eight hours hence. There was nothing for it but to close the, by now, far too familiar Pulau Jarak area and maintain the unpopular periscope watch for the traffic that did not appear.

The next two days were spent on passage towards Pulau Perak and on towards a rendezvous off Pulau Langkawi for the last ever *Tally-Ho* 'dagger' operation. Perhaps, because it was the last one, it went more smoothly than any previous one. The rendezvous position ten miles to the west of Pulau Langkawi was closed without incident and the party of Remarkable IV agents passed over to the junk to be subsequently landed. The normal prohibition on all attacks applied after the completion of the special operation, and it did not expire until 10 November 1944. During this time *Tally-Ho* had moved northwards towards the Butang Group of Islands. Her first operational patrol was mounted on a line joining Pulau Perak and Penang Island.

Two nights were bedevilled by drifting junks. The following day, just after the daily submergence, an urgent summons was received to proceed to a position in the ten-fathom line between Penang and the Dindings. A lower-deck rumour promptly became current that this was to meet with an important target. By surfacing time the following evening the instructions had been cancelled. The only excitement that occurred on the day of the cancellation was that a supersonic transmission (underwater signal) was picked up from HM Submarine *Thule*. She had arrived in Colombo from Britain the previous month and was on her first patrol. She was not close: the range of the signal was all of 23,000 yards.

Even so, the following evening, after an abortive session hunting junk traffic fifty miles north-west of Penang, *Tally-Ho* passed a radio message to Colombo requesting that *Thule* keep clear of the *Tally-Ho* patrol area during the hours of darkness. Ceylon approved this: there was a considerable risk if friendly submarines came too close to one another at night, especially when on the surface battery charging. Submarines had been lost whilst trying to exchange challenges with supposedly friendly boats. As *Tally-Ho* had recently been ordered to a new patrol position the risk had increased.

The next day, Thursday, 16 November, at 0305, well before first light, the voice of Peter Rouse who was officer of the watch brought Bennington running to the bridge: something was stirring astern of *Tally-Ho*. By the time Bennington reached the bridge, the wake of another vessel could clearly be seen crossing that of *Tally-Ho*. Something, or rather, someone, was clearly in pursuit.

'Press the diving hooter: take her down to eighty feet,' ordered

Bennington. His action roused the whole crew and brought them to diving stations as he had intended.

When *Tally-Ho* reached that depth he ordered a supersonic challenge. He was far from pleased: he was ,not accustomed to being pursued. If any pursuing were to be done, Bennington would do it. Equally he was far from accustomed to another submarine creeping up on him without being spotted, even in tricky lighting conditions as at present. He hoped the other vessel was *Thule*, but if it should prove hostile he was perfectly prepared to conduct an attack on an Asdic bearing. Fortunately the message received proved friendly: it *was* from *Thule*.

At least one of the exchanges was derisory in the extreme. Over the hydrophones came the following unofficial communication from P.O. Sid Seymour, Torpedo Gunners' Mate in *Thule*:

'Tell Joe Brighton: up his fat arse!'

Thule was commanded by Lieutenant-Commander Alistair Campbell Gillespie Mars DSO, DSC, RN. Bennington had known Alistair Mars from service before the war and wartime service in the Mediterranean. It was not surprising that a certain rivalry should exist between *Tally-Ho* and *Thule*. The TGM's message to Joe bore witness to that. The crew of *Thule* were only too keen to rub in the fact that they had achieved a recent sinking.

Once identities had been established, Bennington did not stay for an exchange of courtesies but pushed off with all despatch. Neither boat would benefit from staying in the other's company and if they stayed parleying there was a risk that look-outs might relax their vigilance and they both became vulnerable.

The following morning *Tally-Ho* was patrolling the ten-fathom line some forty miles south-west of Port Swettenham, still proceeding south down the strait at periscope depth. At 0928 a small object was sighted on the port quarter. Bennington was called to the bridge and identified the object as a U-boat conning-tower and instantly ordered an alteration of course towards it.

The enemy was also travelling down the strait and appeared to be about 10,000 to 11,000 yards distant. Lighting conditions were a shade tricky. After seven minutes full ahead grouped up, on a near parallel course to the U-boat, Bennington ordered an alteration of heading to 040°. Ten minutes after the first sighting *Tally-Ho*, still at full speed, was on almost a 90° track angle to the path followed by the U-boat and had reduced the range to 7,000 yards. Allowing for an enemy speed of 12 knots – the surfaced U-boat was proceeding quite fast – Bennington fired four torpedoes, aiming each one separately. They were spread over two ships' lengths, which Bennington estimated as 360 feet. As he had time and it was an important target, Bennington let fly a fifth torpedo 1½ lengths astern of the conning-tower. If the U-boat sighted the tracks and went sharply astern, there seemed a very good chance that the single torpedo would settle her fate, assuming the salvo did not. The fifth shot could also catch the target if it turned sharply towards *Tally-Ho* in an attempt to comb the tracks.

If the method of selecting torpedoes for this feat should appear casual it is worth noting that this represented the maximum number of torpedoes to be fired for such a spread and the minimum firing interval. Such things came so naturally to *Tally-Ho*'s captain that an unpractised observer could easily fail to notice the pains he took even when acting swiftly. The moment of firing was followed by the usual nerve-racking wait for the sound of a torpedo hitting. On this occasion, inexplicably, it did not come.

Five minutes after the first firing Bennington took a quick periscope look at the target. He reported to an astounded control room that the enemy had succeeded in combing the tracks of the torpedoes and had somehow passed through the screen unharmed. She was now directly ahead of *Tally-Ho* on a fine angle; *Tally-Ho* was still steering her firing course. Bennington paused only a moment, to ensure that the enemy had steadied on her course, before ordering a sixth torpedo to be fired. He lowered the periscope after firing but snapped it up three minutes later. Still there was no sound of an explosion.

To his surprise the U-boat turned sharply to starboard and increased speed disappearing on approximately the original course. Not one to be put off easily, Bennington turned seaward in pursuit. Mindful of the Japanese custom of calling up air support he made a rapid sky search then lowered the periscope and ordered, 'Steady on 310°. Increase depth to fifty feet. Aircraft in sight, searching.'

The rating keeping the attack log noted the time, 1017. The whole attack had lasted barely twenty minutes since the first sighting. Bennington had ordered depth to be increased as his impression was that the enemy aircraft appeared to have a fairly good idea of *Tally-Ho*'s position. Twelve minutes later *Tally-Ho* was shaken by an explosion, almost certainly that of a bomb. The detonation was not close enough to inflict damage to anything but the nerves. After forty minutes of quiet waiting Bennington ordered *Tally-Ho* to be brought to periscope depth. He took an all-round look and reported, 'Two enemy aircraft in sight, apparently still searching. Down periscope. Increase depth to sixty feet.'

After something like the previous time interval another explosion was heard a shade nearer. *Tally-Ho* stayed down for a further forty minutes before coming again to periscope depth. Bennington's observations this time were a running commentary. 'No aircraft in sight. No. Wait a moment: enemy aircraft turning towards us at close range. Increase depth. Flood Q.'

It was now 1230; the U-boat had effectively occupied the whole of the forenoon. The enemy were perhaps, not particularly accurate but they were persistent, as Bennington recorded in his patrol report:

> From this time until 1600, a large number of depth-charges were heard. The patterns were mainly of four, five and six charges. They were all miles away from HMS *Tally-Ho.*

By 1700 *Tally-Ho* had discreetly moved northwards. This took them back towards the *Thule* patrol area; in the circumstances it was unavoidable. As a precaution, Asdic communication was established with *Thule.* At 1732 *Tally-Ho* surfaced for a blessed breath of fresh air. On the bridge, Bennington reviewed the day. A hell of a lot of torpedoes has been expended without tangible results. Moreover, he wasn't used to wasting time submerged to avoid air attacks. Even so, action had been a great deal preferable to inactivity.

Broad on the beam he watched *Thule* surface half a mile away. He altered course due north, in the direction of Pulau Langkawi. It was politic to put as much distance as possible between the two boats during the hours of darkness. Bennington was still puzzled by the behaviour of *Tally-Ho*'s torpedoes in the forenoon. That the U-boat had succeeded in combing the tracks of the salvo could be explained by luck and an experienced commander but he felt there had been nothing amiss with his aim on the last two that had been fired. He was not accustomed to blaming misses on the equipment available, nor was he accustomed to being let down by *Tally-Ho*.

True, during the work-up period in the early months of 1943, there had been one day when she had seemed wilful and nothing had gone right. On 23 April 1943, on the torpedo firing range at Loch Long, the practice torpedo fired from No. 4 tube had run amok and finished its run in dense scrub 180 yards above the high water mark. As well as that the torpedo from No. 5 tube had broken surface on its discharge. But these had been isolated incidents to be expected on working up and cured like any other teething troubles. It had not been a good week; two days later, in bad weather, at the head of Loch Long *Tally-Ho* had run aground. After this display *Tally-Ho* had appeared to repent of her wickedness and had graciously allowed herself to float off without assistance.

During the work-up period, experiments concerned with establishing facts about the transmission of sound underwater had led to efforts to suppress noise generally inside *Tally-Ho*. This was now proving especially beneficial since the Japanese depended more on sound detection than on Asdic. It had been discovered that sound travelled nearly four times as fast below water as it did in still air — at 4,000 feet per second, to be precise.

Today should be Bennington's last but one in the patrol area and he was determined to sink something before heading homewards. He was by now convinced that the remainder of the present patrol could produce no worthwhile targets. The ten-fathom line swept out from the mainland to enclose Langkawi Island. It was therefore a good place to intercept junk traffic moving south. Just before first light he proposed surfacing there.

If only junks were available; he would sink those.

That day, soon after first light, the business began. In twelve hours *Tally-Ho* sank seven junks, a total of eighty tons. All were heavily laden and on their way south towards Penang. It was an activity that did not appeal to Bennington, but it had to be done. Whenever possible it was conducted with humanity. In the late afternoon five junks in formation were encountered. Bennington ruled that one junk should be left to embark the crews of the others. Their supply lines were by now so extended that the Japanese were desperate for food supplies, and rice had become a munition of war. Bales and sacks of it were carried as deck cargo on most of the vessels sunk.

They were not worth torpedoing. *Thule* developed a technique for ramming them and sank them without expenditure of ammunition. The normal drill was to surface amidst a cluster of them, let fly with the 4-in. gun at point blank range, and submerge minutes later when they were all on fire or sinking and before aircraft or surface vessels could appear. Engaging unarmed and vulnerable targets was not the British seaman's idea of the way to wage war. What made it worse was that the junks were impressed by the Japs and no doubt many of the crews were British subjects.

Every 'junking' called for a highly specialised, rapid surfacing associated with any gun action. Bennington would watch through the periscope till the last possible moment when gun tower and conning-tower hatches were thrown open. He would always notify the target details over the public address system: 'Junk with three masts [or it might be two], range 2,000 [yards], deflection two, right. Aim at the waterline.'

The deflection, here, representing a 2° aim-off to allow for own speed and target speed. The moment *Tally-Ho* was on the surface Jackie Warner would take over firing control and shout orders from the bridge. A voice-pipe was provided for this purpose but was never used in action.

During these operations to shoot up junks, the Oerlikon gun proved its worth. This weapon was of Swedish design and British manufacture. A 20-mm.-calibre automatic cannon, it had an extremely high rate of fire — 450 rounds per minute — as well as a muzzle velocity of 2,725 feet per second. It was, therefore, theoretically possible to fire a whole drum, or 'pan', of ammunition (containing sixty rounds) in eight seconds. The weapon could take ball, tracer, high explosive and high explosive (incendiary) ammunition. Although it had jammed on the occasion of both the ramming and the Aru Bay action, it was at its most effective when engaging junks.

Often the junk targets were so close to *Tally-Ho* that the 4-in. gun had to be depressed rather than elevated to be brought to bear. The vessels were frequently difficult to sink and required the expenditure of much ammunition.

In 1298 Marco Polo had written of junks:

> Some vessels of the larger sort have their hulls fitted with thirteen partitions which are made of thick planks joined together. The purpose of these is to protect the vessel if she springs a leak by running against a rock, for example, or on being struck by a hungry whale – an occurrence which is by no means infrequent.[1]

In 1944 the hazards had changed – *Tally-Ho* saw no hungry whales – but the construction of junks had not, so that they were still often difficult to sink and might keep afloat although holed and on fire. If the junks were well alight, the flames, hard to see in the strong sunlight, would run up the rigging, and the patched sails with their numerous battens would shrivel like fading leaves. *Tally-Ho*'s crew found it heart-breaking that the picturesque sailing vessels – many of them homes for entire Chinese families – should have to be ruthlessly eradicated as military targets. However, war does not afford its participants a choice in such matters. After a final 'junking' session at 1810, *Tally-Ho* moved southwards for her nightly battery charging. The following day was intended to be her last in the patrol area.

At first light, determined to leave no possible target unattended, Bennington moved close inshore to watch coastal traffic between Penang and the Dindings. Nothing was seen until after lunch when a single junk of forty-five tons was sunk and two larger junks

[1] *The Ship* by Björn Landström published by Allen & Unwin 1961

chased. The incident ended with *Tally-Ho* sinking a tonkang of approximately 100 tons. The crew of seven Chinese were embarked to be taken back to Ceylon for questioning by intelligence and, later, put back on a junk in the area where they had been picked up. Had it not been the last day of the patrol it would not have been judged prudent to pick them up. In the present circumstances, *Tally-Ho's* crew were glad of the opportunity to make the humane gesture.

During the night *Tally-Ho* received a radio request from Ceylon that she remain in the area for at least part of an extra day to rendezvous with *Thule* and take off eleven passengers. The eleven to include ten commandos she had been carrying for a frustrated special operation and one seaman who was sick. Bennington was not too pleased at the prospect of overcrowding his boat. However, there was no question of refusing requests from Captain (S) in Ceylon. Determined to complete the transfer of personnel as early as possible in the day, *Tally-Ho* was in the rendezvous position by 0700. The two submarines had to meet in midstrait, out of sight of land. At 1400 *Thule* was sighted on the surface and *Tally-Ho* closed at full speed.

Unknown to Bennington, recent developments aboard *Thule* were complicating the proposed transfer. The sick seaman had died. Like *Tally-Ho*, *Thule* carried no medical officer and was dependent on her captain's medical knowledge. Alistair Mars had been extremely concerned by the seaman's symptoms. They could well have been due to severe heat exhaustion, but they could equally have been symptoms of . . . cholera. To make matters worse some seven members of his ship's company were, by now, exhibiting the same symptoms.

If Mars were to make the transfer, the infection could spread to *Tally-Ho*. If he confided in Bennington, panic could spread to both boats. Mars believed he had no alternative but to refuse to make the transfer while withholding a full explanation of what would seem extraordinary behaviour.

Bennington, suspecting nothing amiss, brought *Tally-Ho* smartly alongside *Thule* within hailing distance, and unwittingly did nothing to make Lieutenant-Commander Mars's task easier.

'Send them over, then,' he shouted.

'Sorry I can't,' Mars called back.

'Why the hell not?' demanded Bennington.

'We have a lot of sickness, it may be something infectious.'

Bennington shouted one further question about the reason for his being kept waiting in enemy waters and then said his goodbyes. He ordered full speed ahead and left, as Alistair Mars later described it, 'in high dudgeon'.

The remainder of 19 November was spent without excitement, moving northwards to begin the long passage back to Ceylon. 'The Road to Mandalay' was played one final time in a gloomy wardroom when the officers took tea. Even Jackie set little store by the gesture.

At first light the following morning the officer of the watch reported masts over the horizon. Instantly everyone's attitude changed as the possibility of a sinking became a reality.

Bennington closed up the attack team and endeavoured to get closer to the possible targets. Almost at once they receded, due it would seem to a mirage distortion. The upper lens of the periscope being close to the surface of the water, the field of vision becomes distended and, under hazy conditions, increases its range. As the distorted line of vision follows the curve of the earth, one can quite literally see over the line of the horizon.

In view of the masts' apparent closeness, Bennington decided to take no chances, so surfaced and made a quick search of the area. An hour or so later the haze began to clear and *Tally-Ho* submerged and proceeded north-west in the direction in which the distant masts had appeared. Just after 1100 a call from the officer of the watch brought Bennington hurrying to the control room. 'Enemy in sight!'

Bennington ordered the attack team to be closed up and took over the periscope. He began a commentary on what he could see which was duly noted in the Attack Log.

'Two vessels in sight: coaster with an escort vessel about a cable length astern of her: almost in her wake. Wait a moment! There's a third vessel – an MTB – it's just appeared from behind the coaster: must have been dead level with it.'

He quickly passed on the bearings of the convoy and Thurlow plotted them against the relative heading of *Tally-Ho* as Bennington altered course to close for a 90° track angle attack. A rapid chase ensued between 1120 and 1150. By this time the plot indicated a target speed of six knots. By now Bennington was close enough to see the three vessels in detail.

'I'm switching target to the escort vessel,' he explained. 'The coaster's only about 250 tons — hardly worth a torpedo. I like the escort vessel, though. Rather like a British *Halcyon*-class sloop. Three 4-in. guns, one on the forecastle, and two aft: one on the boat deck, and a third on the quarter-deck. Awnings spread over the boat deck and quarter-deck: a bit hard to see what's what.'

The attack team in the control room reckoned he could see pretty well.

'She's quite modern; with an open bridge, radar array and a big range finder. The bridge seems to be crowded with personnel,' Bennington added in a dispassionate voice.

In the fore-ends, waiting to pass the firing order, Jackie was feeling more excited than his captain sounded. Probably the party on the escort vessel bridge were visiting staff officers. He smiled optimistically at the thought.

His reflections were interrupted by Bennington's final alteration of course before firing. 'Steer 240°.' Minutes later, 'Standby torpedo tubes 1, 2 and 3. Put me on my director angle.'

Bennington aimed all three individually and Joe Brighton whipped down the tiny firing levers, little realising that these were the last three torpedoes *Tally-Ho* would ever fire in anger.

Minutes after the last projectile had left the tube, Wally Crole reported picking up an Asdic transmission with a range of 1,100 yards. Just after this report came the sound of a very loud explosion. The detonation reverberated for a longer time than the noise of a torpedo striking a steel hull. Bennington judged that they had almost certainly touched off depth-charges or magazine.

At this stage the hydrophones picked up the noise of both coaster and MTB turning towards *Tally-Ho*. Probably the coaster was picking up survivors. *Tally-Ho* went deeper and altered course more than once. The MTB continued her pursuit for almost an hour. *Tally-Ho* had no difficulty in losing her.

At 1309 Bennington had *Tally-Ho* brought to periscope depth and took a quick look through the periscope. The MTB was still

N

searching astern; the coaster was hull down and searching further afield. There was no sign of the escort vessel.

As Bennington watched, coaster and MTB became lost against the wooded background of Great Nicobar. Twisted mangrove roots grew down to below the water line and were confusing when it came to trying to aim at a vessel on the ten-fathom line.

Bennington ordered course away from the coaster and MTB. The patrol was really over now and there was no point in staying longer. His first two torpedoes had been aimed over two-thirds of a ship's length. By comparing the times noted for firing in the Attack Log he was able to deduce that his target had been 250 feet long. This fact, coupled with the observations he already had, enabled him to estimate the escort's size as approximately 1,000 tons. Altogether it wasn't too bad a target on which to bow out. *Tally-Ho* passed through the Sombrero Channel later that day. The 800-mile passage back to Trincomalee was completed without incident.

It may not have occurred to Bennington that had the rendezvous with *Thule* not delayed him an extra day in the patrol area, he would most likely not have achieved his final sinking.

In his patrol on what was, in fact, *Tally-Ho*'s last Far East war patrol, he noted:

There were no defects during the patrol.

HMS *Tally-Ho* has now completed 46,000 miles on main engines at an average speed of 12 knots. Only two defects have ever made it necessary to stop main engines for more than a few minutes. The first, broken silicon explosion rings, resulted primarily from a weakness in design. The second, defective bottom end bearings, was caused by indifferent workmanship and a design defect on the part of the manufacturers.

It is submitted that this is a record that reflects great credit upon the Engineer Officer, Lieutenant P.D. Scott-Maxwell DSC, Royal Navy, and indicates unending devotion to duty on the part of the entire Engine Room staff.

Scott-Maxwell, who agreed with the final words, would have included Vickers Armstrong as well.

CHAPTER TEN

HMS Tally-Ho Comes Home

At 1140 on Thursday, 23 November 1944 *Tally-Ho* entered Trincomalee Harbour. At 1121 'Harbour stations' was piped and the white-uniformed casing party lined up for'ard: Bennington would accept nothing less than the smartest possible turnout as *Tally-Ho* returned from her final war patrol. Probably no one on board felt prouder than the Yeoman of Signals. Stanley Facer had striven hard to sew enough six-pointed stars to the Jolly Roger to represent all the junk actions, to say nothing of a bar for sinking the warship on 20 December 1944. Bennington felt happy observing his crew's pleasure; they were a good crew who had served him well. No doubt they were glad to be returning to Britain — as he was himself.

Having made as thorough a search as he felt was possible of the zone allocated to the 4th Submarine Flotilla of the Eastern Fleet, he was convinced there were no longer worth-while targets to be found. In any case a refit would not come amiss now.

Jackie Warner felt pleasure at the thought of returning home: he had a fiancée back in his native Harwich. For the present he felt he'd had enough of operations where the sea temperature was around 85° F and consequently the temperature inside the boat at least 90° F. He would have no objection to operating elsewhere, in more temperate climes for preference. In any case he was always glad to be back in port and Ceylon still held the delights of Indian gin, curries and exotic fish dishes, as well as swimming from the snowy white beaches. The news that *Tally-Ho* had completed one patrol surplus to requirements for a return to the UK had by now filtered through to him. He was amused and pleased at the thought: it was nice to finish the Far Eastern cruise in style: *Tally-Ho* had never done things by halves.

For the rest of November the boat remained in Ceylon, where

the officers renewed old acquaintances, and the crew enjoyed the glory of *Tally-Ho*'s senior status. Joe Brighton had responsibilities to discharge in port. He was well aware that when *Tally-Ho* sailed, and wherever she sailed, she would do so with loaded torpedo tubes. Come what may, it was his responsibility to ensure that they always functioned with maximum efficiency. The torpedo team's task on reaching port, as always, had been to unload all torpedo tubes and carry out the necessary routine on them. The torpedo team had not changed much; in the fore-ends were Leading Seaman Ianto Griffiths, Able Seaman Herbert Peters (his leg was now as good as ever); the upper deck party was Leading Seaman Cecil 'Jerry' Jerrard and Able Seaman Crooks.

On 1 December 1944 came the welcome order to embark personal gear. The following day HMS *Porpoise* arrived from Freemantle. Those of the crew who had served in her were delighted to see 'the old girl' again. Not least Bennington — it was always a moving moment for any captain to be reunited with a former command. *Porpoise* was old and on the big side for service in these waters, a bit slow to submerge too with her bulky silhouette and high minelaying casing. Still *Proteus* had had all these defects and been older and she hadn't done badly in the Mediterranean. Bennington and all the *Tally-Ho* crew wished her well and 'good hunting'.

On 2 December *Tally-Ho* was ordered to sail. She left Trincomalee at 1750, about the time that she had sailed for her first patrol just one year and six weeks previously. The ship's company had gained a lot of experience in that time. Though the sun was low in the sky, it was still pretty hot. Bennington, on the bridge for leaving harbour, looked towards the depot ship as *Tally-Ho* cleared the boom. A Morse light was winking cheekily on *Adamant*'s bridge. Ginger Facer decoded the following signal:

FROM CAPTAIN IN ADAMANT TO HMS TALLY-HO
   'IT WILL NOW BE SAFE TO GO ASHORE BUT WE SHALL MISS YOU.'

Bennington chuckled briefly. 'Acknowledge,' he ordered, 'and make':

'THANKS WE'LL MISS YOU TOO.'

Tally-Ho then duly took station on *Maid Marion*, as she had done often before, and proceeded to the end of the swept channel.

Tally-Ho's last days in Trincomalee had been marred by a practical joke which misfired. An unknown had laced the wardroom ashtrays with black granules of explosive taken from one of the types of pyrotechnic in use out there. No malice had been intended. Unfortunately for Thurlow, it was he who discovered it by stubbing out a cigarette. Jackie Warner had been present when there occurred what he described as 'a ginormous flash'. Thurlow's hand was badly burned. The depot ship sick bay dressed his wound but Snoopy's ability to take navigational sights, on the early part of the return passage, was seriously curtailed.

At 1010 *Maid Marion* flashed a final message of good wishes and took her leave. The smart little motor launch was soon lost in the fading light, as were the heavily wooded slopes of the hills of Ceylon with their thickly bunched foliage, as *Tally-Ho* set course west-north-west across the Indian Ocean. It took her ten days to reach Aden, her next port of call. The trip was made on the surface and the vessel was well stocked with provisions. It was probably the nearest they would ever get to a luxury cruise. Of course the usual look-out routines were rigorously maintained. Bennington spent much time on the bridge and wore the sun hat earlier commented upon by Ridley. The cook made fresh bread — the loaves were square on section and always saved up on patrol as long as possible, carefully wrapped and the mildewed and cockroach-eaten parts trimmed off. Before a loaf was finally discarded the slices were often as small as 2-in. by 2-in.

The usual security precautions about ditching gash (refuse disposal) were followed but with less conviction than when on patrol. Jettisoned rubbish could easily pinpoint a submarine's presence to aircraft. The risk here, however, was slight. Torpedo routines were practised, just as they would have been anywhere. For Joe there was more time to think. It was a strange life, he reflected; he often wondered it suited them all so well. He had frequently spent the whole four weeks of a patrol without seeing the light of day: his duties never took him up on the conning-tower. So there was no reason why he should go topsides. It was difficult to remain healthy: none of the lower deck or Petty Officers seemed to want to eat much at all, except in the evenings after the rum ration. Some people became constipated – in fact bets on the length of time one could abstain from bowel motions were not unknown. Records of up to a fortnight had been claimed but cheating was not unknown, with clandestine visits to the 'heads'. It was a wonder they all survived; still one didn't often think seriously about that, let alone worry about it.

On arrival at Aden *Tally-Ho* secured to *Ausonia*; and a quarter of an hour later HM Submarine *Vox* secured alongside *Tally-Ho*.

Aden, to Jackie Warner, seemed, even at eight o'clock in the morning, to exude a sense of menace (it had been here *Tally-Ho* had picked up the cockroaches on the outward passage). So her departure the following day was generally welcomed. She had embarked a family of Siamese kittens. All cats are notoriously territory-minded and Snoopy proved itself no exception. Whenever it saw the kittens it beat hell out of them. Fortunately *Tally-Ho* was just large enough for peaceful co-existence – most of the time. In an 'H' boat they would probably have been murdered within a week.

The passage through the Red Sea to Port Said seemed endless. The greatest excitement was when a motor vessel was sighted on an opposing course. Because of a mirage condition it could be seen clearly at an extreme distance, yet the process of closing it took four hours. When *Tally-Ho* was within signalling distance, rather surprisingly the vessel made a challenge. Bennington was on the bridge with the watch-keeping party, drinking cocoa.

'She's made a challenge: shall I reply?' enquired Lieutenant Hamlyn.

'Ah no,' replied Bennington. 'Make . . . Don't be wet. Happy Christmas.'

From Port Suez *Tally-Ho* went on to reach Port Said just in time for Christmas. She was one of 3,320 vessels – over half of them British – to travel the 101 miles of the Suez Canal that year. The Petty Officers took Christmas dinner with the officers on 26 December. In Port Said a plan was put into force by the junior officers which resulted in their First Lieutenant being duty officer almost every day. The officers would sit in a group in the depot ship wardroom for a quick one, making sure Hamlyn was neatly penned-in in a corner. Then, on a pre-arranged signal, they would leap to their feet and rush off exclaiming, 'Last one back on board *Tally-Ho* is duty officer.'

The good-natured Hamlyn never seemed to mind; there was little on shore to interest him — least of all in Port Said. He was keen to get back to England where his wife and son were. Besides, he had witnessed the effects of a 'run ashore' in Port Said. He came upon Thurlow and Warner holding another officer, still fully dressed, upside down under a shower in an effort to sober him up. What made the scene memorable was that hundreds of one pound Treasury notes began to float out of the drenched officer's pockets. It turned out he had been carrying £600 back pay for his ship.

The incident had a happy ending: the notes were all collected, dried on radiators and paid out to unsuspecting seamen. Not for the first time did Hamlyn appreciate that he was missing nothing by remaining a non-drinker.

Tally-Ho sailed from Port Said on 27 December 1944, for Malta. She did not stop in Alexandria where Ludmilla Thurlow was thought still to be. Unknown to Thurlow, by this time she was embarked for England in a troop-ship. There was no question of her being able to tell him: secrecy demanded that even those travelling in a troop-ship be kept in ignorance of its name. By chance Steady had embarked in the same troop-ship and, eventually, would find himself in England before his erstwhile colleagues in *Tally-Ho*.

The submarine proceeded warily across the Mediterranean. Bennington had been sailing these waters since 1935, the year of the Abyssinian crisis. Consequently he was not surprised at this time of the year to experience bad weather. The storm that *Tally-Ho* weathered, between Port Said and Malta, was of such violence that bridge personnel had to be lashed to the periscope standards for safety.

On one occasion Thurlow had just taken over as officer of the watch when Bennington went below. Thurlow was aware that if engine revolutions increased, even slightly, conditions on the bridge would become impossible. Minutes after Bennington went below he heard the engines begin to speed up. Hastily he ordered them throttled back and demanded, 'Who ordered you to increase revs?'

The answer came back, 'The captain.'

'Ben's idea of a joke,' Thurlow wryly supposed.

In Malta there were dubious pleasures available which include Ambite, the local alcoholic spirit, as well as the ready favours of the girls along the 'Gut'. The latter had comparatively little attraction for a ship's company nearing home. Malta was at this time a particularly good place to shop — marvellous silk fabrics were available in the island's markets. Jackie Warner bought several lengths, mindful of dresses for bridesmaids on his return. Rashly he gave most away, having made friends with some local Wrens.

Jackie's adventures in Malta did not stop there. He also, equally rashly, entered the local 'Wrennery' on the pretext of seeing some of the young ladies home after one of the inevitable parties the *Tally-Ho* officers had stumbled upon. Suddenly one of the girls shrieked that the 'Queen Wren' was about to appear on her rounds. Jackie, who was at that time seated on a bed (unoccupied) in a Wren dormitory, realised with horror that the place would obviously be out of bounds to the likes of him. He left by the window — a first floor one — and landed in the arms of a three-badge seaman on sentry duty. He congratulated himself on having escaped unscathed.

Or so it seemed until mid-morning the following day. He was enjoying a cup of coffee with Bennington in the CB [Confidential Books] office, when a Wren CB officer came in and began brightly, 'Do you know? Some frightful man was caught in the WRNS sleeping quarters last night. . . .'

Poor Jackie groaned inwardly: there was no alternative for him now. He 'tendered his reasons in writing': it was not easy to do but he did so, emphasising just how sorry he was and that it would not occur again. His friends were not sympathetic. A fairly typical remark was, 'You're lucky it wasn't the arms of a three-badge *Wren* you landed in.'

The New Year was genially celebrated in Malta and *Tally-Ho* sailed for Gibraltar on 2 January 1945. She left harbour in the early morning, the sun gilding the horizon, the harbour ramparts lined with Wrens and sailors. She was given a raucous send-off, culminating with the words, 'Three cheers for *Tally-Ho*. You lucky bastards! Hip, Hip . . .'.

Lucky they were because it was already known that they were bound for the UK, but it was the first time any of the crew had been called bastards since the Aru Bay action when Lieutenant Adams had been killed.

The passage to Gibraltar proved less eventful than had been *Tally-Ho*'s experience in these waters on her outward passage to the Far East. On 22 August 1943, the day she had left Gibraltar, she had chased two merchant ships off the Iles d'Hyères in the Golfe du Lion, in a newly formed sink-on-sight area. At the end of the chase *Tally-Ho* had fired a total of five torpedoes but no results were observed. Quite possibly that was just as well; earlier that year, on 6 March, Lieutenant-Commander M.R.G. Wingfield DSO, RN, in *Taurus* had sunk the Spanish *Bartolo* off Cap Couronne, in perfectly justifiable circumstances, and had later suffered severely at the hand of the neutral world's Press.

Tally-Ho reached Gibraltar on 7 January 1945. Joe Brighton had had time to reflect on his last visit when *Tally-Ho* was outward bound. He had chipped a tooth and needed a dentist but had had to make do with an obliging rating with a cross-cut file. During that outward stay in Gibraltar, Stoker Petty Officer Ivor ('Bugs') Norman had reported sick: he had later been discovered to be very ill indeed and been flown back to England.

On Wednesday, 10 January *Tally-Ho* left Gibraltar and took station on the Commodore of Convoy MKS 76. The Biscay area held plenty of memories for Bennington. On the outward passage no less than three enemy U-boats had been sighted here. *Tally-Ho* had approached close enough to one to observe the movement of her hull, rocking with the swell, before she vanished into the mist without a single torpedo being fired. It had been a day of bitter frustration, and Bennington had closed his patrol report entry for the day when two U-boats were sighted with the following words:

The misfortunes of the day were thoroughly depressing. Even

the news of the decline and fall of Il Duce occasioned but little hilarity. He might easily have been shot.

On 18 January Land's End was sighted; it was just nineteen months since their last sighting of Cornwall: Trevose Head on 20 July 1943. Later that day, they anchored in Devonport Harbour. The same day the officers dined with Vice Admiral Sir William F. Wake-Walker KCB, CBE, a Lord Commissioner of the Admiralty. The table was arranged so that Jackie Warner was seated next to the great man.

Jackie was considerably alarmed at this prospect, preferring that such an honour should have gone to Bennington. He dreaded the great man's questions, knowing from experience that it was not always wise to utter the first thing that came into his mind. In fact, the Admiral proved far from difficult and Jackie discovered they had more in common than he had suspected. He learned that the Admiral lived not far from where Jackie had been born and Jackie had spent a fair part of his youth poaching his birds and rabbits before joining the Navy.

On 19 January, they secured in harbour at HMS *Dolphin*. HMS *Dolphin*, Fort Blockhouse, at Gosport, Hants, has always been the traditional headquarters of the Submarine Branch of the Royal Navy, so that this could not be other than a return home.

It was with great sadness that the *Tally-Ho* crew later learned that on the day they had secured at HMS *Dolphin*, *Porpoise* had been lost in the Malacca Strait. She was the last and seventy-fourth British submarine to be lost in the Second World War. She had just completed a minelay off Penang — in her service she laid a total of 465 mines — where she had been bombed by Japanese aircraft. The bombs had damaged her oil tanks, one of which had leaked badly, the leak had formed an oil slick, so that the Japanese aircraft had tracked her progress and repeated their attacks until she sank. Her captain and all his crew had been lost with her.

In many of the photographs Bennington appears aloof and unsmiling. He dislikes publicity and, in any case felt no relief at that time that the fighting war was over. It was not that he would have wanted it to continue — quite the reverse — but it had for so long been his life, had taken too much and too many friends from him for relief to be immediate or automatic. He was almost thirty-three years old and still a single man, so that he had, in some respects, less to come home to than the family men in his crew. Whilst he had demonstrated his ability as a wartime submarine commander, his career in the Royal Navy was still a challenge and one that required considerable reorientation. No one could expect to make such a transition instantaneously.

Whilst *Tally-Ho* was at Blockhouse, Rear Admiral Reginald Burnard Darke CB, DSO, the officer commanding, asked for the boat's official badge so that a copy might be hung in the chapel. Bennington sent for Thurlow and asked him to take it to the commander so that a cast might be made.

'I can't,' replied Thurlow. 'You didn't like it and told me to send it to Chiang-Kai-shek.'

'Good God!' Bennington exclaimed. 'Did you?'

'Yes. It didn't seem too important at the time.'

'No, I suppose not,' Bennington conceded. The incident had its funny side but he was blowed if he could see how he could explain it to the Admiral.

He drank a thoughtful gin, went to see the Admiral, braced himself and told the full tale with complete honesty. Inevitably Admiral Darke was not pleased.

'I dislike this sort of levity entirely,' he admonished.

However, nothing could bring the badge back and he accepted the situation. It was some time after the war before a replica was hung in the chapel at HMS *Dolphin*. Bennington was naturally sorry that the incident should have ended thus. Admiral Darke, a most experienced and distinguished submarine officer, had been recalled from retirement in 1940 to take over the important command of Portsmouth. The last thing Bennington would have wished was to offend him.

On 20 January at 0915, 'Hands to divisions' was piped and the *Tally-Ho* ship's company were inspected by Rear Admiral G.E. Creasy CB, CBE, DSO, MVO, as Flag Officer of Submarines. Later the same day *Tally-Ho* left for Blyth. En route she made an unscheduled stop in Harwich. Intelligence had reported that mines had been dropped in the east coast area she was about to enter. Jackie was delighted. He made a lightning visit to his family and fiancée. He also profited by the trip ashore to dodge Customs by taking all his 'rabbits' with him. He now regretted he didn't still have all the silks he'd bought in Malta.

Tally-Ho resumed her passage to Blyth, arriving on Thursday, 25 January, and securing to Ice House jetty. Bennington was welcomed with a cordial hand-shake by Captain G.P. Claridge RN, the commander of the submarine base, whom Bennington knew well. An official photographer recorded the scene. Blyth, where there was snow on the ground, was a far cry from the Malacca Strait or the Mediterranean. There was snow on the bridge of *Tally-Ho*, too, when the officers were photographed in a group there the following day. Although the weather was cold, the recption accorded *Tally-Ho* in Blyth was unmistakably warm. *Good morning*, the Daily Mirror publication for submariners, produced a special supplement 'Yoicks *Tally-Ho*.' In it appeared pictures of a WRNS reception committee being entertained and pictures of some of the officers and crew members. When it was all over the fore-ends crew got down to the task of unloading the torpedo tubes.

On 29 January the first leave party went ashore. It did not include Lieutenant Thurlow, who now aware that his wife was on her way to Britain, was naturally anxious for news. When he received a telegram on a different subject, in his disappointment his immediate impulse was to crumple it and throw it away. On taking a second look, he read the words: 'CONGRATULATIONS ON YOUR DSC STOP BENNINGTON'.

Very soon after that his pleasure was complete when he received a telephone call from Steadman saying he was in Britain and that Ludmilla was well and would be landing soon at Bristol.

February 1945 proved a good month for the *Tally-Ho* officers and crew. On 7 February a group picture of the officers appeared in *The Tatler and Bystander*. On 20 February a citation appeared in the *London Gazette* of a final share of awards for *Tally-Ho*'s officers and crew. Wartime security was relaxed to the extent of permitting mention of the submarine's name. The citation began with the words: For outstanding courage, skill and devotion to duty in successful patrols in HM Submarine *Tally-Ho*. . .

The awards began with a second bar to Bennington's DSC,

which he regarded as an award to all his crew.

Tally-Ho went to Wallsend-on-Tyne for repairs in February 1945. Some of the crew had begun to appreciate the publicity that was now centering on their boat. They began to feel something of celebrities. There was even talk of a short Admiralty film being made featuring *Tally-Ho*. Bennington was opposed to the idea: whenever possible he avoided anything at all which might be concerned with publicity.

Soon after this the VIP treatment stopped abruptly and the *Tally-Ho* team broke up. Bennington entrusted the boat's Jolly Roger, with its record of all the sinkings, to Yeoman Ginger Facer. Then he took his leave of his officers and crew before they dispersed to take up new postings.

Bennington's own posting was an important one: he became Senior Submarine Officer on the Staff of the Deputy Comptroller of the Admiralty, with the responsibility for submarine diving trials and acceptance inspections.

Many of the crew members were posted to Loch Ryan, Galloway, Scotland, where captured German U-boats were being assembled and inspected. Here some of the officers and crew of *Tally-Ho* succeeded in meeting the crew of the two German U-boats they had unsuccessfully attacked. The U-boat attacked twice on 17 May 1944 during the fifth patrol, some 40 miles north-west of Port Swettenham, had been German and had just embarked a cargo of Malay tin to take back to Germany. When Scott-Maxwell confronted the former German senior ratings with the knowledge that their craft had been seen, under way, with all crew members mustered on the casing, they were first astonished and then rather sheepishly admitted the details of the attack. It was clear that the Germans had believed they were too far from home to be spied on effectively. Scott-Maxwell was amazed to think that he had discovered the very submarine among one of several 'trots' of captured U-boats under his charge at Loch Ryan.

The U-boat attacked on 16 November 1944 on the last patrol was also German. She had been attacked north of Penang Island and had succeeded in combing a salvo of five torpedoes. Joe found a former German Petty Officer who claimed that a German aircraft had spotted *Tally-Ho* and attempted to warn the U-boat by bombing the torpedo tracks. Although this episode sounded a shade far-fetched, there had been aircraft about and explosions were reported in the patrol report. It is even possible that the German Petty Officer was confusing the 16 November attack with that of 17 May 1944, when Bennington *had* reported an aircraft apparently flying down the torpedo tracks. The matter afforded interesting speculation.

In Northern Ireland trials were run on some of the U-boats — particularly the type XXI (high under-water speed/electric). One of them, U.1407 salvaged and refitted after being scuttled, came to Britain as HMS *Meteorite*. On board her was Scott-Maxwell who as Engineer Officer served in her from September 1945— February 1946. She was powered by a revolutionary new turbine developed by the German Dr Walter. A submarine's diesel engines had, hitherto, always required to be run on the surface since they needed oxygen to combine with diesel fuel for combustion; normal practice was to use the oxygen in the atmosphere by running on the surface with the conning-tower hatch open. Dr Walter's invention did not rely on atmospheric oxygen but used the oxygen from its fuel — hydrogen peroxide.

The development work began in Northern Ireland and culminated, in 1954, with the launching of HMS *Explorer* at Vickers Armstrong; this was the first British submarine to use hydrogen-peroxide propulsion. It had taken nearly twenty years since Dr Walter's first experiments, and by then Scott-Maxwell had left the Royal Navy and was working with Vickers Armstrong at Barrow-in-Furness. Post-war experiments and development work also led to the adoption of the Schnorkel breathing system, in its British form of 'Snort'.

After the end of the very successful Far Eastern commission, the *Tally-Ho* crew members met together in strength only once more. An Investiture was held at Buckingham Palace on Friday, 20 July 1945. Bennington having been there twice before (many of his crew had been *once* before), did not arrive early and remembers that this caused some passing annoyance to a Palace official. In all, sixteen of the officers and crew were present and, after the ceremony, they were photographed together, in the Palace forecourt.

The *Tally-Ho* crew and officers were decorated *en masse* and it was probably a record number of decorations for one ship. While they waited before the awards were made, Bennington exchanged conversation with a high-ranking army officer. When the time came to move, Bennington looked round and said, quietly, 'Right! Come on you buggers'.

It was his own way of getting things done, and it was effective. The *Tally-Ho* party moved as one man with parade ground precision.

The army officer remonstrated: 'I say, you can't talk to your men like that.' Bennington smiled slightly. He knew he could talk to them any way he chose and that they would follow him *anywhere*. After all, he had proved it. He was only sorry he would not have the chance to command them again.

> *Home is the sailor, home from sea,*
> *And the hunter home from the hill.*
> Robert Louis Stevenson.

AFTERMATH

With the coming of peace some of the officers and crew of HMS *Tally-Ho* left the Royal Navy.

HMS *Tally-Ho* appeared on the disposal list in 1961. Her last use was as a floating class-room. Post-war she had not lain idle; she went all over the world on good-will visits – even back to Trincomalee. In 1950 she became a film star, appearing in the film *Morning Departure.* She was sold to Thomas W. Ward (ship breakers) on 23 February 1967 and broken up by them in 1968. Today her bell is kept safely in the Submarine Museum at HMS *Dolphin* and her official badge hangs in the chapel at *Dolphin.*

Captain L.W.A. Bennington DSO*, DSC**, RN (Retd) served post-war on the Ruck-Keene Committee investigating the problems of escape from sunken submarines. The panel included Lieutenant-Commander W.O. Shelford OBE, RN (the author of *Subsunk*), instructors from the Royal Corps of Naval Constructors and, in Bennington's own words 'Doctors of all sorts'. They interviewed survivors from British, German, United States, Danish and Norwegian submarines.

After that Bennington went on to other commands: in 1948 he was training the Chinese Navy; in 1949 he was in the light Fleet Carrier HMS *Vengeance* when she conducted experimental trials in the Far North. He found it more congenial than had been the Arctic working-up patrol in *Tally-Ho.* In 1951 (aged 39) he was promoted Captain, and as Captain (S3) commanded the depot ship HMS *Montclare* at Rothesay. Four years later, he was the Queen's Harbour Master and Captain of the Naval Dockyard at Malta. His last posts in the Royal Navy were with the Fleet Air Arm establishments, the very last (1959-1960) being HMS *Daedalus*, where his command included responsibility for training the Fleet Air Arm Field Gun Team which races annually in the Royal Tournament. Under Bennington they did not lose.

In 1960 he retired from the Royal Navy to take up a post in the world of commerce. He is well known in connection with his work in yachting circles. No longer a bachelor, he has a son at university.

J.C. (Joe) Brighton DSM* retired from the Navy in 1948 after twenty-five years of service, eighteen years of service being spent in submarines. After that he spent seven years in HM Coastguard in Cornwall, Devon and Sussex. Today he lives in quiet retirement, not six miles from where he was born, in his native Norfolk.

Tan Sri Sir Claude Fenner KBE, CMG, PMN, DPMB continued his secret work behind Japanese lines throughout the war. When to remain a civilian (he was Assistant Superintendent of Police) was clearly courting trouble, he became a 2nd Lieutenant in the Intelligence Corps (Indian Section). Later he was promoted (acting) Major and finally Lieutenant-Colonel. He was awarded the MBE for his war work.

He remained in Kuala Lumpur in the police after the war and retired in 1966 as Inspector General of Police in Malaysia. He had previously been Head of Special Branch. Today, knighted by both Great Britain and Malaysia, he is Chief Representative for the Rubber Growers Association in Kuala Lumpur.

L.D. Hamlyn OBE, FIL, although on his own admission a reluctant recruit to the submarine world, received his OBE for post-war work on the development of submarine escape techniques. This included personally making escapes from extreme depths not previously attempted. Today, although he has retired from the Royal Navy, his work for the Royal Naval Personnel Research Committee (of which he is Assistant Secretary) is still concerned with submarine crews, in particular their health and efficiency and escape in emergencies. A fluent Italian linguist he enjoys translating technical papers in his spare time.

Kenneth Lockyer remained in the Navy until 1958 acquiring the nickname 'Tanky' (storeman). He served in so many different submarines that today, he says, they are mixed up in his mind. But he will never forget the night he was on the bridge of *Tally-Ho* when she was rammed. Today he is employed by a firm of wholesale meat suppliers.

P.D. Scott-Maxwell DSC*, a 'hostilities only' officer, was demob-

o

ilised in March 1946 and went to Vickers-Armstrong at Barrow-in-Furness. Today he is chief executive of Vickers Australia Ltd. His work is still connected with submarines and has ranged from the old 'H' and 'L' class to Polaris.

J.M. Steadman DSC died suddenly in London whilst the author was still searching for him. After returning to this country in 1945 he went back to General Service from the Submarine Branch. Later he retired in favour of civilian life. Around 1961 he was keeping a public house at Whitstable. Steady flew the white ensign over it and was careful to explain that, by a right of prescription, he was entitled so to do. He was only 52 at the time of his death and had left *Tally-Ho* just before his 25th birthday.

Snoopy (the cat) never missed a patrol and always had to be aboard forty-eight hours before sailing, locked in the captain's cabin. After the war, looked after by Captain Bennington's mother, it lived happily until the age of twelve.

Rear Admiral A.G. Tait DSC, RN is still a serving officer. In 1955 he commanded *Tally-Ho*. As Captain of the Britannia Royal Naval College at Dartmouth he received Prince Charles when he attended the college in 1971.

Captain C.T.M. Thurlow DSC returned to the Mercantile Marine after the war and achieved Captain's rank.

Lieutenant-Commander S.A. Warner MBE, DSC, RN (Retd) remained in the Royal Navy, his last appointment being at HMS *Vernon*. When he retired he had been decorated with the MBE for his peace-time work on diving techniques. Today he is continuing that work as a Civil Servant. He lives in Hampshire and believes he is the first *Tally-Ho* officer to become a grandfather.

NB. Sadly, since publication of the first edition, Captain Bennington, Sir Claude Fenner and Peter Scott-Maxwell have all died. The author, privileged to share their friendship, mourns their passing.

ENEMY WARSHIPS AND NAVAL VESSELS SUNK BY
BRITISH SUBMARINES IN THE FAR EAST DURING THE
PERIOD 1 JANUARY to 31 DECEMBER 1944.

Date	Name	Type	Position	Submarine	Tons	
11-1-44	*Kuma*	Cruiser	Off Penang	*Tally-Ho*	5,700	
12-2-44	*Choko M*	Net tender	Off Penang	*Stonehenge*		889
15-2-44 (Reginaldo Giuliani)	UIT 23	U-boat ex-Italian	Malacca Strait	*Tally-Ho*	1,140	
15-4-44	Special Mine-Sweeper No.7	—	Andaman Sea	*Storm*		630
22-4-44	*Gio Kokuan*	Salvage Vessel	Andaman Sea	*Taurus*		558
17-7-44	I 166	U-boat Jap	Malacca Strait	*Telemachus*		1,635
9-9-44	Special S/M Chaser No.8	—	Malacca Strait	*Porpoise* (mine-lay 8.7.44)		130
3-9-44	U 859	U-boat (German)	Off Penang	*Trenchant*		1,366
6-10-44	Special S/M Chaser No.2	—	Malacca Strait	*Tally-Ho*	100	
4-11-44	Special Mine-sweeper No.5	—	Malacca Strait	*Terrapin*		615
20-11-44	Special Mine-layer No.4	—	Nicobars	*Tally-Ho*	297	

(1) Total sunk by *Tally-Ho*: 7,237

(2) Total sunk by all other British submarines: 5,823

Note: during this period *Tally-Ho* sank over 20% more than the rest of other British
     submarines put together.

The total tonnage sunk by *Tally-Ho* was also an impressive proportion of that by all
British submarines (see overleaf Appendix 2).

(1) By *Tally-Ho* (a) Warships/Naval Vessels   7,237

             (b) Merchant Vessels   5,386

                              12,623

(2) By remainder of British submarines

         (a) Warships/Naval Vessels   5,823

         (b) Merchant Vessels   45,287

                              51,110

i.e. *Tally-Ho* sank nearly a quarter of the total tonnage of warships and enemy naval vessels
sunk by British submarines, or

$$\frac{12,623}{51,110} \times 100 = 24.6\%$$

JAPANESE MERCHANT SHIPS OVER 500 TONS SUNK BY BRITISH SUBMARINES IN THE FAR EAST DURING THE PERIOD 10 NOVEMBER 1943 to 10 NOVEMBER 1944.

Date	Name	Type	Position	Submarine	Tons
10-11-43	Kisogawa Maru	Water Tanker	Malacca Strait	Tally-Ho	1,914
15-1-44	Ryuko Maru	Passenger Cargo	Andaman Sea	Tally-Ho	2,962
21-2-44	Daigen Maru No.6	Cargo	Malacca Strait	Tally-Ho	510
8-3-44	Shobu Maru	Cargo	Malacca Strait	Sea Rover	1,950
28-3-44	Yasushima Maru	Cargo	Malacca Strait	Truculent	1,910
3-5-44	Amagi Maru	Passenger Cargo	Andaman Sea	Tantalus	3,165
12-5-44	Kasumi Maru	Cargo	Penang	Taurus (Mine-lay 18.4.44)	1,400
22-5-44	Kosho Maru	Cargo	Malacca Strait	Sea Rover	1,365
28-5-44	Tyokai Maru	Cargo	Malacca Strait	Templar	2,658
10-6-44	Hiyoshi Maru	Cargo	Malacca Strait	Tantalus	535
12-6-44	Kainan Maru	Cargo	Malacca Strait	Stoic	1,133
18-6-44	Eiko Maru	Cargo	Malacca Strait	Storm	3,011
26-6-44	Harukiku Maru	Passenger Cargo	Malacca Strait	Truculent	3,040
23-7-44	Kiso Maru	Cargo	Mergui Archipelago	Storm	554
22-8-44	Sugi Maru No.5	Cargo	Andaman Islands	Statesman	1,983
2-9-44	Toso Maru No.1	Cargo	W. Siam	Strongbow	800
5-9-44	Shiretoko Maru	Cargo	Sunda Strait	Tantivy	1,799
10-9-44	Taketun Maru	Tanker	Penang	Porpoise (Mine-lay 8.7.44)	3,029
18-9-44	Junyo Maru	Cargo	W. Sumatra	Tradewind	5,063
12-10-44	Manryo Maru	Cargo	Malacca Strait	Strongbow	1,185
28-10-44	Sumatra Maru	Cargo	Phuket harbour	Trenchant ('Chariots')*	4,859
2-11-44	Hachjin Maru	Cargo	S. China Sea	Tantalus	1,918
19-11-44	Nichinan Maru	Cargo	Malacca Strait	Stratagem	1,945
10-11-44	Shoei Maru	Cargo	Sunda Strait	Stoic	1,985

(1) Total sunk by *Tally-Ho*   5,386

(2) Total sunk by all other British submarines   45,287

Note: the above figures do not include junks which were usually under 500 tons.

* 'Chariots' were 2-man human torpedoes. After this particular operation the 'charioteers' were safely re-embarked aboard their parent submarine.

CREW LIST OF HMS *TALLY-HO* ON 1 JANUARY 1944.

Initials/Surname		Rank	Duty	Awards	Service No.
OFFICERS					
LWA	Bennington	Lt. Comdr. RN	Captain	DSO, DSC	
JM	Steadman	Lt. RNR	First Lieutenant	MID	
CTM	Thurlow	Lt. RNR	Navigation Officer		
PD	Scott-Maxwell	(T'y) Lt(E)RN	Engineer Officer	DSC, MID	
SA	Warner	Sub-Lt. RN	Torpedo & Gunnery Officer		
MA	Clark	Lt. RN			
SEAMAN BRANCH					
CH	Ridley	Chief PO	Coxswain		P/JX 130594
RC	Underhill	Elect'l Artificer	Electrics/Torpedo Tubes	MID	D/MX 47688
JC	Brighton	PO (TGM)	Torpedoes	DSM	C/J 109201
SR	Facer	Yeoman of Signals	Visual Signals	DSM	D/J 112356
SF	Fensome	PO (LTO)	Electrical Specialist		P/JX 130575
F	Crossley	PO (Cook)	Galley		D/MX 50805
JH	Houlston	SPO			C/KX 81428
GB	Osborne	PO (Teleg)	Chief Telegraphist		D/JX 136937
VG	Backman	L/Telegraphist	Asdic Operator	DSM	D/JX 129189
HJ	Barker	L/Seaman	Gun Layer		D/JX 217340
WG	Crole	L/Seaman	Oerlikon Gunner		C/JX 154167
A	Simpson	L/Seaman	2nd Coxswain		P/JX 136636
RE	Griffiths	L/Seaman	Torpedoman		D/SSX 26673
C	Jerrard	L/Seaman	Torpedoman		P/JX 135997
G	Charnock	L/Seaman	Torpedoman		D/SSX 19551
S	Hawkey	L/Seaman	Quarter Rating	DSM	D/JX 127066
A	Sutton	L/Seaman			P/SSX 17788
J	Flynn	L/Signaller	Visual Signals		P/ESDX 1654
LT	Parker	L/Steward	Wardroom Steward		D/LX 24163
HC	Peters	Able Seaman	Torpedoman		C/JX 335185
AM	Leckie	Able Seaman	Torpedoman		P/JX 144931
EE	Fulford	Able Seaman	Torpedoman	MID	C/LDX 4444
DA	Harvey	Able Seaman	Torpedoman		D/JX 234588
F	Ross	Able Seaman	Torpedoman		C/SSX 17283
JT	Benyon	Able Seaman	RDF Operator		P/JX 368282
DART	Whitehead	Able Seaman	RDF Operator		P/JX 392227
B	Ryan	Able Seaman	RDF Operator		D/SSX 21004
ST	Lisk	Telegraphist	Asdic Operator		D/JX 196382
JT	Palmer	Telegraphist	Asdic Operator		P/JX 321444
P	Dillon	Telegraphist	Asdic Operator		C/PK 162243
JA	Cotter	Able Seaman	Submarine Detector		D/JX 212776
CS	Love	Able Seaman	Submarine Detector		P/JX 219317
W	Hopewell	Able Seaman			C/JX 317151
ST	Melling	Able Seaman			C/SSX 21012
K	Lockyer	Able Seaman			C/SSX 32490
D	Edwards	Able Seaman			D/JX 416872
SA	Watts	Able Seaman	Torpedoman		P/JX 215108
A	Coney	Able Seaman			D/JX 417369
ENGINE ROOM BRANCH					
JM	Powell	CERA		DSM	D/MX 53617
DJ	Hughes	CERA			RNR D/X/2962
AW	Bulless	CERA			C/MX 76035

JS	Heath	CERA	P/MX 53748
A	West	CERA	D/MX 73402
RR	Charnock	CERA	D/MX 75063
JJ	Wheeler	SPO	D/KX 80147
WEP	Betts	L/Stoker	C/KX 91285
FF	Blake	L/Stoker	P/KX 100613
GW	French	L/Stoker	P/KX 119760
FJ	Hall	Stoker	C/KX 151870
JE	Neale	Stoker	P/KX 104750
GA	Rennie	Stoker	C/KX 113055
H	Judge	Stoker	P/KX 108073
WE	Illsley	Stoker	P/KX 119781
RGW	Tanner	Stoker	D/KX 144949
WD	Williams	Stoker	D/KX 139754
JH	Gale	Stoker	P/KX 112475
EJ	Wiseman	Stoker	C/KX 121559
HA	Windridge	Stoker	P/KX 135747
DA	Gay	Stoker	C/KX 111192
R	Rodgers	Stoker	P/KX 163242
H	Bullen	Stoker	C/KX 166023
V	Pearce	Stoker	D/KX 161124

Note: decorations and awards shown are those obtained by 11 January 1944: many of the ship's company received later awards.

List of abbreviations:

PO	Petty Officer
TGM	Torpedo Gunners' Mate
LTO	Leading Torpedo Operator
CERA	Chief Engine Room Artificer
MID	Mention in Despatches

LIST OF DECORATIONS WON BY
TALLY-HO CREW ON HER FAR EASTERN CRUISE.

Bar to DSO	Comdr. L.W.A. Bennington	1	(1)
2nd Bar to DSC	Comdr. L.W.A. Bennington	1	(1)
Bar to DSC	Lt-Comdr. L.W.A. Bennington	1	
	T/Lt. (E) P.D. Scott-Maxwell RN	1	(2)
DSC	Lt. S.A. Warner RN	1	
	Lt. J.M. Steadman RNR	1	
	Lt. C.T.M. Thurlow RNR	1	(3)
Bar to DSM	ERA 2nd Class J.M. Powell	1	
	CPO (TGM) J.C. Brighton	1	
	T/AB S. Hawkey	1	
	L/Teleg'phist V.G. Backman	1	(4)
DSM	A/LS H.J. Barker	1	
	ERA 4th Class J.S. Heath	1	
	C/Stoker W.S. Adams	1	
	T/A/LS A. Sutton	1	
	T/A L/Stoker J.E. Neale	1	
	A/CPO C.H. Ridley	1	
	EA 2nd Class R.H. Underhill	1	
	L/Stoker E.C. Fulford	1	
	L/Stoker G.W. French	1	
	ERA 4th Class A. West	1	(10)
		21	

Mention in Despatches

T/Lt. (E) P.D. Scott-Maxwell RN	1	
Lt. J.M. Steadman RNR	1	
ERA 3rd Class D.J. Hughes	1	
ERA 3rd Class A.S. Bracher	1	
T/A/LS C. Jerrard	1	
T/AL/Stoker J.E. Neale	1	
AB G. Bruce	1	
Stoker 1st Class H.J. Dale	1	
Stoker 1st Class W.E. Illsley	1	
ERA 4th Class A.W. Bulless	1	
CPO J.C. Brighton	1	
PO/LTO S.F. Fensome	1	
P/O Cook F. Crossley	1	
Stoker PO J.J. Wheeler	1	
T/LS H.J. Barker	1	
Stoker 1st Class D.A. Gay	1	
T/LS G. Charnock	1	
AB W.G. Crole	1	(18)
Total	18	
GRAND TOTAL	39	

Note: Ranks quoted are those at the time the citation appeared in Supplements to the *London Gazette*.
Decorations listed are those obtained whilst serving in *Tally-Ho* and exclude those won in previous service.

ATTACK ON ENEMY U-BOAT (on surface)
(U IT 23 – *REGINALDO GIULIANI*)

15 February 1944   04°N 100°E

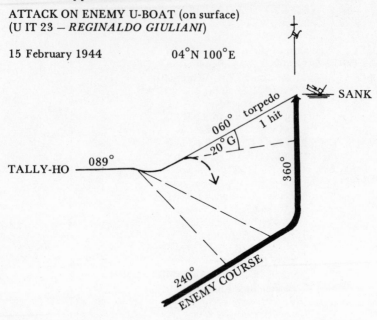

'0522 steadied on 060° and fired
three torpedoes at "the first
U-boat" on the surface.'

Enemy course	360°
Own course	060°
Enemy speed	14 knots
Track angle	120°
Director angle	20° Green
Range on firing	3 000-3 500 yards

'Almost as soon as *Tally-Ho* started to alter course to 060° both port
look-outs reported an object which they thought was another U-boat on the
port bow. The officer of the watch (Lieut. M.G. Clark) examined the object
and also came to the same conclusion that it was a U-boat. The Commanding
Officer could only spare a few glances in the direction indicated and saw
nothing, but nearly missed the firing angle in so doing.

    After firing, course was altered 90° to starboard and the submarine dived
to 80 ft at the same time.'

L.W.A. Bennington
patrol report

FIRST ATTACK ON ENEMY U-BOAT OFF KUALA SELANGOR
17 May 1944   03°27′N 100°56′E

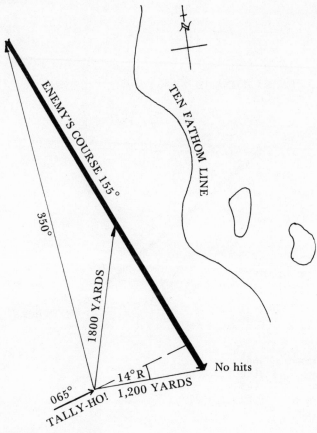

Range on firing	1 200 yards
Enemy course	155°
Own course	065°
Track angle	90°
Enemy's speed	12 knots
Director angle	14° Red

SCALE

| 1,000 | 0 | 1,000 | 2,000 | 3,000 | 4,000 |

YARDS

'1449 fired 5 torpedoes spread over 2 ships' lengths. Torpedoes were aimed individually. Missed. Immediately after firing altered course to 130° and increased depth to 45 ft.'

SECOND ATTACK ON ENEMY U-BOAT OFF KUALA SELANGOR
17 May 1944 at 1509   03°27N 100°56′E

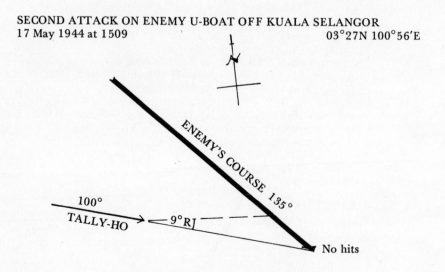

Enemy's course	135°
Own course	100°
Track angle	145°
Enemy's speed	12 knots
Director angle	9° Red

'Two Loud explosions were heard after firing (first attack) these could have been aircraft bombs or torpedoes. Returned to periscope depth. The U-boat was still steering 135° and appeared to be undamaged but her crew had mustered on the upper deck.

At 1509 fired the remaining bow torpedo. Missed.'

ATTACK ON JAPANESE U-BOAT OFF PENANG
16 November 1944   05°46½'N 100°02½E

'0928 Course 141° at 3 knots. Sighted small object (U-boat) conning tower, port quarter, altered course 100°.
Estimated enemy course 128°, range 10-11 000 yards, altered course 040° full speed.
Fired 5 torpedoes, individually aimed, allowing for enemy speed of 12 knots. The first 4 torpedoes spread over 2 ship's lengths (360 ft), the fifth 1½ lengths astern of conning tower.
Enemy turned stern on 5 minutes after firing and sixth torpedo was aimed with a director angle of zero. The enemy resumed original course 3 minutes after firing.
The sixth torpedo also missed.'

Enemy course	128°
Own course	040°
Track angle	92°
Enemy speed	12 knots
Director angle	16° Red
Range on firing	7 000 yards

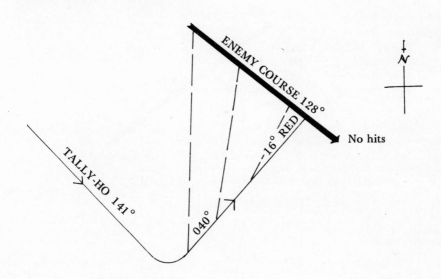

ATTACK ON JAPANESE MERCHANT SHIP IN POSITION 03°N 100°E
21 February 1966

'At 1410 on 21 February merchant ship sighted approaching from south east
and very close inshore. It appeared to be 2 000-2 500 tons.

Enemy course 304° at 1412 approximate range 1800 yards. Altered course
to 300°. Range plot gave target speed of 7 knots.

At 1437 altered course to 034° and closed at slow speed on a 90° track.
1447 fired 5 torpedoes spaced 1½ ships' lengths. There was one hit and the
enemy sank within 4 minutes.'

L.W.A. Bennington
patrol report

Enemy course	304°
Enemy speed	7 knots
Own course	034°
Track angle	90°
Director angle	9½ Greer
Range on firing	1 300 yards

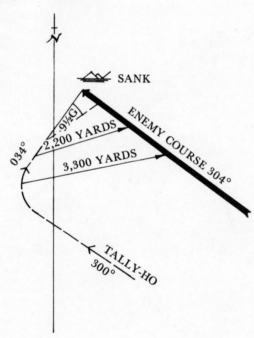

ATTACK ON JAPANESE MERCHANT VESSEL (estimated 7 000 tons)
15 January 1944 at 0054   09°29′N 92°41′E

'During a submerged patrol off Sawi Bay in the island of Car Nicobar on 14
January 1944 *Tally-Ho* sighted a merchant ship with one escort. Six
torpedoes fired spread 2½ ship's lengths, one hit, vessel sank.'

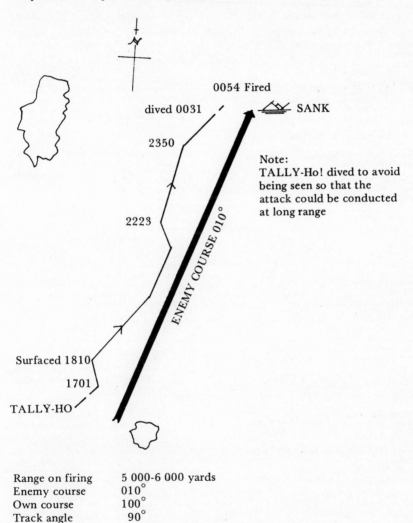

0054 Fired

dived 0031

SANK

2350

Note:
TALLY-Ho! dived to avoid
being seen so that the
attack could be conducted
at long range

2223

ENEMY COURSE 010°

Surfaced 1810

1701

TALLY-HO

Range on firing	5 000-6 000 yards
Enemy course	010°
Own course	100°
Track angle	90°
Enemy speed	9 knots
Director angle	13° Green

Index

The ranks and decorations shown are those gained by the end of the Second World War: many of the persons listed went on to gain higher ranks and further honours. Place names are those current at the time of the narrative, thus Port Swettenham (Malaya), instead of Port Klang (Malaysia), as it is now.

The index does not include references to appendices (except diagrams).